Sport &
Christianity

Sport &
Christianity

*A Sign of the Times in
the Light of Faith*

*Edited by Kevin Lixey, L.C.,
Christoph Hübenthal, Dietmar Mieth,
and Norbert Müller*

The Catholic University of America Press
Washington, D.C.

Originally published as Dietmar Mieth, Norbert Müller, Christoph Hübenthal, *Sport und Christentum: Eine anthropologische, theologische und pastorale Herausforderung* (Matthias-Grünewald-Verlag, 2008).

Library of Congress Cataloging-in-Publication Data
Wissenschaftliches Symposium "Zur christlichen Sicht des Sports" (2007 : Akademie des Bistums Mainz)
[Sport und Christentum. English.]
Sport and Christianity : a sign of the times in the light of faith / edited by Kevin Lixey ... [et. al.].
p. cm.
Includes bibliographical references and index.
ISBN 978-0-8132-1993-6 (pbk. : alk. paper)
1. Sports—Religious aspects—Catholic Church—Congresses.
2. Sports—Moral and ethical aspects—Congresses.
I. Lixey, Kevin, 1968–   II. Title.
GV706.42.W5713 2007
796.01—dc23
2012011700

Contents

vi   Contents

Foreword

Did you ever wonder what the Fathers of the Church had to say about the sports of their time? Would you like to know what Pius XII had to say about sport when meeting with coaches from Princeton, Stanford, Michigan State, and Penn State colleges—all of whom were affiliated with the military Central Sports School? Are you aware that a papal condemnation of doping dates back to 1955? Would you be surprised to read that John Paul II—the sporting pope—compared modern sport to a "sign of the times"? Did you know that some Catholic priests officially form part of national Olympic teams as sport chaplains? To sum it all up: "Is there such a thing as a Catholic perspective of sport?"

Up until now, finding an answer to these questions would have been quite difficult in the English language. Although for many years the Catholic Bishops' Conferences of Italy, Germany, and Poland have had a national office for sport that in the past few decades has discussed aspects of sport from a Catholic theological and pastoral perspective, there is little of such investigation to be found in English.

Thus, the following publication seeks to change the status quo. This volume contains the English translation of the European seminar "Sport and Christianity: Anthropological, Theological, and Pastoral Challenges" that was held March 1–4, 2007, in Mainz, Germany.

The seminar was a unique and historic collaborative effort between the Vatican's "Church and Sport" office and the Scientific Commission of the Church and Sport working group of the Catholic German Bishops' Conference. As a few years have passed since these seminar proceedings were published in German, this edition has been updated. It includes two additional chapters: one on sport in the magisterium of Cardinal Ratzinger/Benedict XVI and a final chapter that offers some practical points regarding pastoral action in this field.

Although it is not proper to speak of a "Christian sport" per se, it is, however, fitting to speak of how Christianity specifically enlightens sporting activities by offering discernment criteria and by broadening sport's horizons, enabling sport to remain open to the deeper questions of human existence. For this end, various theological elements were examined, beginning with sport in sacred Scripture, the early Church Fathers, and recent pontiffs. These findings were complemented by an approach to sport in light of the Second Vatican Council, with its emphasis on interpreting and responding to the signs of the times, which must include the social dimension of sport as a world phenomenon. Rather than drawing together a series of conclusions, this publication seeks to provoke debate and ongoing reflection on the relationship between Christianity and sport in its anthropological, theological, and pastoral dimensions.

Especially in the United States, there seems to be growing interest in joining forces in order to defend the dignity of the human person and to recover and maintain sport's recreational and formative dimension. Consequently, I envision this book as a sort of bridge that not only crosses the divide between the German and English languages, but also can serve to unite Christians, people of other faiths, and people of goodwill in this common mission of safeguarding and enlightening sport.

LESZEK J. SIBILSKI, *The Catholic University of America*

Preface

Allow me to share some considerations with the reader of these seminar proceedings, now being published in the English language. I would like to simply highlight some of the points made throughout this work. I realize my selection is very subjective, but nonetheless it serves as an overview to the following chapters.

First of all, the introduction to this study is offered by Bishop Josef Clemens, a longstanding member of the Roman Curia, who worked for more than twenty years as the personal secretary to Cardinal Joseph Ratzinger, and since 2004 as Bishop has been the secretary of the Pontifical Council for the Laity. He raises two important points that I would like to draw to your attention. The first point refers to the operations of the new Church and Sport section of his Vatican dicastery, whose task it is to coordinate the Church's worldwide initiatives in this area according to the aims established by the Holy See. Here you can find out more about the goals and projects of this office, which was established in the Vatican in 2004 at the request of the Servant of God, John Paul II. It suffices to say that the seminar in Mainz in 2007 and the publication of these proceedings in German and now in English are concrete ways we wish to lend our support to these efforts. Bishop Clemens also mentions his desire for the eventual publication of a comprehensive document on sport for the benefit of the Universal

Church. This appears to me to be a very sensible proposal as the Universal Catholic Church has an obligation to provide an orientation to people in this vast field of sporting activity so that they might properly discern this universal cultural phenomenon from a Christian perspective. In whatever shape or form this document might assume, it will certainly be a challenge, as it is not easy to analyze a phenomenon that includes a plethora of meanings and experiences with a document of universal relevance. Nevertheless, there is undoubtedly a need for the wide world of sport to receive competent advice and orientation, especially with regard to its inherent moral, religious, and cultural questions.

After this general introduction, the book is divided into three main sections. The first section offers an anthropological investigation of some fundamental considerations of the human person and his or her final destiny and how this relates in a general way to sporting activity. The second is a theological approach that considers this phenomenon from the perspective of the Church's magisterium and from current theological reflection. The third part of our discussion considers some pastoral responses to this phenomenon while looking at both the challenges and the opportunities it presents to the Church today.

In chapter 1, Professor Karen Joisten offers a very original approach with her presentation of four historical mindsets (*Gedankenkreis*) that help us to understand a person's worldview and self-perception. The first is the mindset of Ancient Greek civilization—which Father Koch references (cf. chapter 4); the second is the mindset of the Middle Ages and its relation to knighthood, which I have complemented with a corresponding image of ascetic monasticism (cf. chapter 8); the third is the modern framework of thought, which was not presented in detail since it is well known by all; and finally the trans-anthropological or the postmodern mindset. This last way of thinking is characterized by the paradox of solipsism, in which a once communal experience of sport is now isolated into individual workouts and personalized sport consummation. A further analysis of this phenomenon is also taken up again by Father Maier's analysis of egoism in sport (cf. chapter 10).

In chapter 2, Father Barrajón presents different models that could be used to overcome the residue of dualism that continues to resurface today in sport. He first described the bioanthropological model, which can be opposed to the Platonic or Cartesian model, but which remains within its own limits. Then we have the model of Hans Urs von Balthasar, which stresses in a special way the development of the person as a bodily whole. Here the person's steady development and determination to find meaning in his or her activity overcomes any sort of dualism, although it can reach its completeness only through the Christological definition of the concept of "person."

Christoph Hübenthal draws attention in chapter 3 to the "anthropological difference," that is, the difference between that which is pre-given in the person and that which the person creates through his actions. When discussing the parameters of sport he points out several phenomena: that of the game itself, that of cultural achievement, and that of the rules. In addition to this he refers to how the experiential background of sport points to something beyond it: the aesthetic dimension of sport. On the one hand he finds in this dimension the locus of the "question of meaning." On the other hand he also discusses the so-called effects of presence in live sport, which are also to be taken into consideration. Through a person's immediate experience of sport, joy, and gratefulness can be produced or felt by the individual. The person who experiences these emotions enters the dimension of immediate perception. (And I would add to this statement: "in the awareness that all immediate experience can be mediated.")

The second section of the book begins with chapter 4, where

Father Koch provides an academic approach that, in a certain way, differs from the usual theological or biblical approach to sport. He focuses especially on the meaning of the biblical and patristic metaphors in ecclesial literature that are drawn from the realm of sport. With the intellectual rigor from his years of investigation, he offers the reader a better understanding of the historical meaning of these agon or sports metaphors in order to avoid misunderstanding and misconstruing these comparisons. He clearly argues that the sports metaphors used in the Bible (especially by Paul in his Letters to the Corinthians) are nontransferable to our present day. In other words, we cannot say that the popular metaphors that were taken from the well-known phenomenon of the athletics of antiquity, and eventually found their way into Scripture, are sufficient grounds for inferring that this has any retroactive relevance for the understanding of sport per se (yesterday or today) or for a Christian appreciation therein. These sports metaphors are always directed toward the understanding of a Christian way of life, and not vice versa. Nonetheless the Church Fathers retain as valuable criteria in the "discernment of spirits" the distinction between a "cult of the body" and a "culture of sport." Whereas some Fathers adopted a negative stance toward the body that was already present in Ancient Greece, others manifested a general appreciation of the body—such as Tertullian, who approved frequenting the bathhouses. Nonetheless, all of the Fathers reject the rituals and the cults that linked sport to the pagan religion.

Chapter 5 inaugurates an investigation of sport in the writings and speeches of recent pontiffs, by considering Pius XII. In the aftermath of World War II, Pius XII was especially concerned with the role of sport in the lives of Catholic youth of Italy, and encouraged the sporting activities that were carried out under the leadership of the Church through its Catholic youth and sport associations. Father Lixey suggests that Pius XII had a broad vision of "pastoral care" that considered youth sport as an opportunity for developing certain natural and Christian virtues. In this way, Pius XII highlights sport's educational dimension. In his ethical evaluation of sport he stressed primarily the natural law and the Decalogue, but he also pointed out dimensions that transcend it, like the salvific dimension of human existence. He warned against losing sight of the innate and higher meaning of one's own corporality and insisted on not allowing the loftier goals of the human person to be forfeited to insignificant ones.

In chapter 6, Bishop Carlo Mazza investigates sport in the magisterium of John Paul II, one who obviously spoke about sport from the perspective of an insider—as one who practiced it. This personal experience explains a certain enthusiasm about the phenomenology of sport that overflowed into his speeches. It can also be noted that John Paul II always placed his analysis of sport within the framework of the modern development of culture. I would only mention here the concept of a "global age." It was John Paul II who took the concept of "world" out of its old Latin paradigm of *mundus*. Today we call the world a globe, especially in the period of globalization. The two levels of criteria that were used by John Paul II should also be mentioned: the criteria of the truth of creation and the criteria of the salvation and redemption of man. He has united these concepts and created a socioethical concept of person that is understood in a complex and holistic way.

Bishop Josef Clemens offers us in chapter 7 a post-Mainz seminar reflection on the theme of sport in the speeches of Cardinal Ratzinger/Pope Benedict XVI. He takes many points from a unique interview that the then Cardinal Ratzinger gave on Bavarian radio before the World Cup (of soccer/football) in June of 1978. Bishop Clemens complements this chapter with some of Benedict XVI's more recent papal addresses on sport throughout his first five years of his pontificate, thus providing us with a unique addition to this English text that the German publication did not have.

In the first part of chapter 8, I stress the necessity of communication of the language of the Church and the levels of ecumenical extension, in the effort to lead an authentically religious and moral life in sport. In my own reflections, I acted on the assumption that in order to implement a Christian vision of sport, what we are in need of today are certain premises. This is an inductive process, a meticulous discernment of the "signs of the times." We do not want to impose on the culture of sport deductive reasoning. Rather we are trying to build and develop this culture "from below" by further developing its already existing views. In fact, this is the fundamental approach of the cultural sciences that is taken up by Stephan Goertz (cf. chapter 9) and presented in a much clearer way than I do here. In the second part I try to exemplify how these things reflect beyond themselves in the sense of an analogy by making some connections between different types of sport experiences. Analogy means at the same time similarity and dissimilarity. We should never forget the dissimilarities. Some examples I mention are competition without aggression and commerce, the understanding of the indivisible body over which one does not try to dominate according to the principle "divide et impera." Furthermore, I make reference to the general promotion of life, the analogy between training and asceticism, that is, the perfectibility of the person, who develops as a process in sport, the teaching of understanding between people, the conscience of the contingency of failure and guilt, the possibility of valuing the Second Tablet of the Ten Commandments and the Golden Rule. I also associate the First Tablet of the Decalogue with the obligation to observe Sunday as a day of rest in order to offer the possibility to understand sport from the perspective of a "mystical phenomenon", that is, as a phenomenon of the experience of limits.

The third part seeks to describe some of the pastoral aspects of sport from the twofold perspective of its challenges and its opportunities. After this, it moves toward a consideration of this phenomenon from a more practical nature.

In chapter 9, Stephan Goertz presents some deep insights into the concepts of "body turn" and "cultural turn," which can no longer be ignored today and have to be interpreted from the perspective of being signs of the time. Goertz describes sport exclusively from a social perspective, that is, as a game rooted in the social fabric of a culture. He speaks about the sport that prefigures the games of life, the sport that takes semi-religious shapes, and the sport that contains in itself irreplaceable forms of knowledge and experience. If these phenomena are regarded as a challenge, it becomes clearer how great is the need of resolving the antagonism between different anthropological approaches and of assimilating the differences in perspectives of social forms and possibly also of different views of moral and religious solutions. Here, and through this book, there is a strong emphasis and consensus on the Christian approach to sport.

In chapter 10, Father Maier in a unique way shows how sport can be seen as a field of opportunity for a "good shepherd" and how only one who is engaged in this activity can best understand this field of pastoral care and all that it entails. His reflections, which are based on decades of experience, constitute a kind of personal "testimony" in which he presents the antagonism between the image of a sportsman, a keyword for many challenges, and the implications of this person's image of God. With the help of this image the ad hoc language of sport was replaced by a completely different language, the language of forgiveness, of mercy, and of acceptance. I found it extremely interesting that he included in his paper testimonies of athletes about their own lives and about the questions they want to be answered by the Church. In this way we had the chance of getting acquainted with a different inductive element.

Lastly, in chapter 11, Norbert Müller presents some reflections based on his work in the deduction of the document "Sport and Christian Ethos: A Joint Declaration," which was fruit of the work xvi *Dietmar Mieth*

between Catholics and Evangelicals involved in sports ministry. It is an invitation to join forces in safeguarding the foundational value in sport and also complements the thoughts of Father Maier in considering other pastoral opportunities such as those afforded to coaches, trainers, and volunteers for pastoral work among the youth via sport.

This short summary makes clear how far-reaching our analyses were. Our focus was always on exactness and was full of intensity. This is why I believe we gained some important insights from this conference. If we want to sketch a Christian vision of sport for its various sectors, what we are still missing is that which I mentioned above—the amplification of inductive inputs. For this purpose, it would be necessary to present cultural and sociological visions in partial controversy with our Christian vision in order to provoke debate and reflection. Secondly, the question on the context of our Christian view leads us into the realm of a plurality of approaches that have to be maintained and shown their own proper value. I believe there are a series of controversies in this field that are clearly raised in the critical remarks of Father Maier against Gunnar Drexel, a Tübingen scholar in sport sciences. I also know how controversial the individual phenomena of sport ethics are. For now we must be content with presenting these present findings in the hope of now extending this discussion to the international level.

DIETMAR MIETH

Acknowledgments

This book began life as papers that were presented at a unique international seminar of Catholic sport theologians held at the Catholic Academy in Mainz, Germany, March 1–4, 2007. This seminar was organized by the scientific committee of the Church and Sport working group of the German Catholic Bishops' Conference with the collaboration of the Pontifical Council for the Laity's Church and Sport section. The editors wish to thank the contributors for their papers, which were originally published in German under the title *Sport und Christentum: Eine anthropologische, theologische und pastorale Herausforderung* (Mainz: Matthias-Grünewald-Verlag, 2009). Special thanks go to Anna Cranz, Maria Katharina, and Moser Matthew Specter for their help with the translations from German to English. The editors wish to thank Professor Leszek Sibilski of the Catholic University of America for making the initial contact with the Catholic University of America Press. Lastly, we are indebted to Bishop Josef Clemens of the Pontifical Council for the Laity and James Kruggel at CUA Press for their encouragement and guidance.

Sport &
Christianity

Bishop Josef Clemens

Introduction

The Christian Mission within the Field of Sport

I would like to touch upon four general points in this introduction. The first regards the establishment of this new Church and Sport section within the Vatican. A second point, closely connected to the first, is that of the seminar "The World of Sport Today: A Field Christian Mission" that was held in Rome in November of 2005. After this, I will share with you some of the future projects and tasks of the section. Lastly, I will offer some remarks about the providential nature of this present seminar, "Sport and Christianity: Anthropological, Theological and Pastoral Challenges."

The Church and Sport Section within the
Pontifical Council for the Laity

Although the roots of sporting activity can be traced back to the dawn of humanity, never before as today has sport become so established as a mass phenomenon. In fact, its unique capacity to gather throngs of people on a planetary scale makes it one of the most universally recognized components of popular culture. For some, sport is experienced as a kind of "ecstasy" from the humdrum of daily life. For others, sport has acquired an importance that goes beyond that of mere amusement or entertainment and has become a way of life itself, or a surrogate for religious experience.

The Church has always shown particular concern for the many different facets of human existence, and the same can be said of sporting activity. We can call to mind the encounters of Pius XII with Catholic sports associations in 1945 and 1955 and other encounters of professional athletic teams with various pontiffs. Yet, of all the pontiffs of the twentieth century who have addressed the world of sport, John Paul II stands out for the great attention he paid to sport and to the body. Not only did he speak about sport, he even practiced it both before and after becoming pope (skiing, swimming, and canoeing). This is why in his meetings with sports men and women, his speeches on the subject have always had a special value. Athletes saw him to be a man who shared firsthand their sporting experiences.

Not only this, but the establishment of a new section within the Vatican dedicated to the rapport between the Church and sport can be seen as the direct legacy of the late Pope John Paul II. As a longtime member of the Roman Curia, I would like to share with you how this new section for sport came into existence.

The origin of this new section traces its roots back to the Great Jubilee of 2000, in which there was a special Jubilee for Sport. After having participated on Saturday, October 28, at a special convention on the theme, "During the time of the Jubilee, the Face and Soul of Sport," the next day, Sunday, October 29, John Paul II celebrated a special Mass and preached a homily to the vast crowds of sports men, women, and children who packed into Rome's Olympic Stadium.[1]

Of the many speeches and addresses John Paul II has given to

1. John Paul II, "Homily at the Mass for Sports Men and Women" (October 29, 2000), *L'Osservatore Romano*, English ed., no. 44, November 1, 2000, 1.

athletes, this homily stands out as a sort of Magna Carta for the Christian mission within the field of sport. The Holy Father, commenting on the passage of St. Paul "Do you not know that in a race all the runners compete, but only one receives the prize? So run that you may obtain it!" (1 Cor 9:24), observed:

Playing sports has become very important today, since it can encourage young people to develop important values such as loyalty, perseverance, friendship, sharing and solidarity. Precisely for this reason, in recent years it has continued to grow even more as one of the characteristic phenomena of the modern era, almost a sign of the times capable of interpreting humanity's new needs and new expectations. Sports have spread to every corner of the world, transcending differences between cultures and nations.[2]

The Holy Father then pointed out that with this growth in sport's popularity and its worldwide attraction comes the need for an adequate response on the part of the Church and others. He noted: "Because of the global dimensions this activity has assumed, those involved in sports throughout the world have a great responsibility. They are called to make sports an opportunity for meeting and dialogue, over and above every barrier of language, race or culture. Sports, in fact, can make an effective contribution to peaceful understanding between peoples and to establishing the new civilization of love."[3]

Building upon the positive points that can be found in sport, the Holy Father then laid out very clearly the challenges that face all people of goodwill in sport, as well as the need to work to together. He observed: "The educational and spiritual potential of sport must make believers and people of good will united and determined in challenging every distorted aspect that can intrude, recognizing it as a phenomenon opposed to the full development

2. Ibid.
3. Ibid.

of the individual and to his enjoyment of life. Every care must be taken to protect the human body from any attack on its integrity, from any exploitation and from any idolatry."[4]

Lastly, in this same homily, the Holy Father then gave us a blueprint for sport, describing how he sees, within a Christian perspective, the sporting ideal that the Church should promote and uphold:

> A sport that protects the weak and excludes no one, that frees young people from the snares of apathy and indifference, and arouses a healthy sense of competition in them; sport that is a factor of emancipation for poorer countries and helps to eradicate intolerance and build a more fraternal and united world; sport which contributes to the love of life, teaches sacrifice, respect and responsibility, leading to the full development of every human person.[5]

At the end of his homily, the pope exhorted every Christian "to become a strong athlete of Christ, that is, a faithful and courageous witness to his Gospel," for Christ is "God's true athlete" and the "more powerful" man.[6]

In a certain sense, this homily laid out the principal tasks and aims that the Church's mission within the field of sport must entail. In fact, just three days after this jubilee for sport, a written request was made by the then secretary of state, Cardinal Angelo Soldano, to the president of the Pontifical Council for the Laity for an investigation on how an office for sport could be established within the Holy See.[7] It was noted that such a section within the Pontifical Council for the Laity might fit well alongside its already existing Youth section, as sports go hand in hand with youth. After a period

---

4. Ibid.   5. Ibid.
6. Ibid., 2.
7. Regarding the Pontifical Council for the Laity, see www.laici.va, and John Paul II, *Christifideles Laici: On the Vocation and the Mission of the Lay Faithful in the Church and in the World* (Vatican: LEV, 1988).

of preliminary research, investigation, and debate on various proposals, the Church and Sport section was officially erected in 2004 with a letter from the secretary of state, Cardinal Sodano, which was dated January 23, 2004 (Protocol No. 543 564). The crucial sentence of this correspondence states: "I therefore have the honorable duty of informing you that the Holy Father, in addition to the existing Youth section, establishes the Section for sport within the Pontifical Council for the Laity." Therefore, we are proud to have as a real spiritual father and patron of this new Church and Sport section none other than the Servant of God, John Paul II. Along with this comes the responsibility on our part of safeguarding and passing on this rich patrimony that this great pope has bequeathed to the world of sport during his long and proficuous pontificate.[8]

In June of 2004, Reverend Kevin Lixey, L.C., came from the United States to begin the work of this section, which was envisioned as a point of reference within the Holy See for all national and international sports organizations, serving as a kind of "observatory" for the world of sport at the service of evangelization. Consequently, it was given the following specific goals:

• To ensure more direct and systematic attention to the vast world of sport on the part of the Church that fosters a renewal of pastoral work in and through sports.

8. To illustrate the magnitude of his pontificate, I would like to share some figures and statistics. Pope John Paul II (*1920, 1978–2005) published 102 major doctrinal documents (13 encyclicals, 12 formal apostolic letters, 11 apostolic constitutions, 41 apostolic letters, and 25 letters *motu proprio*). He received, in 1,330 special audiences, representatives of public life, including 38 heads of state in formal state visits. He granted general audiences that a total of 16.155 million visitors attended. These figures do not take into account the participants in the Eucharistic celebrations and at other meetings during his 140 apostolic trips within Italy and 95 abroad (1,205,312 km). In his travels he gave a total of 3,251 sermons and speeches. The texts published during the entire span of his term of office (1978–2005), which can be found in *Insegnamenti di Giovanni Paolo II,* amount to 82,339 printed pages. Truly a pontificate of superlatives!

- To diffuse the teachings of the Church regarding sport and to promote the study and research of various themes of sport, especially those of ethical nature.
- To promote initiatives that can serve to evangelize the world of sport, especially those that foster the witness of an authentic Christian life among professional athletes.
- To promote a culture of sport in harmony with the true dignity of the human person through youth education (schools, oratories, parish centers, lay movements, and other associations).
- To favor collaboration among the various sporting organizations and associations on the national and international level, serving as a point of reference and dialogue with the various national and international sports entities.

Without dwelling on each of these goals, I would like to comment on what a unique opportunity is placed before us. As our initial analysis reveals, the world of sport—or perhaps more precisely, the human person engaged in sport—has need of the light of Christ and a *super partes* moral voice that can serve as a guide. We have seen how money and ambition can drive athletes, coaches, and even parents to push themselves and others beyond their natural limits and often to the detriment of their health. The Church has always defended the human person from threats imposed by secular society, and it must also uphold the dignity of the person from a sporting environment that seeks to use people as means to an end, such as for economic gain or for fame.

In fact, the initial positive reaction of the international sports world to the institution of this new office proves this point. National and international governmental and nongovernmental organizations have expressed their appreciation of the Church's genuine interest and concern for the modern sport phenomenon, as shown in this new attention on the part of the Holy See. Furthermore, the

Church's effectiveness and credibility in the world of sport is enhanced by the fact that the positions and concerns voiced by the Holy See are expressed by a nonpartisan institution with no nationalistic or financial interests. As an "expert in humanity," the Church takes positions on fundamental and ethical issues that are acceptable to many, if not all. All of these factors position the Holy See via this sport section to become a global player among the international sporting institutions.

Some exceptional events that have occurred in these past few years, such as the pontificate of Pope John Paul II and the election of Pope Benedict XVI, have had worldwide resonance. The pontificate of the "sporting" pope, perhaps unprecedented in history, will not be easily forgotten among many sports men and women, managers and trainers, and sports associations. Today, we can humbly recognize a new receptiveness to questions of faith, and also to their ethical consequences. It is no coincidence that many famous sports men and women have asked to be received or greeted by the new pope as well. All of these factors present a *kairos* for the Church's mission within this field that can perhaps be considered a sign of the time.

What can be expected for this section in the new pontificate of Pope Benedict XVI? It is already apparent that the pontificate of Pope Benedict XVI will be marked by a period of more scholarly concentration and reflection, and less external activity. The publication of his first encyclical, *Deus Caritas Est,* already gives this impression from both its content and its style.

Pope Benedict XVI noted in his homily in St. Peter's Square on the day of his inauguration that "the purpose of our lives is to reveal God to men. And only where God is seen does life truly begin. Only when we meet the living God in Christ do we know what life is." And he added in an almost hymnlike manner, the now much-quoted words: "There is nothing more beautiful than to be surprised by the Gospel, by the encounter with Christ. There is nothing more beautiful than to know Him and to speak to others of our friendship with Him."[9]

With these words, Pope Benedict lays out a program that is focused on the essential and with a special emphasis on a positive interpretation of the Christian faith by its followers. The pope wants to affirm that faith is not an elaborate system of laws, of commandments and prohibitions! Faith is not a collection of various "nos." Rather, the Gospel is a rich and fulfilling "yes"! In this sense, faith says "yes" to properly understood and exercised sporting activities. It is a "yes" pronounced with conviction, which conveys standards and principles that uphold the good of the person against any alienating aspects.

Review of the First Vatican Sport Seminar

I would like to briefly comment on our first seminar, "The World of Sport Today: A Field of Christian Commitment Received," which was held in Rome November 11–12, 2005. The seminar sought to provide an panoramic perspective of the world of sport today, with both its positive and negative aspects, in order to make a preliminary assessment that would help establish the agenda for the sports section for the years to come. It should be noted that the participants, who came from all over the world, were very enthusiastic regarding the establishment of this new section. The proceedings of this seminar have been published and are available through the Pontifical Council for the Laity in Italian and English.[10]

---

9. Pope Benedict XVI, "Homily during the Inaugural Mass of His Petrine Ministry" (April 24, 2005), *L'Osservatore Romano*, English ed., no. 17, April 27, 2005, 9.

10. Cf. Pontificium Consilium Pro Laicis, *The World of Sport Today: Field of Christian Mission* (Vatican: LEV, 2006).

A Look at Future Tasks of the Church and Sport Section

Let us now look at the projects that this sport section will undertake in the immediate future. We are elaborating a sort of *vademecum* for all Catholics engaged in this field. Whether this would be something published by the Pontifical Council for the Laity or something that would be under the care of the secretary of state is not certain. Yet given the large number of Catholics who are engaged in this field, whether as volunteers, players, or fans, we feel that this enormous pastoral challenge and opportunity must be properly evaluated. Thus, we feel that such a document could be useful for helping Christians to discern that which Pope John Paul II alluded to in a positive way as a "sign of the times."

We also intend to establish an international library for the pastoral field of sport within the library of the Pontifical Council for the Laity in Rome. We especially hope to make more readily available the ample papal magisterium on this theme, especially in the speeches of Popes Pius XII and John Paul II, which are explored in this book in subsequent chapters. We are also assembling a collection of important documents and statements that deal with sport-related issues that have been produced by offices of sport ministry affiliated with various bishops' conferences around the world. It should be noted here that Germany is one of a dozen countries that have some type of delegate or Church and Sport office dedicated to the pastoral ministry of sport.

We also want to promote and favor the international exchange of ideas and best practices among these same national offices as well as with other Catholic sport associations. This network can also be useful for joint pastoral ministry at major world sporting events, such as the Olympics or World Cup, where many of the heads of these national sport ministry offices also oversee the chaplaincy work at these same events.

Additionally, we seek to raise awareness of pastoral opportunities in this field in our contact with bishops from around the world who come to the Vatican every five years *in visita ad limina.*

We are in favor of strengthening European and international Catholic youth sport associations such as FICEP (Fédération Internationale Catholique d'Éducation Physique et Sportive) and FISEC (Fédération Internationale Sportive de l'Enseignement Catholique) in their identity as Catholic associations of the lay faithful,[11] which through their affiliates on the national level are suitable partners and collaborators in the work of this section. What is more, given the common commitment of many Christians in sport, these sport associations and the works of other ecclesial communities provide opportunities for ecumenical cooperation, and as such, make a valuable contribution to the promotion of Christian unity.

Lastly, as an institution of the Holy See, we intend to participate in international conferences and hold periodic international seminars and other meetings in order to foster a worldwide reflection on various sports related themes.

The Christian View of Sports: Anthropological, Theological and Pastoral Aspects

After a long excursus about the establishment of the Church and Sport section, we now arrive at the heart of the matter: this present seminar. We might ask: Why is the Pontifical Council for the Laity here in Mainz? What do we seek to obtain from these present anthropological and theological investigations? What expectations do we have?

As mentioned above, this seminar can be viewed as a concrete response to this last point. Yet, we need not start from zero. Rather, we need to build upon the foundations that have been laid by the

---

11. Cf. *Code of Canon Law* numbers: CIC 215, CIC 312 § 1; 322.

work of the national bishops' conferences in this field, such as the Church in Germany. By means of this present seminar, we hope to initiate, at least at the European level, a discussion about some of the elements that constitute a "Christian vision of sport."

In our first Vatican seminar on sport (2005), we sought to take a kind of inventory of the current state of affairs of the world of sport in order to formulate what specific contribution the Holy See could make to this phenomenon. From this preliminary survey, one could conclude that sport is at very critical moment in its history.

Recently in Italy, we perceive this all the more with the latest eruption of episodes of violence that have occurred at sporting events (i.e., the murder of policeman Filippo Raciti in February 2007 in Catania, Italy) and the latest cases of doping in the cycling world, which have also brought this scourge front and center in the media. On the other hand, we have seen the great media interest regarding the "Clericus Cup"—the annual international soccer tournament among Catholic seminarians and priests studying in Rome at the pontifical universities.

For these reasons (and others) there seems to be a special interest in or openness to the pastoral work of the Church in this area of sport. I consider this seminar in Mainz and this publication of its proceedings to be a concrete response to this *kairos*. We have sought to elaborate the anthropological and theological bases for developing this special pastoral ministry as a response to the sporting phenomenon. Because of this, the Pontifical Council for the Laity is very grateful to this scientific commission of the Church and Sport research group of the German Bishops' Conference for organizing this unique event. In fact, the Church and Sport research group of the German Bishops' Conference has throughout its many years of existence held various seminars of study and has produced various documents on sport. Thus we are indebted to the Catholic Church in Germany for this extensive patrimony of research and for bringing us together for this rich discussion.[12]

12. As a few years have passed since the Mainz seminar, allow me to add, in retrospect, the more recent words of Pope Benedict XVI, in which he encouraged the Pontifical Council for the Laity in their efforts to address the world of sport with these words: "Through sports, the ecclesial community contributes to the formation of youth, providing a suitable environment for their human and spiritual growth. In fact, when sports initiatives aim at the integral development of the person and are managed by qualified and competent personnel, they provide a useful opportunity for priests, religious and lay people to become true and proper educators and teachers of life for the young. In our time when an urgent need to educate the new generations is evident it is therefore necessary for the Church to continue to support sports for youth, making the most of their positive aspects also at competitive levels such as their capacity for stimulating competitiveness, courage and tenacity in pursuing goals. However, it is necessary to avoid every trend that perverts the nature of sports by recourse to practices that can even damage the body, such as doping. As part of a coordinated, formative effort, Catholic directors, staff and workers must consider themselves expert guides for youth, helping each of them to develop their athletic potential without obscuring those human qualities and Christian virtues that make for a fully mature person." Cf. Benedict XVI, "Message to the President of the Pontifical Council for the Laity on Sports, Education and Faith" (November 3, 2009), *L'Osservatore Romano,* weekly English ed., no. 46, November 18, 2009, 5.

Part 1 Anthropological Aspects

At the anthropological level, interest in the well-being of the human person moves Christians and non-Christians alike in a their common concern and appreciation for sport, which they do not wish to see ruined by an unhealthy obsession for victory and financial gain. Thus it is opportune to join forces in order to defend the dignity of the human person and to uphold the good that can still be found within sports. Here, a reflection on the fundamental elements of Christian anthropology can contribute to this field. What is more, this anthropological reflection could serve as a bridge between Christians and people of other faiths within the world of sport.

While it is true that Jesus Christ encouraged us to fear that which could do harm to the soul more than that which might harm the body, Christians do not totally despise either the flesh or the temporal realities of this world. Rather, ever since the first centuries of its existence, Christianity has fought against Gnosticism and other heresies that despise the body and has promoted instead the inherent good of creation and the fundamental dignity of the human person himself as created body and soul in the image of God. Thus, this first section gives voice to these ideas, drawing from the Christian truth that the human person is created in the image of God.

Chapter 1 works from the premise that the manner in which we consider our athletic heroes reflects the way we consider ourselves and vice versa. Under this light the author surveys four exemplary mindsets that have characterized the god-world-man relationship, including the trans-anthropological mindset typical of our age.

In chapter 2 the author claims the necessity of considering the human person as a unity of soul and body in order to overcome anthropological dualism, that is, à la Plato and Descartes. The author marshals evidence from the views of Arnold Gehlen and Hans Urs Balthasar to prove the merits of a unified or integral anthropology. He concludes with a exposition on a theological approach to the person that enriches our understanding of human action (like that of sport) because these personal encounters are with other animated bodies that manifest the call to communion of the self: body and soul.

Finally, chapter 3 explores this pre-given disposition toward play in the human person, which is to be harmonized with their personal freedom and responsibility. Consequently, activities such as sport are characterized as spheres of transitive action, but also of intransitive action, as these same actions freely and creatively constitute who the person is. This unique double-sidedness to sportive actions and precisely the intransitive dimension identifies the moral and aesthetic aspects of being human. The author explores how both dimensions can open this sphere of activity to religious questions that pave the way for a Christian interpretation of sport and its ultimate meaning.

Karen Joisten

1 Man, Mortality, and the Athletic Hero

Yesterday and Today

By considering the title of this chapter, we can see two lines of thought that are indivisibly intertwined: that of man and that of sport.[1] We gain access to man from an interpretation that is predominant to a specific intellectual-cultural mindset, while we gain access to sport via its admired athletic heroes on whom the public eye rests. Thus, we shall formulate a theory that will serve as a kind of guideline for our further elaborations. The theory is: the manner in which man—consciously or subconsciously—cares for himself is, if thought about more deeply, the manner in which he will treat himself and his mortality. This is an adaptation of the phrase "the manner in which we see a person will be in accordance to the manner in which we behave toward a person—and vice versa" to the phrase "the manner in which man considers himself will be in accordance with the manner in which he treats himself and hence will be the manner in which he engages in sport," and it will get its

1. I shall use the modern term "sport" on the grounds of readability as a generic term in this article. This incorporates the numerous heterogeneous contests, games, and exercises that should be clearly differentiated from a historic perspective.

full meaning as this chapter develops.[2] My elaborations therefore suppose a hidden but detectable connection between the manner in which man engages in sport and the manner in which he deals with his self and his mortality.[3]

The consideration that sport can be interpreted as a kind of mirror of society in which the intellectual-cultural positions of an epoch are especially pronounced goes hand in hand. In the course of our focus on sport, we will bring into focus the admired sportsmen—the athletic heroes of a specific era—and by them try to uncover the immanent, undivulged stances of each epoch toward life and death (and by this to man himself). Leisure time, games, and sport competitions are explicitly or implicitly amended through their confrontation with the athletic idols of their time. For man has always looked to the role models and heroes of his day to gain orientation, and this is mirrored back to him and influences him.

So as not to go too far astray due to the vastness of the subject

2. This idea that man's self-consideration is founded in his consciousness of his mortality and the corollary that the manner in which man understands himself will be the manner in which he engages in sport ties in with the approach in the book by Peter Kemp, *Das Unersetzliche. Eine Technologie-Ethik* [The irreplaceable: Ethics of technology] (Berlin: WiehernVerlag, 1992). Kemp transforms this idea to fit our context: "With modern technology man has new possibilities to treat others as means to an end. Technological manipulations have no integral limitations. These limitations therefore must be imagined elsewhere. For this reason ethics are neither science nor technology but visions of experience and narrative imagination of what man and his world are. Ethics constitute the idea of man, inextricably linked to the understanding of society and nature. Consequently the principle arises: the manner in which we see a person will be in accordance to the manner in which behave toward a person—and visa versa" (275). Considered in our context, the sports hero incorporates an idea of the person inextricably linked to an understanding of society and nature but especially linked to his or her consideration of mortality.

3. See my elaborations in an essay concerning the athlete's attempt to conquer death: Karen Joisten, "Wenn Gott den Ball versenkt," in *Abseits denken: Fussball in Kultur, Philosophie und Wissenschaft,*" ed. Andreas Hütig and Johannes Marx (Kassel: Agon Sportverlag, 2004), 8–86, and my essay on the philosophical reflections on man in the thought of Pierre de Coubertin, "Der Mensch im Spiegel der Olympischen Idee," in *Olympischer Dreiklang: Werte-Geschichte-Zeitgeist,* ed. M. Messing, Olympische Studien Series 6 (Kassel: Agon Sportverlag, 2004), 21–34.

matter, we shall choose a typological approach by establishing four basic ways of viewing the god-world-man-relationship. In doing so, we shall pursue the question of the interpretation of mortality in the light of four ways of viewing the athletic heroes of each epoch. We shall set off with the help of Max Scheler, who in his essay on *Man's Place in Nature* establishes three (*Gendankenkreis*) "circles of thought" or mindsets: the Jewish-Christian mindset, the Ancient Greek mindset, and that of "modern science and of genetic psychology."[4]

Nearly eighty years have past since Scheler and our ways of thinking have changed. This is why we shall add a new mindset to those already mentioned, which we will call the "trans-anthropological" mindset.

The Ancient Greek Mindset

The Ancient Greek mindset can be labeled as cosmos-centrist, in which the metaphysical question of a reality in the entirety is of central importance. The question that arises is a question about the beginning, the *arche*, from which all being originates and to which it returns in the end. The manifoldness of being in its en-

4. Max Scheler, *Man's Place in Nature*, trans. Hans Meyerhoff (Boston: Beacon Press, 1961) 2. Scheler expresses these circles of thought in the following way: "If one were to ask an educated European what he thought, when confronted with the word 'man,' three disparate mindsets [*Gendankenkreis*] would start competing with each other. On the one hand the Jewish-Christian mindset revolving around the tradition of Adam and Eve of Genesis, the paradise and the fall of man. On the other hand the Ancient-Greek mindset in which self consciousness assumed a distinguished position. In this theory man constitutes himself by his possession of 'reason' .... And thirdly, the mindset of modern science and of genetic psychology that has long come to be considered as traditional, in which man is understood to be a very late and final outcome in the development of the planet earth; he is a being that only differs from prior shapes found in the animal world, by means of the levels of complexity of the mixture of energies and abilities, that already occur in subhuman nature. These three mindsets lack any form of unity. This is the reason why we are in the possession of a scientific, a philosophical and a theological anthropology, which are independent of each other—We do not however possess a uniform idea of man."

tirety is shown as a system or cosmos that is constituted by the beginning and so has an inherent relationship with it. This system is something holy and powerful, in which the immanent and the transcendent are not yet divided.

The cosmos is inhabited by gods and men. If we refer to what Hesiod writes in his *Theogony:* Zeus, the highest ranking of the gods of Olympus, has divided all the particulars of the cosmos between the mortals and gods, so giving them "the honours in equal parts."[5] The Greeks admired their Olympic gods and were awed by them. In accordance with Bruno Snell, we can show clearly that the Homeric man was "free before his gods: he is proud when the gods grant him a gift, but at the same time, humble, as he knows that everything great comes from the gods."[6] Consequently, according to Homer, it is "not the poor and weak who are nearest to god but, on the contrary, those who are strong and powerful."[7]

If we regard only the view of the Hellenic period, by which time brutalization had grown considerably, the accounts of the athletic competitions in which the athlete is the quintessential embodiment of the "strong and powerful man" who is "nearest" to god are extremely dramatic. They show a much higher readiness to use violence to an extent that we would find offensive, or even repulsive.[8] The athlete does not only use every possible means to gain

5. The exact wording: "And he was reigning in heaven, solely holding thunderbolt and smoldering lightning, having overcome by might his father, Chronos; and he distributed good and fairly to the immortals their portions and declared their privileges." Hesiod, *The Theogony, Work and Days, and The Shield of Heracles,* trans. Hugh Evelyn-White (Stillwell, Kans.: Digireads Publishing, 2008), 16.

6. Bruno Snell, *Die Entdeckung des Geistes: Studien zur Entstehung des europäischen Denkens bei den Griechen* (Göttingen: Vandenhoeck & Ruprecht, 1993), 38.

7. Ibid., 37.

8. We can find a description of Pankration (a type of floor-wrestling) in the elaborations of Pausanius: "Pankration was fought with every part of the body, with the hands, feet, elbows, with the knees, neck and head, the Spartans even fought with their teeth. And yes, it was valid to gouge the opponent's eyes. Furthermore, the all encompassing fighting system allowed the fighters to straddle the leg; one was

his triumph. He also puts everything on the line—as his own life is at stake. This use of violence and the uncompromising way in which these competitions were dealt with—though it is not found in such a concentrated form throughout the whole Greek period—do leave us troubled. However, we must not be too quick in passing judgment. These competitions also served the purpose of establishing a sort of relationship with the gods and of educating the individual for warfare, as training for battle was vital for survival. Consequently, the purpose of these competitions was to showcase virtues, such as steadfastness, courage, and bravery, that gave each individual the most glory and highest honor in competition as well as in battle.[9] So it was most important during the agonistic fighting techniques to display the virtue of *arete*, to triumph and to leave the fight as the champion.

Accordingly, Norbert Elias writes: "The moment of decision over either triumph or failure was at the centre of the attention of the competition and not its due course."[10] Let there be no misun-

---

also permitted to grasp the opponent's foot, nose or ears and dislocate fingers and arms, and throttle him. If the pankrationist managed to floor an opponent he was permitted to sit upon him and direct merciless blows toward his head, face and ears, push him and yes, trample on him. Needless to say, the most horrific injuries came about in these coarse fights, and yes the fights were often ended fatally." Pausanius, *Pausanius's Description of Greece*, trans. James G. Frazer (London: Macmillan, 1898), 155–56.

9. Norbert Elias notes that "Fighting, in games as in war, was centered on the ostentatious display of the warrior virtues which gained for a man the highest praise and honor among other members of his own group,—for his kin-group or his city—among other groups." Cf. Norbert Elias, Stephen Mennell, and Johan Goudsblom, *Norbert Elias on Civilization, Power, and Knowledge: Selected Writings* (Chicago: University of Chicago Press, 1998), 173.

10. And it continues: "It was about endurance, muscular strength and dexterity. Serious injuries to the eyes, ears and even to the cranium were common, just as swollen ears, broken teeth and noses beaten flat. There are reports of boxers which consented to entering the fight. The former dealt the opponent a blow to the head who survived this. When he lowered his guard, the latter struck him with his taut hand and perforated his abdominal wall with his strong nails, and disemboweled him, thus killing him." Ibid., 174.

derstanding of what this means: it was imperative for the athlete to win. Rather than losing, it was better to meet death in battle, at least if we are to believe the oral tradition that Philostratus II put in writing (around AD 200). It reads: "the most desirable of all is to triumph with the price of one's life." As we know, the champion was endowed with the most glory and highest material honors and esteem. Or, as Philostratus put it, a champion is one who can "pass into the realm of the contented." This perception is aptly defined by the words of Hannah Arendt:

> Now the task and potential strength of mortals lies in that they are able to create things: compositions, deeds, words ... those who are deserving will be allocated a place in the everlasting cosmos by which mortals themselves can find the appropriate place for them, in a system in which everything is everlasting except they themselves. Through undying actions which leave unfading traces in the world as far as humankind stretches, mortals can attain a kind of human immortality of their own and thus prove that they are also of a divine nature.[11]

From this point of view man can follow either that which is beastly in him or that which is best in him. He follows the divine within himself if he endeavors to leave behind an imprint of his life. He does so if he lives a life in a manner in which he distinguishes himself through "compositions, deeds, words." If he succeeds in doing so, he will not live or die like an animal but gain immortality: "to exist and last through time," to lead a deathless life—as the Greeks believed was given to "nature and the Olympic gods." Hence the difference between man and mere being runs through mankind as a clear divide: only the "'best'...,who must prove themselves as the 'best' repeatedly...by favouring 'everlasting fame before mortal things,' are more than mere beings. Whereas those countless who are content with that which nature endowed

---

11. Hannah Arendt, *Vita activa: oder Vom tätigen Leben* (Munich: Piper, 1992), 24.

upon them live and die like animals."[12] Bearing this in mind, let us ask again: Why could the athlete face this risk of losing his life in such a manner? What understanding did he have of himself? What understanding did he have of life and death? Then the answer becomes apparent: he put his life at risk because he wanted to win everything, that being immortality. It was his chance to pull himself out of the swamp of a mere bestial existence and attain a home in the everlasting.[13] In doing so man makes himself divine by fashioning his immortality. He makes himself the best, the highest, and the most fulfilled man he can ever endeavor to be, and in doing so he performs, so to speak, the process of immanence of transcendence within himself.

The picture we have painted so far remains incomplete, as it refers mainly to Ancient Greek history. However, if we move on using larger strides, we see that the main focus that lay on *arete*, and consequently on physical training, is joined by an additional factor. One did still hold on to *arete*, as it was still of importance. However, as Heinz Schöbel elaborates:

The focal point was now set to benefit intellectual values. The term *kalokagathia* was coined, meaning a conjunction of the good and beautiful. The ancient Greeks viewed it as their educating ideal. It demanded that the free citizens of a polis were to meet the classical ideal of the physical

12. Ibid., 23; she continues: "Mortal man was born into the eternal life of nature and under the heavens of the immortal and unaging deities, the only thing perishable in an eternal cosmos, in which the mortal and the immortal met, but in which there was no eternity or dominion of an eternal god" (25). Immortality therefore must not be seen as an equivalent to eternity, as Arendt points out correctly. The "discovery" of eternity takes place with Plato, put more precisely, it is the discovery of the "actual antagonism between eternity and immortality" (25). Man relies on human community in some form, or in the words of Arendt, on "the plurality of human society."

13. Pindar emphatically warned against an athlete's quest for immortality, as such an incorrect projection of man would lead to equality with the deities. In other words, he admonishes that man might forget to be human and might try to make himself in to a deity.

mean, or better said, it required them to have perfect proportions, to be well trained and to have shapeliness and chasteness as well as strength of character.[14]

It is from this that our understanding of man, his body and mind united in harmony, stems. It is here where we can find the ideal that tries to unite physical beauty with an intellectually accomplished mind. And this is where the athlete emerges as the one trying to learn the virtue of *kalokagathia* and hence as the one who is trying to unite body and mind.

If you understand Plato to have established this ideal, you will without a doubt find passages in his writings as proof that the training and education of the body (via gymnastics) should be seen in close connection with the development and formation of reason (the soul). If, however, you also take his discovery of infinity into consideration, then a divide of immanency and transcendence and the following juxtapositions are implied: on the one hand that which is outside time, the timeless, the ideas, and on the other hand, the fleeting and mortal, the shadows that are projections. Hence, probably unwillingly, Plato has made way for the contempt-of-body concept. Following Plato, it may be the case that it was still as important to nurture the body as it was to nurture the mind, and both were to interact harmoniously. Nevertheless the soul, or better said, that part of the soul allocated to reason, is now seen as that which is true in man, which defines man. Subsequently, the soul has moved up in the hierarchy and has gained a more recognized position. It gives man the chance to separate his soul from his body when he dies, and as such man can come to be with the "good gods in eternity."[15]

14. Heinz Schöbel, *Olympia und seine Spiele,* 7th ed. (Berlin: Uranaia, 1988), 19.

15. If man, the philosopher, tries to free his soul from the physical in his life and attempts to let go of physical conditions and circumstances, thus concentrating on his self, man is able to, according to Plato, be in the position of happy hopefulness that his soul will advance to that which is similar, to the invisible, to the divine, to the immortal and the reasonable after his death. According to what we read in the

The Christian Mindset

Now that we enter a mode of thought in which God and man are fundamentally adjoined. As man is understood to be made in God's image, the self-assurance of man is certainty stemming not from a single autonomous ego, but rather from the indication of that which is divine in man. Man is obliged to emulate this divinity in its entirety in order to be able to see God as the way to the epitome of truth. In this concept, in which the inseparable tie between man and God could be called a "religious a priori,"[16] man is always an "auto-theonom" because of the previously stated nature of being and perfection of physical proportions through which the inseparable tie between him and God can be construed.[17]

If we consider the understanding of man in the Christian mindset (before we bridge over to sport) we can directly tie it to Plato's line of thought: it is from his point of view that a common, maybe the most common, way of understanding the Christian position emerges—which may in fact not be genuinely Christian. This understanding, which can be aptly worded as "contempt of the body," is an equivalent to the Platonic tradition that sees the soul as the defining characteristic of man. New Testament Christians, in their reading and understanding, could not easily abstain from using basic Greek principles and concepts.

Phaedo, when death befalls man, it seems that that which is mortal in him dies, the immortal, however, and the eternal continue unscathed. This is why the conception of immortality of the Greek athlete, in regard either to their *arete* or to their *kalokagathia*, which assured them immortality here on earth, is transformed into Plato's conception of eternity.

16. I owe this expression to Bernhard Jansen, who used it to underline Augustine's point of view. Cf. Bernhard Jansen, "Zur Lehre des hl. Augustinus von dem Erkennen der Rationes aeternae," in *Aurelius Augustinus: Festschrift der Görres-Gesellschaft zum 1500,* ed. Martin Grabmann and Joseph Mausbach (Cologne: Bachem, 1930) 120.

17. Cf. Saint Augustine's "I desire to know God and the soul. And nothing more? Nothing more whatever." Augustine, *The Soliloquies,* trans. Rose Elizabeth Cleveland (Boston: Little, Brown, 1910), 10.

They saw the world through the ancient Greeks' eyes, thus with the Greek world of conception and vocabulary of concepts. It is because of this that they could not grasp the Hebrew conceptions, the Old Testament, and consequently overlooked these. Alois Koch stressed this:

The scriptures of the New Testament are worded in the Greek language: they were read and interpreted by man dating back to the first Christian centuries. These were predisposed by a Greek conceptions and vocabulary. However, in contrast to this it can be proven that the world of conceptions and the world of vocabulary predisposed by Greek views are not sufficient for the understanding of man but in fact, require the fundamentally determining Hebrew concepts and vocabulary of the Old Testament as well.[18]

It is here that a second view of the understanding of man emerges from the shadows of existence. This second understanding sees body and soul in fundamental unison, in an integral entireness. In this understanding the Christian position incorporates man as a whole, in stark contrast to the strong differentiation that Plato makes.

Let us look at two exemplary quotations: the first is a quotation taken from the theologian Othmar Schilling:

In no way can the soul be seen as the most crucial element of man and the body to be considered by all as repulsive ballast. Instead both body and soul are God-willed, God-created and God-filled realities. Both are distinct features of God's creation and God saw that it was good. Here the idea of "man" is man in his concrete reality and not Plato's immaterial ideal in the heavenly realm. It is man's concrete existence in reality that corresponds to the understanding that God has of him and thus as an "image of God."[19]

---

18. Alois Koch, "Das biblische Menschenbild und seine Bedeutung für die Wertung der Leiblichkeit und der Leibesübungen," in *Begegnung: Christentum und Sport*, ed. Willi Schwank and Alois Koch (Aachen: Meyer und Meyer 2000), 2:55.

19. Othmar Schilling, *Das biblische Menschenbild* (Cologne: Wort und Werk 1961), 24.

The other quote stems from the Encyclical *Deus Caritas Est,* where Pope Benedict XVI, describing the unity of body and soul, writes:

This is due first and foremost to the fact that man is a being made up of body and soul. Man is truly himself when his body and soul are intimately united; the challenge of eros can be said to be truly overcome when this unification is achieved. Should he aspire to be pure spirit and to reject the flesh as pertaining to his animal nature alone, then spirit and body would both lose their dignity. On the other hand, should he deny the spirit and consider matter, the body, as the only reality, he would likewise lose his greatness.[20]

The understanding of the Christian perspective is visible in both quotations. It views the human person as an inseparable unity, body and soul as one entity. Hence, both parts set man apart, and not just this body or that soul. Consequently, continual unity is man's goal: the aggregation of these two parts is the essential goal of man and not its wrongful disjunction.

But how did it come about that from this first manner of understanding a contempt for the body became so predominant? Why was one, at least according to public opinion, more aware of this view? Is the allusion to hidden Platonism enough to answer these questions?

We shall again concentrate on sport while we try to answer our questions. Let us focus on the eyes of the people in the world as it was during the Middle Ages. Whom did they admire? Whom did they acknowledge? Who was their athletic idol or role model?

In a society regulated by classes of peasants, citizens, nobility, and clergy (spiritualists), there may have been sports pursued by the noblemen, those pursued by the citizens, and those played by the peasants in the countryside. However, it was surely not the athletic activities of the peasants or monks (nor their personal hygiene) that were admired. It was the knights and their compe-

20. Benedict XVI, *Deus Caritas Est,* no. 5 (Vatican: LEV, 2005), 14.

titions. These tournaments were massive sporting events during which knights and noblemen showcased their culture of knightly disciplines, and competitions were at the climax of great and important social events.[21]

Now it is not our main interest to describe these competitions in full detail. But we shall draw a very rough outline of these events with Johannes Rothe's "Seven points of agility" that each knight had to master. In his "Knight's manual" (*Ritterspiegel*), which was published roughly around 1400, he offers the following seven points: riding; swimming and diving; shooting different types of weapons; climbing; participation in tournaments; wrestling, fencing, and long jump; and what he called "suavity," which encompassed dancing, the playing of board games, and appropriate table manners.[22] Here it becomes apparent that the knight represents an ideal, which focuses primarily on total moral and physical skill and virtue.

Bearing in mind the reality—better said, the actual realization of this ideal—and the fact that, in time, the institutional Church became more and more outspoken against the holding of these tournaments, consequently, it is my suspicion that this might have given one the impression that the Church was against sporting activities as a matter of principle.

It seems that reality looked completely different, as Michael Krüger shows us on the basis of R. Barber/J. Barker:

Tournaments took place constantly. Knights and their knightly delegations were travelling to participate in these the whole year round. The Church condemned these tournaments as they caused the demolition and

---

21. Martin Vogt, "Der Sport im Mittelalter," in *Ge-schichte des Sports aller Volker und Zeiten*, ed. G. Bogeng (Leipzig: Seemann, 1926), 190; see also Michael Krüger, *Einführung in die Geschichte der Leibeserziehung und des Sportes*, vol. 2 (Schorndorf, Germany: Hofmann, 2005), 174.

22. Michael Krüger, *Einführung in die Geschichte der Leibeserziehung und des Sportes*, vol. 1 (Schorndorf, Germany: Hofmann, 2004), 183.

depredation of gardens, meadows and paths in the villages and towns and in course of their duration several casualties and deaths were to be reported. From the Church's point of view, tournaments were prohibited since the Council of Clermont in 1130. Men that lost their lives during the tournaments were not entitled to a Church burial. However this anathema could not be enforced.[23]

So it is not surprising that the tournament knights were thought to have committed all seven deadly sins, namely: haughtiness, envy, wrath, greed, gluttony, sloth, and lust—as claimed by Jacob of Vitry, bishop of Akko.[24]

If we choose to view the Christian perspective of sport in the Middle Ages from this angle, it becomes clear that it is not intend-

---

23. Cf. ibid., 187, where he writes: "However further arguments could be found amongst the clerics and monks which were against tournaments and its participating knights. 'And what kind of glory would this be, the glory of the unholy, of villains, of cowards?', a Dominican monk scolded. 'As they prove themselves in places and times of peace not of war, and prove themselves against friends, not foes. To what use can gold adorned weaponry be put, which only encourages the enemy ... and moreover which they cast away in order to flee more rapidly from their adversaries, as we saw not long ago.... What kind of glory lies therein that such are seen as glorious and seek plaudit and reward in prohibited combat, as are tournaments and suchlike, whilst showing themselves fearful and cowardly and eager to flee during works of virtue, as in righteous wars and in defense of their own country. They allow enemies to play havoc in their lands, to pillage and to depredate, to burn down towns, to destroy castles and drag off prisoners." And on 188 he continues to write: "In other words the knights and nobles were reproached for their tournament amusements which had no purpose than the pursuit of vain glory and they were reproached for their neglect of their real duties, imposed upon them by god. These duties demanded that they protect people and country from enemies, from pillaging and destruction. Not only did the tournament knights not engage in their duty of national defense, they themselves, as is pointed out elsewhere, participated in the pillaging of the land and the harassment of countrymen in the course of these tournaments.'"

24. Cf. ibid., 188: "They felt haughtiness for their hunger for glory; envy, as they did not want to accept the higher glory of the other tournament knights; wrath, as they engaged in combat when the atmosphere was petulant during the tournaments; greed, as they coveted the other knights' horses and armaments ... ; gluttony, as they partook in feasts; sloth, because of their behavior in face of failures during a fight, and finally lust, as they wanted to please courting women when they wore their insignia during the tournaments."

ed to seek for the ideal itself, but is more of a critical appraisal, to be seen in close context to reality. One does well to suppose that the real, specific practice of the sport of that time prohibited the development of and support for a sport and an athletic ideal that squared with the Christian understanding of man as the unity of body and soul. One clearly saw that the sport as it was practiced during the tournaments did not serve the purpose of further deepening man's body-soul unity nor of being good or becoming so. As it was practiced then it perpetuated man's lesser aspects. Nor did the monasteries and convent schools offer, not even in a modified form, an "alternative." "Some cloisters had simple baths or washrooms that were intended for personal hygiene but no specific training was undertaken at the convent-schools in gymnastics or swimming. Children's games and simple exercises were sometimes tolerated, but easily cast aside under the influence of the fundamentalist reform movement in the Church."[25] It is possible to get the impression that Church authorities neglected to create their own athletic ideal and to support it decisively as an alternative, due to their justified criticism of the realities being practiced at that time and the way these were admired. This is perhaps an interest that is only recently starting to be nurtured.

The Scientific-Anthropocentric Mindset

After the cosmos and the God-man relationship, in the third scientific model of anthropocentrism, the focus is on man himself. Man no longer assumes his understanding of his being within a Cosmo-centric or Theo-centric system of ontology or metaphysics, in which the divine or God himself is the *fundamentum inconcussum,* but replaces it with the consciousness of self and primarily construes himself as a thinking self or ego. Man understands him-

25. Ibid., 188.

self as increasingly rational, consequently seeing himself more and more before the backdrop of modern scientific developments. This turn toward the individual, which manifests itself in the modern works of Descartes, Kant, and Feuerbach, has led to a larger riff between theology and philosophy. Man no longer understands himself as an image of God, but God is construed as an image of man. This concept is aptly worded by Ludwig Feuerbach in his "Philosophy of the Future." In the first paragraph he writes: "The aim of the modern era was the realisation and humanisation of God—the transformation and denouement of theology towards anthropology." And in the second paragraph he states: "modern philosophy makes man including nature, the foundation of man, to the exclusive, universal and most significant object of philosophy—and it defines anthropology, including physiology, a universal science."[26]

If one tries to use "anthropocentrism" as the umbrella term for an era, in an ideal understanding it would incorporate early modernity (fifteenth–eighteenth centuries), including humanism, the Reformation, the Baroque period, and the Enlightenment. The founding principle of this period are the renouncement of a rigid scholastic tradition and the affirmation of self-determination in the light of reason. Visible external signs of this movement are the founding of numerous universities that express the empirical ideal of intellectual and scientific education as well as the establishment of the Philanthropinum school in Dessau in the year 1774, which finds its roots in French modernity, and is to be understood as the epitome for the imperative to perpetuate man's reason and the progress of science. Hence the achievement of felicity and perfection of man takes the first place.

In consequence to this anthropologization and its stark scientific tone, man now sees himself more in a rational and a matter-

26. Ludwig Feuerbach, "Grundsätze zur Philosophie der Zukunft," in *Feuerbach-Studienausgabe*, vol. 3, ed. Erich Thies (Frankfurt: Suhrkamp, 1975), 248 and 319.

of-fact way. As such he begins to view his own mortality in respect to his physiological determinants. It is in this refocusing that the health aspect of sport is given special attention, as sport advocates the perpetuation of health and the quality and span of man's life. In consideration of this, the study of the doctors of Ancient Greece and their health doctrines was revived. Especially the works of Hippocrates, Galen, and Celsius were newly interpreted, as all these ancient Greeks stated that proper, health-conscious behavior, diet, and physical hygiene were of fundamental importance for the prevention of and recovery from illness. These views included appropriate and substantial forms of exercise, games, and gymnastics.[27]

It is in this context that an especially critical eye was turned on inadequate gymnastics. The famous doctor Mercurialis plays an important role, as beginning in the year 1569 he wrote the six benchmark books *De Arte Gymnastica,* which achieved great effect.

An external sign of the rising interest for systematic health research in connection with physical ability and the possibilities of physical ability is the publication of numerous specialist and nonfiction books: from guides about swimming, equestrian skill, fencing, and wrestling to educational books that described the appropriate behavior of gentlemen and ladies (*galant homme*), which included physical-motor skills and qualities, especially dancing and playing "Jeu de Paume."[28]

There is also a development of modern sports "which include … aspects such as the determination of the winner of a competition according to specific rules which are rationally feasible and comprehensible similar to the tournaments held during the Middleages which were already strictly regulated. Bureaucratic institutions also developed as they were necessary for the undertaking

27. Krüger, *Einführung in die Geschichte,* vol. 1, 209.
28. Cf. ibid., 200.

of such events and in general the recognition of the merit principle also developed regarding physical exercise and competitions."[29]

The ideal—or better said, the guiding principle—for education of man was, at least during the Baroque period, the ideal of the *galant homme*, the gentleman who was understood as the harmony of body and mind. The men and ladies of court had to have a good intellectual and physical education and thus had to be in the true sense of the word fully "refined" if they sought to be acknowledged at court. All peasant qualities and mere physical accomplishments were considered coarse, unnatural, and contemptible, and thus one tried to distance oneself from them. The education was primarily practiced in schools exclusively for the nobility or princes, termed "knight-academies." The education in these schools chiefly targeted, alongside the intellectual advancement, the physical education "according to the ancient Greek model of educational doctrines which concentrated equal parts to intellectual and physical education. Therefore the daily timetable included numerous hours of gymnastics and game lessons. Exercises that were already practised by the knights in their training were utilised."[30]

Disregarding the differentiations needed to distinguish this period from the Enlightenment (for instance: Jean Jacques Rousseau gives preference to man in his natural state as opposed to the socially constructed), it becomes apparent that this new anthropological principle, while distancing man from God, consequently positions man at the center of focus. As man now perceives the world and himself from his own perspective, the truth that was once grounded in God is now grounded in man. In this way the sovereignty of reason is established. A self-conception of man that completely entrusts itself to the leadership of reason becomes possible, and through this, in turn, sport develops in a modern manner.

29. Ibid., 200.
30. Ibid., 208.

The Trans-anthropological Mindset

In the fourth model, which can be termed the trans-anthropological mindset and is perhaps the most intellectually challenging, man is concerned, after the disappearance of God, with the task of overcoming his own self. The characteristic anthropocentric man-world relationship has become obsolete and the world becomes the governing institution, a manifold interbranched, dendritic, and intertwined network constituting a vast web that is scarcely surveyed. This manner of relationship between man and the world can be described with the help of the image of the rhizome, of an underground rootstock, which was first coined by the French philosophers Gilles Deleuze and Felix Guattari. The rhizome does not posses a main root, but illustrates the multiple branched and intertwined root formation, the dispersed, meandrous, and labyrinth-like mode of thinking and understanding of the world that lacks a fixed center and an origin. "Principles of connection and heterogeneity: any point of a rhizome can be connected to anything other, and must be. This is very different from the tree or root, which plots a point, fixes an order."[31]

The process toward the trans-anthropological mindset was carried out step by step. Hence initially "the modern theory of man [lost] its centre of organisation" during the nineteenth century, as evidenced by Ernst Cassirer who observes: "In its stead stands an anarchy of different approaches ... theologians, scientists, politicians, sociologists, biologists, psychologists, ethnologists and economists—all these people deliberated the subject from their respective point of view. It was impossible to unite or affiliate these particular views and perspectives."[32]

31. Gilles Deleuze and Félix Guattari, *A Thousand Plateaus: Capitalism and Schizophrenia*, trans. Brian Massumi (London: Continium, 2004), 7.
32. Ernst Cassirer, *Versuch über den Menschen* (Hamburg: Felix Meiner, 1996), 144.

Friedrich Nietzsche had the "mad man" proclaim the death of God, thus verbalizing the factotum of the receding effect of Christian faith, eventually resulting in the "transcendental homelessness" as it is generally referred to by Georg Lukacs, leaving man radically thrown back on to himself, having lost any foothold or orientation. This is so colorfully put into words by the mad man: "Whither do we move? Away from all suns? Do we not dash unceasingly backwards, sideways, forwards in all directions? Is there still an above and below? Do we not stray, as through infinite nothingness? ... Does not empty space breathe upon us? Has it not become colder? Does not night come on continually, darker and darker?"[33]

Along with the loss of faith there is also a loss of traditional ties and tradition per se. The type of knowledge through which experiences of the past had been handed down from generation to generation begins to wane as well. Therefore, Walter Benjamin writes: "We have become impoverished. We have given up the heritage of mankind, one piece after the other; having often had to pawn it for a fraction of its worth, to gain a penny in advance for today."[34] The total sellout of human tradition reveals itself to be the sellout of the "enduring words that like a ring are passed from generation to generation."[35]

Sensation, rapid change, effectiveness, volatility, speed, and timeliness all now come to the fore. To the loss of faith and relation in the twentieth century, the loss of literary culture is accrued in the twenty-first century. In the course of transition from the Gutenberg-culture to an electromagnetic culture—which is representative for our century—technical images and a digital world emerge in lieu of

33. Friedrich Nietzsche, *Die fröhliche Wissenschaft*, vol. 3 of *Sämtliche Werke: Kritische Studienausgabe*, ed. Giorgio Colli and Mazzino Montinari (Berlin: Deutscher Taschenbuch Verlag, 1980), 481.
34. Walter Benjamin, "Erfahrung und Armut," in *Gesammelte Schriften*, vol. 2, pt. 1, ed. R. Tiedemann and H. Schweppenhäuse (Frankfurt: Akademie, 1977), 219.
35. Ibid, 214.

scriptures and books alike. Time and space unravel in this electro-magnetic culture: "In this new world, space and time are dissolved and the self is retained while immersed in a web that follows the currents of the universe."[36] If one is completely serious in under-standing the world as a digital, multiple dendritic network, the di-chotomy of texture, deep structure, syntax, and semantics become obsolete. What remains is the colorful texture of the technical im-ages, behind which—or rather underneath which—there is nothing anymore:

Hence the novelty of what is modern in our time is precisely characterised by the impossibility of relation and explanation. An explanation would entail forging relationships and giving reasons which would support that which is to be explained. But the novelty of what is modern in an electro-magnetic culture in which there is no deep structure and only superficial area, is ... precisely the absurdity of wanting to explain it. Enlightenment has expired and there is nothing new that remains to be explained. There is nothing mysterious in it, it is transparent as mesh. It has no depth.[37]

Let us now consider man, taking into account the rough con-touring of the intellectual–cultural situation in the trans-anthro-pological mindset. How does he react to this intellectual-cultural situation in the twenty-first century? How does he react to the stress that the trans-anthropological mindset has subjected man to? In other words: what will happen to man in trans-anthropo-centrism after having before placed all focus upon himself in the scientifically saturated anthropocentrism? Put plainly: after the death of God, the death of traditional relationships and knowl-edge acquired through experience, the loss of time and space, of values and the omnipresence of technical images, man has—in

36. Elizabeth Neswald, *Medien-Theologie: Das Werk Vilém Flussers* (Köln: Böh-lau Verlag 1998) 9.
37. Vilém Flusser, *Die Schrift. Hat Schreiben Zukunft?* 4th ed. (Göttingen: Im-matrix, 1992), 148.

a figurative sense—begun to kill himself. He has turned his back on himself, he has abandoned himself, and he is now endeavoring with every possible means—whether biotechnology, artificial intelligence, or media-theory research—to create something new and different: a trans-human. The envisaged trans-human differs fundamentally from given man, by which the "trans" not only implies an enhancement but also a novelty, a progression in quality. Two tendencies can be discerned within this mindset.

One of the tendencies endeavors to overcome man in favor of a trans-human meta-body. We can see here, in alignment with the ideal of youth and physical fitness, an extreme handling of the body that manifests itself in exaggerated forms of the fitness craze and the having-to-stay-active with all means possible. The alternative tendency strives to overcome man in favor of the trans-human meta-intellect. Here an extreme esteem is given to mental activity. It is in accordance with the liberation from physical ties or respectively the reduction to a minimal of their bothersome influence (perhaps in the shape of an intelligent machine, i.e., a spiritual machine with humanoid abilities). Both tendencies share the mutual interest of demolishing the physical constrictions and limitations of man to become, equitable to deification, unlimited, without horizon and immortal at last. In this context the athletic ideal of our time can be understood as the epitome of the realization of the trans-human meta-body. Aided by the media-staged mega-spectacles, he rises into the Olympus of mass communication as the abstract of superhuman grandeur, a godlike figure, a projection of a god. "No longer is the greatest footballer of our time (Diego Maradona) held responsible for a treacherous and game-deciding act of hand-play, but God himself is made responsible, by referring to the 'hand of God.'"[38] The athletic hero is under-

38. Gunter Gebauer, "Die Mythen-Maschine," in *Sportphilosophie,* ed. Volker Caysa (Leipzig: Reclam Verlag, 1997), 312.

stood not as an autonomous, responsible individual here, but as a person who, put in the words of Gebauer, is without "inner consistency, which would be necessary for making decisions and to anticipate the consequences of his own actions."

Consequently today's athletes adrenalize their bodies to achieve peak performances in the vortices of media power and myth machineries trying to comply with one of the preestablished myths.

One of the new elements [of our time] is that myths arise before the heroes do. In the old conception of heroes the events took place first. Then when the gun smoke had cleared the legends were spun. With the benefit of hindsight the event was declared to be (in the majority of cases by the victors) to have been an unheard-of occurrence. That was the time the pedestal was erected on which the hero took his place. The new formula reverses the traditional order: myth is the outset. The entire myth-machine is fashioning run of the mill legends. Mythical disguises are churned out in an assembly-line manner: instant-myths for disposable heroes with the life-span of a week-end in the German football-league.[39]

Thereby it is my impression that this new form of hero not only distinguishes himself by extraordinary performances but also can be characterized by a special quality to which in turn the spectators can behave in an either renunciative-dissociative or empathic-affirmative manner. Thus a cagey and distant idol now appears who can be approached by no one except the spectator himself—that is, at least in his dreams.

Conclusion

These exemplary approaches in the stated circles of thought may be attributed to specific periods; however, this would not take reality into consideration. These circles of thought overlap, coincide, and permeate one another even today. Naturally they call

39. Ibid., 304.

upon us to consider each of them separately, but also to contemplate them as a whole. To contemplate them as a whole is to apply to them a concept of man that is capable of integrating all these circles of thought. My proposal, which I unfortunately cannot elaborate on here, is that of interpreting man as one on a homeward journey and to clarify the particular possibilities and limitations of each mindset by a reciprocal contemplation considering the anthropological principle concept.[40] The omnipresence of sport today—and the media playing no small role in this—gives it top ranking in the construction of our culture. It is here that the system of values, and moreover the attitudes, spanning the entire spectrum of emotion, affections, and the intellect, crystallize. Sport is made into a form of medium, to be understood literally as a go-between and an intermediate between the particular and the diverse, between that which is personal and that which is public, between the solitary and the conjoint. Put into more concise words: sport thus becomes a medial space to which man and community relate and align themselves, since the modalities of molding the self are dependent on the range of available shapes, which are already present in a community. If therefore an individual pursues a sporting event in front of the television in his sitting room, he ultimately primarily pursues himself inasmuch as he is part and member of the sporting community, and he has been shaped and is still being shaped significantly by it.

Just as few people have the ability to pull themselves up by their own bootstraps, few are able to detach themselves from the sporting community. However, we are able to advocate for instance a specific conception or understanding of man. Let us recall the previously postulated principle: "The manner in which we see a person will be in accordance to the manner in which we behave

40. For a further analysis, see Karen Joisten, *Philosophie der Heimat—Heimat der Philosophie* (Berlin: Akademie Verlag, 2003).

toward a person and visa versa." And also let us recall the paraphrased version that has been worded to attenuate our cause more concisely: "The manner in which man sees and construes himself will be in accordance with the manner in which he treats himself and hence will be the manner in which he engages in sport." It is here that the two sides of the medal, that is, the idea of man and the accompanying side of ethical behavior, become apparent. In the conceptual design of an idea of man, man envisages an understanding of himself that always incorporates an ethical relevance. For in the realization of that which is man, man has, in a narrativeinterpreting manner, directed reality to a "vision" toward which he should actively strive. Hence this perspective becomes a type of mental outline, the horizon within which human existence and that which ought to be done are given their proper framework to prosper and develop.

These are the outlines we have to discuss. It is for these that we must give an account.

Pedro Barrajón, L.C.

2 Overcoming Dualism

The Unity of the Human Person in Sport

In addressing a group of professional soccer players, John Paul II took the occasion to underline the value of the body and its proper relation to the spiritual dimension of man:

It is good to recall, regarding this that already the Christian thinkers of the first centuries, with little biblical data, affirmed the unity of the human person, and vigorously opposed a certain ideology, then in vogue, that was characterized by a clear devaluation of the body, and misguided by an erroneous over exaltation of the spirit. "What is man—asked an author of the end of the 2nd century or beginning of the 3rd—what is man, is not a rational animal composed of a soul and of a body? The soul, then, taken by itself, is not then, a man? No, this is the soul of a man. Then is the body a man? No, but it must be said that this is the body of a man. Because of this, neither the soul, nor the body, on their own, is a man, but rather, he who we call by this name is that which is born from the union of these" [*De Resurrectione, VIII*, in Rouet de Journal, *Enchiridion Patristicum*, 59n147]. Thus, when the Christian thinker of this century, Emanuele Mounier, says that man is "a body in the same degree that he is spirit: entirely body and entirely spirit" [see E. Mounier, *Il Personalism*, Rome, 1971, 29] he is not saying anything new, but simply restating the traditional thought of the Church.[1]

As John Paul II points out, Mounier is restating the traditional thought of the Church, but this doctrine has often been overlooked and at times even compromised by either a tendency to value only the soul and what is spiritual in the human being, and want to have nothing to do with the body—and subsequently with sport— or the opposite tendency, that of reducing a person to the purely material being and subsequently neglecting his or her spiritual dimension. Yet, neither is it easy to simply maintain this balance between the two, and this holds especially true for the world of sport.

However, in his first encyclical, *Deus Caritas Est,* Pope Benedict XVI offers us a crucial anthropological principle:

Man is truly himself when his body and soul are intimately united; the challenge of eros can be said to be truly overcome when this unification is achieved. Should he aspire to be pure spirit and to reject the flesh as pertaining to his animal nature alone, then spirit and body would both lose their dignity. On the other hand, should he deny the spirit and consider matter, the body, as the only reality, he would likewise lose his greatness. The Epicure Gassendi used to offer Descartes the humorous greeting: "O Soul!" And Descartes would reply: "O Flesh!" Yet it is neither the spirit alone nor the body alone that loves: it is man, the person, a unified creature composed of body and soul, who loves. Only when both dimensions are truly united, does man attain his full stature. Only thus is love—eros— able to mature and attain its authentic grandeur."[2]

In this paragraph, which is found at the beginning of the Holy Father's encyclical on love, we find the anthropological key that we use to assist us in resolving the question regarding dualism that is

1. John Paul II, "Discorso ad atleti italiani ed argentine" [Speech to Italian and Argentine soccer players—authors translation] (May 25, 1979), in *Insegnamenti di Giovanni Paolo II,* vol. 2, pt. 1 (Vatican: LEV, 1980), 1216.
2. Benedict XVI, *Deus Caritas Est* (Vatican: LEV, 2006), 14.

put before us. To begin this task I will first recall what some great philosophers have said regarding this, namely Plato and Descartes, who were inclined toward the solution of anthropological dualism. Then I will explore two attempts, one philosophical (Arnold Gehlen) and the other theological (Hans Urs von Balthasar) to overcome in different ways this dualism. After this I will show how the doctrine of the Church, as grounded in biblical teaching, has always maintained a holistic and unitarian vision of the person. Lastly, taking advantage of the insights offered by John Paul II in his catechesis on human love, I will offer another perspective of resolving this theme of dualism with that which has been called the theology of the body.

Pope Benedict, with the above-quoted passage, presents a type of anthropological axiom: man as the task of becoming who he is. And this can be done only to the degree in which he finds a profound unity between body and soul. This unity, however, is full of tension, and not at all easy to reach. Yet it is a task that is always possible even though it is intrinsically difficult because, after original sin, the law of sin reigns in our members (Rom 7:23). The body tends toward the part of eros, while the spirit tends toward a unification that doesn't take into consideration the demands of the body. It comes head to head with the search for an arduous unity. This unity is sought after in what constitutes the goal and vocation of the human person: love. In fact, the unifying point within the person is love. Any anthropological theory that does not leave room for love, as that which formally makes up the person, will be marked by a great void; something will be missing. In fact, love is the door that opens to the mystery of the human person. Here, it is beneficial to recall the words of Pope John Paul II in his first encyclical, *Redemptor Hominis:* "Man cannot live without love. He remains a being that is incomprehensible for himself, his life is senseless, if love is not revealed to him, if he does not encounter love, if he does not experience it and make it his own, if he does not participate intimately in it."[3] The most personal act is that of love, of agape. But it is the person who realizes the action of love. The theme of the unity of the human person thus leads to the theme of the mystery of the person, which, in the Christian perspective, finds its origin in the divine and creative love and is called to participate in this eternal love in union with God and the saints.

Overcoming the Dualism of Plato and Descartes

The fundamental unity that we find in a human does not deny that he or she is also a dual being: "man is truly himself when his body and soul are intimately united."[4] It cannot be denied that the human person has two components; as Joseph De Finance says, man is "a citizen of two worlds":[5] "man is entirely spiritual and entirely natural; entirely animal and entirely rational."[6] Yet this intersecting of spirit and matter, this belonging of man to two worlds, has been underlined so much by some authors such as Plato and Descartes that man becomes an uncertain mixture of these two substances.

Plato was a dualist, but with clear monistic-spiritualistic tendencies in that he favors the value of the soul to the detriment of the body, which remains in the realm of the shadows, nearly vanishing altogether. For Plato, man's soul is, after the gods, the divinest thing and most truly his own.[7] The result of this is Plato's clear division of reality into two worlds, that of the visible world and that of the invisible, which is "the realm of the pure and everlasting"

3. John Paul II, *Redemptor Hominis* (Milano: Ancora, 1979), 20.

4. Benedict XVI, *Deus Caritas Est*, 14.

5. Joseph De Finance, *Citoyen de deux mondes: la place de l'homme dans la création* (Rome: Univerisità Gregoriana Editrice, 1980), 17.

6. Ibid., 18.

7. Plato, *Laws* (V, 726), in *The Collected Dialogues of Plato*, ed. Edith Hamilton and Huntington Cairns, 14th ed. (Princeton: Princeton University Press, 1989), 1314.

and "immortal and changeless"; the soul is the only human aspect that is capable of consorting with this realm of the absolute.[8] Its task is that of being recollecting in itself, in order to escape from the visible world so that it can live in the world that is truly proper to it, that of the invisible, where it finds itself truly at home. In this sense, the soul has for Plato a clear mediating function as it is that which is capable of putting the sensible world in communication with the world of ideas that are revealed to the soul. When the soul leaves itself, it becomes dispersed in the world; when it remains in itself, then it is free from the sensory and able to rise to the realm of the intelligible. Furthermore, the cosmic soul is the source of life and movement; it is unbegotten, incorruptible, and immortal. It is not moved by another but is moved by itself. This is also immanent to the movement of the cosmos, to which it confers perfect movement. This also gives a natural rhythm to all life and individual souls. This also calms the tension of the ideas by rendering them present in the sensible.

The individual soul is distinct from the body and belongs to the spiritual order. But, as it is in contact with the sensible world, it lives the drama of wanting to be freed from the insipid (*anous*) life in the body.

For Plato, the soul is capable of the bringing together these two worlds: it is in the soul where the body with its limits meets the unlimited world of intelligence. It is fixed between two worlds. The soul is at the very limit of life, creating a state of dispersion that the soul must put back into order. It is also at the very limit of knowledge, because knowing for Plato consists in the vision of the Idea.

The soul is the great protagonist of life on the individual and universal level. In Plato, the soul lives in a process of emanation

---

8. Plato, *Phaedo* (79d), in *The Collected Dialogues of Plato*, ed. Edith Hamilton and Huntington Cairns, 14th ed. (Princeton: Princeton University Press, 1989), 63.

(*aporroia*) and return (*epistrophe*). This downward movement process is necessary, and the soul, the ultimate substance after the One and the nous, interacts in an unintentional and random way. On the other hand, the movement of return is free and intentional: it is not controlled by the fateful process of necessity (*ananke*), but rather, is a bipolar process that moves between freedom and necessity.

Platonic dualism, then, is a spiritual dualism inasmuch as the balance clearly turns in favor of the soul. The body, on the other hand, is the "guard post of the soul,"[9] the "cage of the soul,"[10] or the "tomb of the soul."[11] In spite of these expressions, the Platonic vision of the body is not completely negative. Rather, it simply overvalues the soul to the point of leaving the body in the twilight zone.[12]

After Plato we find another great dualist philosopher in René Descartes. He sought to found his philosophy upon an infallible point, and his famous *cogito, ergo sum* provides him the foundation upon which to build a system of knowing that could not undergo any further critical doubts. But such a method as this creates clear division between the *res cogitans*, which is that which pertains to thought and to the soul, and the *res extensa*, which is that which pertains to all material reality, including the human body. The division between these two realities makes the body seem as a reality completely exterior to thought. Descartes's explanation is totally contrary to our modern day conception of the personal dimension of the body. In fact, he links the body to the soul by means of the pineal gland. The Cartesian perspective presents us,

---

9. Ibid. (62b), 45.
10. Ibid. (82e), 66.
11. Plato, *Gorgias* (493a), in *The Collected Dialogues of Plato*, ed. Edith Hamilton and Huntington Cairns, 14th ed. (Princeton: Princeton University Press, 1989), 275.
12. Cf. Pascal Haegel, *Le corps, quel défi pour la personne?* (Paris: Fayard, 1999), 401–5.

on the one hand, thought and consciousness and, on the other hand, a body that is like a corporeal machine. Certainly it is a wonderful machine, as it is made by God and possesses functions that other animals do not have, but in the ultimate analysis it is only a machine.

Cartesian dualism holds in high esteem the value of knowing of the *res cogitans* but only while reducing the body to a purely mechanical function, creating a slippery slope that can easily lead to either the depreciation of the body or a mechanical vision of reality, where others who come after Descartes will deny the spiritual nature of consciousness.

The Cartesian philosophy that follows, which has had a notable influence in the philosophical approach in the West—and above all in Europe—places the unity of man and its consequent attempts to overcome this dualism at the very center of the anthropological debate. The efforts to overcome this dualism are numerous. As previously mentioned, I will deal only with the efforts of Arnold Gehlen, who is not completely successful in arriving at a perfect synthesis of that which is spiritual and that which is material in the human person. Afterward, I will present the more theological perspective of Hans Urs von Balthasar.

The Philosophical-Anthropobiological Attempt of Arnold Gehlen

The philosophy of Arnold Gehlen could be placed within what is commonly called today: anthropobiology, which seeks to study man on the basis of scientific data provided by biology, which in turn is reflected upon philosophically. It concerns, we could say, a vision of man constructed from below (from base to vertex). All of these anthropobiologies unanimously show, contrary to those who today uphold the so-called animalism, that the position of the human being in the world is unique and singular.

Helmuth Plessner is considered one of the founders of anthropobiology. He has shown how human biology reveals a typically human characteristic that he called "eccentric." Man is the only animal capable of turning inward upon himself by means of the actions of his intelligence and will, and of having an objective knowledge of reality, of having self-dominion over his actions, of suspending instinctive action.

On the basis of some of Plessner's findings, Gehlen elaborates "one of the broadest attempts in the 20th century to constructing a philosophical anthropology characterized by the mutual implications of body and soul in the being and actions of the human person."[13] According to Gehlen, man is a being "who is missing something," someone unfinished (*Mängelwesen*). He lacks biological specialization (*Unspezialisiertheit*). Man is also missing some basic instincts that other animals have. The human being is a being without instincts (*Instinktlos*), or at least with a strong reduction in instinct. This instinct reduction is in itself very dangerous: "it is a miracle that the human is not extinct." The question that rises then is how is it that this atypical animal is placed above the rest, when the logical consequence of the instinct should be the loss of the species? In fact, man does not possess super-specialized organs. If anything, he is a premature mammal according, to the expression of Portmann. While most animals have need of a few days in order to activate their kinetic system, man has need of at least three years. But, in contrast to other animals, a child will have a range of movement much more extensive after these three years. Moreover, human organs are "geologically" more ancient. The distinguishing bodily characteristics that are specifically human are as in the fetal state that are transformed into a permanent state. In this sense, man is a "super-embryonic" animal.

13. Leopold Prieto, "El hombre, el animal y la antropología," *Ecclesia* 19, no. 1 (2005): 56.

There exists an essential difference between a human being and an animal. An animal remains totally indifferent before that which does not stimulate it. Nor does an animal perform noninstinctive actions, that is, actions that are merely expressive or communicative. The animal cannot go against its instinct; but man can. Human impulses are not periodic like those of an animal. For Gehlen, the differences between man and animal are presented not only at the level of intelligence, but also at a biological level: anatomy, sensory motor apparatus, sense physiology, and pulse mechanisms. In contrast to animals, there exists in the human person a type of hiatus between impulse and action. A human does not automatically give in to impulse. In fact, he or she can even go against an impulse, which is a biological coup d'etat.

In searching for an answer to what is the specific difference between man and animal, Gehlen does not have recourse to the presence of a spirit, but prefers to uphold that it is precisely this lack of instinct that opens the way to this new mode of existence. As such, man must face his life as a task that lies before him. The lack of instinct helps man to regulate his life, by giving it an overload of information that he must process and simplify. He does this by establishing institutions, a culture, a morality that are capable of organizing human life. This lack of instinct thus gives man the opportunity to "complete" himself, and to open himself up to a world that is no longer limited to that of an animal. Whereas an animal is not conscious of the existence of an entire world but only a part of this, man's environment is the entire world. For the squirrel there exist the ants that crawl up the tree; for man there also exist the mountains far off in the distance, the sun and the stars … things that seem superfluous to him from a biological point of view.

Since man's instincts are precarious, his life is easily filled with tensions that cause him to have recourse to his intelligence and to create social institutions that render his existence more stable.

Man's capacity for inward reflection (his capacity for imagination, thought, and language) is a question of survival if man is to reach a status of harmony in life. A particular form of using his intelligence is language, which enables man to adapt himself to reality, overcome his impulses, and be in control of situations with a minimal effort.

Arnold Gehlen, along with the other anthropobiological attempts, seeks to understand the depths of human nature and a human's unity through the study of biological data. His findings catch a glimpse of some of the spiritual elements of man, but the unity that is sought is too biological, and the true emergence of the spirit is not evident.[14]

The Theological Attempt of Hans Urs von Balthasar to Overcome Dualism

One theologian who has sought to resolve the dualism present in man is Hans Urs von Balthasar. In addition to the body-spirit dualism, he identifies two other dualisms: that of male-female and that of individual-group.[15] These tensions are rooted in the fundamental fact that man is in the image of God, and moreover, in the image of the Trinity. Before Balthasar, the philosopher Enrich Przywara had already pointed out this is part and parcel of the enigmatic and mysterious character of the human being. Balthasar observes that in all three dimensions "man seems to be built according to a polarity, obliged to engage in reciprocity, always seeking complementarity and peace in the other pole. And for that very reason he is pointed beyond his polar structure."[16]

These three fundamental tensions are preceded by one still

14. Arnold Gehlen, *Der Mensch. Seine Natur und seine Stellung in der Welt* (Wiesbaden: Aula, 1986), 146.

15. Cf. Babini Ellero, *L'antropologia teologica di Hans Urs von Balthasar* (Milan: Jaca Book, 1988).

16. Hans Urs von Balthasar, *Theo Drama: Theological Dramatic Theory: The Dramatis Personae Man in God* (San Francisco: Ignatius Press, 1990), 2:355.

more basic: the tension between man's worldliness and his super-worldliness. In fact, it is specifically within this worldly dimension of man where there emerges in a certain sense his super-worldliness. Balthasar frequently expresses this fundamental tension with the figure of the Centaur and the Sphinx, mythical animals that are depicted with certain traits that manifest a superiority above their animal nature. This situation reveals that the human being is "more" of a being than an animal because he is found beyond that which can be contained in a purely conceptual affirmation. For man, finding this unity is made all the more difficult as much as his life is played out in a realm that Balthasar calls "dramatic." Man lives in a movement that begins with a first original act and continues in a progression toward the final act. This drama is played out on a stage—that of the world and of history. Because human life is a continual action and always in movement, a static description of this situation, that which is essentialist, is not possible; life is a drama. Only in the final act will this rupture, the fragmentation and the split that afflicts man, be definitively overcome. Additionally, in this drama, man is not the sole actor (God enters the scene with the mystery of the Incarnation), but rather a co-actor (*Mitspieler*).

After this basic tension, come the other three tensions. We will reflect on the first, that tension between spirit and body. On the one hand, man contains in himself all the other kingdoms (mineral, vegetable, and animal) that precede him in the hierarchy of being, so to speak. But on the other hand, although man is profoundly united to these kingdoms, at the same time, he keeps a certain distance and transcends them. As Balthasar notes, "the spirit needs the physical-spiritual infrastructure (although, nonetheless it transcends it) in order to perform its specific operation, reflection."[17] Man remains immersed in the material, but at the

---

17. Hans Ur von Balthasar, *Theo Drama: Theological Dramatic Theory: The Dramatis Personae Man in God*, vol. 2 (San Francisco: Ignatius Press, 1990), 359.

same time he seems like a stranger to it as he longs for a world that was initially lost. Balthasar, following the line of thought of ancient philosophy, especially that of Neoplatonism, sees in this soul-body dualism something positive inasmuch as it is a sign of man's transcendence over the world, his domination of it. However, with the Pauline teaching, he admits that this dualism becomes dramatic because it implies a contest between "flesh" and "spirit" (cf. Rom 7), which is a reflection of the drama of human misery. In this world the human person must walk on the "frontier" but as often happens this frontier can become a no-man's-land.

This situation of being on the frontier burdens man with the task of realizing himself in two different movements: a descending movement that entails an ongoing incarnation of that which is spiritual and an ascending movement that entails a growing dominion of the spirit over the sensual nature. These two movements create a dynamic synthesis that is also at times "dramatic." In Balthasar's synthesis, balance is achieved through recourse to a conception of man as created in the image of God, which is the original image of God (*Urbild*), which avoids this descending movement being a fall (as some Gnostic philosophies and theologies uphold) or a complete abandonment of the sensible world for a false spiritualization. In this double movement (from matter to spirit and vice versa) there remains unresolved the enigma of death, which can be given a satisfactory resolution only in Christ.[18]

Only Christ is capable of resolving these difficulties of this first tension as well as the other two (man-woman and individual-group). In this sense, Christ accomplishes for man a personalizing function. It is he who makes possible for man the transition from a spiritual subject to a person. In fact, Balthasar notes that the spiritual subject knows that he shares in a human nature that is

18. Ibid., 2:364.

identical in all individuals, but "they do so in a way that, in each instance, is unique and incommunicable,"[19] even if he does not know exactly who he is. This can come to be known only through a gratuitous communication and revelation that will come from the Absolute. In this sense, only he who created man can reveal to man his personal identity and can make possible the passage from the spiritual subject—within which this above-mentioned polarity consists—to that of the person. God's call to man renders him a person, conferring on him the profound understanding not only of his own identity but also that of his own mission.

"In Christ, however, every man can cherish the hope of receiving personhood from God, becoming person, with a mission that is likewise defined in Christ."[20] Christ can accomplish this "personalizing mission" in man because he is "the unique, singular, archetypical case in which there is a full identity between the subject and his mission."[21] In Balthasar, as in a majority of other contemporary theologians, anthropology takes its starting point in Christology: Christ fully reveals man to man.[22] The personalization wrought in Christ entails also a "socialization" inasmuch as the person is inserted into his Body, the Church. To become a person, a participant in communion with God, is also at the same time to live the mystery of communion to the greatest degree. *Homo christianus* is *homo ecclesiasticus*, and this happens by means of the greatest possible individualization, which is the greatest and most genuine expression of his proper identity. Openness to the communion offered in Christ implies also openness to the greatest pos-

19. Cf. ibid., 3:204.

20. Ibid., 3:220.

21. Ellero, *L'antropologia teologica di Hans Urs von Balthasar,* 178.

22. Vatican Council II, "Pastoral Constitution on the Church in the Modern World: Gaudium et Spes," in *Vatican Council II: The Conciliar and Post Conciliar Documents,* vol. 1. 1988 rev. ed., ed. Austin Flannery (Dublin: Dominican Publications, 1988), 922.

sible singularness and uniqueness. Balthasar sees this as being realized in the great figures that accompany Christ, such as Peter and Paul, James and John, and above all, in Mary. It is also seen in the figure of the saints, who, with their strong personalities and theological uniqueness, were all creators of points of communion and freedom within the Church.

Balthasar sees the victory over anthropological dualism in the process of personalization that God works in man through Jesus Christ. The spiritual subject must integrate in a dynamic and dramatic way the weight of the material that he carries in himself, and he can free himself from these tensions only by inserting himself in Christ through grace. Only in him is a personalization realized that is capable not only of resolving in a dramatic way these different tensions, but also of showing the true identity of man and the call that God makes to him through the revelation of a mission and through this openness to communion with God and with others.

Corpore et Anima Unus

Having presented two attempts at a unified or integral anthropology, I deem it useful to now briefly consider the biblical and magisterial teachings in order to show how the Church has always given key importance to the theme of the unity of man and consequently the overcoming of dualism.

This important Christological reflection came in the first centuries of the Christian era, because if Christ was, as upheld by faith, true man, it was not only useful but absolutely necessary to know in the best possible way human nature and its most profound identity. A noteworthy synthesis of the longstanding magisterium about this can be found in number 14 of *Gaudium et Spes*, where it affirms: "Though made of body and soul, man is one. Through his bodily composition he gathers to himself the elements of the material world; thus they reach their crown through him." The Latin words used at the beginning of this phase are very precise, "corpore et anima unus," and speak clearly of the fundamental unity of the human being while still being made up of dual components. Duality (of components) but not dualism. In this sense, duality simply recognizes that man is the convergence of corporal (material) elements and others that are spiritual. The negation of any duality ends in reductionism: material reductionism when it denies the spirit; spiritual reductionism when the value of the body is negated. Maintaining the equilibrium of this unity in diversity is not easy, but it is the only path to take in order to arrive at an integral understanding of the human person.

The unity of man is a fundamental biblical assertion. The clear unifying anthropology of the Old and New Testaments is a indisputable biblical reality. "Research of the Old Testament and of the history of religions characterize Hebrew thought as predominantly synthetic and unitary (holistic)."[23] It is clear that "man is not the object in the Old Testament of an abstract, essential, or generic definition as those coined by philosophical tradition."[24] The analysis of the various terms to indicate man in the Old Testament (*nefes, ruah, basar*) shows that they always refer to the entire man in his totality, even though each term can add a specific nuance in a certain context. The same can be said for the anthropology of the New Testament. While the text uses multiple terms to indicate the human person (*psyche, pnuema, sarx, soma*), he or she is always an indivisible whole; the body-soul opposition does not exist except as they are the integrating elements of an anterior unity.

This fundamentally holistic conception that accepts the duality or plurality of components was threatened by certain currents

23. Johann Metz and Francis Fiorenza, "El hombre como unidad de alma y cuerpo," in *Mysterium Salutis*, vol. 4, ed. J. Feiner and M. Löhrer (Madrid: Ed. Cristianidad, 1970), 666.
24. José L. Ruiz de la Pena, *Imagen del hombre. Antropologia teologica fundamental* (Santander, Spain: Sal Térrea, 1988), 25.

in thought such as Gnosticism. Before these, the Church reacted vigorously by reappraising the value of the body as locus of salvation in continuity with the theology of St. John and St. Paul. Some writers of the first centuries, such as St. Irenaeus, heartily underlined this unity. For Irenaeus, "the entire man, neither only the spirit, nor only the flesh, is in the image of God and man and his world advance towards their recapitulation in Christ."[25] However, there have been epochs in which the value of the soul was highlighted to the point that the value of the body appears to have been completely forgotten. This uncertainty was finally resolved during the Council of Vienna, where the Thomistic doctrine was accepted affirming that the rational soul is truly and essentially per se the form of the human body. This was upheld against those, such as Peter Olivi, who maintained that the plurality of the substantial forms in man was equivalent to the loss of his fundamental unity in his identity.

The Council of Vienna had come to make its own the thesis of St. Thomas Aquinas that stated that the soul was the singular form of the body (*unica forma corporis*).[26] This formula expresses in a clear way the radical unity of man while not denying a plurality of dimensions. Karl Rahner, commenting on this formula, affirms that in the Thomistic position, man "is not composed of body and soul but of a soul and 'prime matter' that is to be understood as a substructure from which all the soul's full potential for substantial self-realization—that is to say, its metaphysical information—is dispensed in reality according to the passive possibilities inherent in the prime matter, thus communicating to reality that which is the soul itself."[27] This means that soul and body are not two sepa-

25. J. Metz and F. Fiorenza, "El hombre como unidad de alma y cuerpo," 682–83.

26. Thomas Aquinas, *Summa Theologica*, vol. 1 (pt. I, Q. 76, ad 1, 3), trans. and ed. Dominican Fathers of the English Province (New York: Benzinger, 1947), 372.

27. Karl Rahner, "Para un teologia del simbolo," in *Escritos de Teologia*, vol. 4, ed. J. Feiner et al. (Madrid: Taurus Ediciones, 1964), 302.

rate substances that unite in an artificial way, but rather, there exists a fundamental unity that is "entirely soul and entirely body at the same time, in such a way that that which is affirmed for the soul and that which is affirmed for the body can be predicated for the entire human being."[28] For St. Thomas, soul and body are two metaphysical principles that give life to the original unity of man in such a way that every human activity is *operatio totius hominis*.[29] In the teachings of St. Thomas, "it is for the soul's good that it was united to a body";[30] the body is not the prison of the soul, nor its mere instrument, nor a consequence of original sin. In order to know reality, man must use his body (the senses). Human corporality is not that which necessarily opposes the soul. On the contrary, this corporality is that which situates man into history and makes him a member of the human race, and capable of opening up to others. Because of this, "corporality plays a very important role in the theology of St. Thomas Aquinas where the incarnation of grace is an essential element in the redemption of man and the dispensation of this redemption."[31]

The inheritance of this Thomistic doctrine, which makes a philosophical and theological system out of this biblical teaching, has been welcomed into the doctrine of the Church as that which sustains the unity of the human person, created in the image of God, "a being at once corporeal and spiritual."[32]

---

28. Johann Metz, "Seele," in *Lexikon fur Teologie und Kirche*, vol. 9, ed. Michael Buchberger (Freiburg: Herder, 1964), 570.

29. Thomas Aquinas, *Tertium Sententiarum Librum*, vol. III (D.31, q.2, a.4), in *Thomae Aquinatis Iuxta Editionem*, ed. Joannis Francisci Bernardi de Rubeis (Madrid: Tipographia Viduae Elisaei Sanchez, 1769), 350.

30. Aquinas, *Summa Theologica* (pt. I, Q. 89, 1c), 453.

31. Metz and Fiorenza, "El hombre como unidad de alma y cuerpo," 691. Regarding this theme in St. Thomas, see also Nicola Pende and Raimondo Spiazzi, *Unità e grandezza dell'uomo* (Brescia, Italy: Morcelliana, 1956).

32. *Catechism of the Catholic Church*, no. 362, pocket ed. (London: Geoffrey Chapman, 1994), 88.

Recognizing a Unity of Identity in the Gift of Self

To finish, I would like to make reference to the rich magisterium of John Paul II regarding this theme. In his famous catechism on human love, he sought to offer a fitting anthropology on the basis of a biblical analysis united to the phenomenological method.

In the first cycle of his catechetical teaching, the focus was on the original moment of creation of man and woman in order to have a clear understanding of what constitutes "human identity." The result of this was the elaboration of a theology of the body and an integral vision of the human person, seeking to grasp not only a part of the human person, but rather the *integrum humanum*. Within the complex reality that is the human being, it is the essential unity that is being sought—what constitutes the very essence of the human person—in spite of its diversity and complexity.

John Paul II provides a twofold analysis of the definition of man as based on the first two chapters of Genesis: the objective one of the first chapter and the more subjective one of the second chapter. After discovering his original solitude, which enables him to also realize that he is the subject of a covenant and partner with the Absolute, as well as "a body among other bodies," the first man then finds himself in front of a woman, the first human "you," This encounter reveals to man his identity as image of God, but with the added peculiarity of being an image that is in the communion of persons. He is essentially the image of an indescribable divine communion of persons. The encounter of the human "you" with the divine "you" reveals to man his call to partake of this vertical communion with God and this horizontal communion with the other. This call to communion is recognized in the very body of the other. In fact, it is the body that reveals the person and this profound vocation to communion.

If the body reveals the person, this means that the body that is discovered in the other (and in some way also in oneself) is perceived as an animated body and as the body of a person. The encounter with the other manifests the call to communion that is made efficacious with the sincere gift of oneself. The act of giving oneself is an integral gift, that is to say, it is of both body and soul, of the person. The gift would not be true if it were to hold back one of these components that constitute the integrity of the human person. Man perceives this call to communion as a call to give himself or herself as a sincere gift, and this gift, if it is sincere, must comprise the entire person, in his or her integrity. In this way, the human person understands himself to be unitary being, image of God, who lives his vocation in communion with, and in imitation of, the same Trinitarian God who is infinite and perfect communion.

In this sense, the exchange of the gift of self, made in marriage, is a privileged moment to recognize oneself as a personal being, profoundly united. In this exchange of gifts, the other is accepted as he or she is, in all of their masculinity and femininity, as a personal, bodily, spiritual, integral, whole. Anything contrary to such an acceptance would signify the privation of the gift or the reduction of the other to a mere object. The giving of oneself is also the accepting of the other in such a way that the act of giving becomes the act of accepting and the accepting is transformed into a gift. This giving and receiving is present in Genesis 2:23–25, where God gives the woman to man and man accepts this. The woman, in turn, gives herself, and her self-recognition is fulfilled in this act of giving herself and accepting the gift of himself that the man offers her in return. In the moment in which she is accepted by the man as the Creator willed, she rediscovers herself. Precisely because she accepts the gift and her gift is likewise accepted by man, the dignity of their self-giving is secured; she offers all of herself in all of her personal reality—and all of her femininity—and in doing so she "reaches the intimate depths of her person and the full possession of herself."[33] This discovering of oneself fuels further self-giving and becomes a fountain of a new gift of self. In this way, the woman is entrusted to the man, to his eyes, to his conscience, to his heart. In turn, he must secure in the process of this exchange of gifts a reciprocal sharing of the giving and receiving of the gift of self, which creates in this way a communion of persons.

By receiving the acceptance from the woman, the man enriches himself and is enriched by her; he is enriched by means of her gift, but also by the fact that he also becomes a gift for her. In doing so, he is exalted, so to speak, in his humanity and achieves a greater depth of self-possession (dominion). He gives himself, but at the same time he receives the gift of the woman, and the woman accepts his gift. Both discover themselves in the other in the sincere giving of themselves. The giving of oneself to the other does not result in the loss of self, but rather in the discovering of oneself, and in personal happiness, which is all the more inasmuch as it is the happiness of the other, and thus a happiness that is shared. In this communion of persons, both grow in such a way as to be able to give of themselves anew with greater depth and sincerity.

This analysis of the exchange of the gift of self speaks of a total gift, of body and soul: it is a gift of the person. It is the person in fact who is given and received—the human being in his or her integrity who is given and received. The dualistic tension between body and soul is resolved in the degree in which this tension is overcome in the unity of the person. Thus a further deepening in the understanding of the theme of the person is of great value in order to grasp man's essence from a philosophical and theological point of view.

We can know make a short summary of our thoughts before

33. John Paul II, "Wednesday General Audience" (February 6, 1980), *L'Osservatore Romano* weekly English ed., February 11, 1980, 1.

concluding. We began with an analysis of the dualist temptation, which has been a recurring temptation throughout the history of thought and predominant in some of the great philosophical systems, such as those of Plato and Descartes. After that we considered some attempts to overcome this dualism. One attempt, which came from philosophy—that of the anthropobiology of A. Gehlen—gave us some valuable elements to better understand from the point of view of biology and philosophy the peculiar nature of the human person but left much to be desired in its inability to account for the spiritual component. Another attempt was theological—the thought of Han Urs von Balthasar, who maintained that in order to overcome the tensions that are created by the bipolarities found in man (body-spirit; man-woman; individual-group) it is necessary to refer to the personalization that God works in Jesus Christ, in which the spiritual subject is capable of becoming a person.

We also recalled how the biblical conception of the unity of the human person is grounded in the Bible and has been supported by the magisterium, in particular at the Council of Vienna (1312), which accepted the Thomistic thesis of the soul as the unique form of the body. This thesis comes to us today in the well-formulated phrase "corpore et anima unus," as expressed in *Gaudium et Spes* and in the *Catechism of the Catholic Church.*

Lastly, we have pointed out the originality of the effort of John Paul II of presenting a unified anthropology through the theological analysis of Scripture, namely those passages that speak of the beginning of creation, before the fall, where there clearly emerged the call to communion of persons of man and woman. This communion is realized by the exchange of the gift of self, where each person becomes aware of his or her own personal identity and that of the other, manifesting the profound unity of the person and the call to live their vocation of communion in both the vertical and horizontal sense.

There are other ways of overcoming this dualism. However, the unifying vision that is forwarded by Christian anthropology is an undisputed theological acquisition upon which must rest further anthropological reflections such as those that regard human activities among which is that of sport.

We turn again to those words of Pope Benedict XVI with which we began our reflection: "Man is truly himself when his body and soul are intimately united." We found this profound unity of soul and body in the person, image of God, and called in Christ to live in communion with him. Because the action par excellence of the person is the act of love, love is consequently, as an action of the person, the unifying act of the human being and that which manifests to all that his being is an image of the God who is love.

In a parallel way, we can conclude that man is truly himself in sport when both body and soul are united. "Body, spirit and soul form a single unity and each component must be in harmony with the other," stated Pope Benedict in an audience with the Austrian Olympic ski team. He went on to say: "You know how necessary this interior harmony is in order to reach sporting goals at the highest levels. Consequently, even the most demanding sports must be rooted in a holistic view of the human person, recognizing his profound dignity and favouring an overall development and full maturity of the person."[34]

34. Benedict XVI, "Non siate solo competitori sportive..." [Be not only competitive athletes...] (October 6, 2007), *L'Osservatore Romano*, Italian ed., no. 41, October 12, 2007, 4.

Christoph Hübenthal

3 Morality and Beauty

Sport at the Service of the Human Person

The subtitle of this chapter, "sport at the service of the human person," may provoke the question as to why sport should have "to serve" the person. Ought not all of our activities serve the maintenance, the promotion, and the perfection of the human person? And if they don't, aren't they—almost by definition—inhuman patterns of behavior that should strictly be disapproved of? Every type of human practice must serve the person, and sport should not be an exception. Hence, the moral demand hidden in the subtitle of this paper seems to be rather trivial and doesn't seem to require further discussion.

But perhaps it is not the normative question that is at stake here, but rather the empirical one: "How is this to be achieved?" In responding to this question, we usually point to the multiple functions of sport, for example the role it plays in the preservation and restitution of physical health, its recreational value, its educational function, its contribution to the social integration of marginalized groups, its importance to the cultivation of team spirit or fairness, its role in promoting a good understanding among nations and in overcoming cultural differences, or its role in instilling a sense of discipline, and even its ascetic effects. Such individual and social functions usually will be mentioned when we want to indicate how sport can be of service to mankind.

However, we should be careful, since for many (if not for all) of these, functional equivalents can be found. That is to say, other means exist that serve the same purpose, possibly in a much better way than sport ever does. For instance, if I wish to remain healthy, a good nutritional diet and regular visits to a doctor can be enough. Peace in the world will, if at all, be achieved by political means rather than by great sporting events. Discipline and asceticism are also characteristics of the life of an artist, scientist, or monk. So, in terms of its functions sport may be interchangeable with other activities.

There is another important point to be mentioned here. The functioning of an activity is always determined in relation to a given purpose. Purposes, however, can often become dubious or even highly problematic. In sport this is also the case. History shows us that it has often been used for political, military, or economic purposes and frequently appears to be an expression of mere self-interest or even inhuman ideologies. To insist that sport is at the service of the human being simply by fulfilling certain functions is not to realize that each human activity can be manipulated and misused even for the most horrible goals. In talking about the functions of sport in a responsible fashion, it is important to ask the questions, who stands to gain from the performance of sport and why?

Since the question "how can sport serve mankind?" apparently cannot be answered by simply pointing at its functions, once more we encounter a normative problem. An appropriate solution to it obviously requires convincing standards by which we can evaluate the different purposes of sports. To find such standards, we are to select from two different approaches, that is, a religious or an anthropological one. The first starts from a religious (or ideological) idea about the essence and destiny of the human being. Subsequently, this image of man can serve for rather unambiguous criteria that help to determine whether or not a certain practice corresponds with the assumed human essence. If, for instance, someone opts for a Christian point of view, she believes that the human being is equipped with an unalienable dignity since it is created in the image and likeness of God.[1] Therefore, each activity that violates or harms human dignity is to be disapproved of. Whenever, on the contrary, human dignity is given an appropriate expression, the practices in question will be warmly endorsed from the Christian point of view. By use of the powers of discernment, then, these criteria easily can be applied to all kinds of sports activities.

On the other hand, as we said, one can make use of an anthropological approach. In this case, one doesn't start from a certain image of man, but tries to acquire some general knowledge about the human being by careful observation and reflection. If such knowledge, at least in part, turns out to be normatively substantial, one is provided with sound criteria to judge human behavior. Of course, such an approach requires some advance knowledge, since one must have, at least, an initial idea of what is worth observing or reflecting on in order to achieve the intended results. Yet, this approach is characterized by a greater independence than any ideological or religious bias. This is exactly the reason why its outcome should ideally be communicable across all cultural or religious boundaries.

In what follows, this second, anthropological approach will be developed. This, however, is not because I would assume that from a Christian point of view nothing sensible can be said about sports. On the contrary! According to the old maxim *gratia supponit naturam et perficit eam,* the initial independent anthropologi-

1. See Gn 1:26.

cal analysis can, afterward, shed a much brighter light on the universal validity of the Christian vision than a theological approach (that begins with a strong claim on the general human relevance of the Christian perspective) could ever do. To put it bluntly, only the anthropological approach can demonstrate the unconditionality of the question that the human being is to herself and to which the Christian message wants to give an appropriate answer.[2] The anthropological approach therefore has to fulfill a subsidiary function for the developing of a Christian vision of sports.

Preliminary Anthropological Considerations

We must start our anthropological considerations with a brief historical reckoning. During the first half of the nineteenth century, the philosophy of mind had reached an intellectual level that was hardly known before. Remember, for instance, German Idealism and names like Johann Gottlieb Fichte, Friedrich Wilhelm Joseph Schelling, and Georg Wilhelm Friedrich Hegel. From the middle of the century, the natural sciences underwent a comparable development. Charles Darwin, Marie Curie, Ernst Koch, Wilhelm Conrad Röntgen, and Max Planck are just a few of the celebrated researchers of this period. The immense progress made by the humanities and the natural sciences by the end of the nineteenth century compounded the difficulty of answering a question that, one hundred years ago, Kant already had declared to be the top of all "world-philosophical questioning," that is, the question "What is man?"[3]

To answer this question at the beginning of the twentieth century, one had obviously to combine a complex amount of philo-

2. Thomas Pröpper, *Evangelium und freie Vernunft: Konturen einer theologischen Hermeneutik* (Freiburg: Herder, 2001), 22. "If there were not this unconditionedness inside the human being, and if this unconditionedness would not be actualized, God couldn't have unconditional concern for human beings."

3. Immanuel Kant, *Logik*, in *Werke in sechs Bänden*, vol. 3, ed. W. Weischedel (Darmstadt: Wissenschaftliche Buchgesellschaft, 1983), A 24–25.

sophical and scientific knowledge. That's why Max Scheler stated: "The growing number of specialized disciplines dealing with the human person, even though they may be valuable, rather hides the essence of man than enlightens it."[4] In such a situation anyone who raised the question apparently had to overcome all the disciplinary specializations once again and closely relate philosophical with scientific knowledge. By doing so, one hoped eventually to solve a problem that Descartes had considered and that even Kant had been unable to resolve: the problem of how to explain the anthropological double aspect of corporality and inwardness in just one and only one theoretical framework. It was philosophical anthropology that was entrusted with that task. Helmuth Plessner put it like this: "The important thing is not to overcome this double-aspect since it is an (undeniable) phenomenon. The important thing is rather to eliminate the fundamentalization of this double-aspect and to invalidate it as a principle which splits the scholarly endeavour into natural sciences, i. e. measurement, and the humanities, i. e. analyzing oneself."[5]

From that moment on, it was the famous philosophical-anthropological approaches that narrated with great emphasis man as a sensuous and spiritual being that, on the one hand, is imbedded in its natural environment and, on the other, nevertheless is keeping a peculiar distance to its psycho-physical network of conditions. "World-eccentric nucleus of being,"[6] "anthropological gap,"[7] "eccentric positionality,"[8] and "anthropological difference"[9] are just some of the famous ciphers that indicated the refracted indirect-

4. Scheler, *Man's Place in Nature*, 9.

5. Helmuth Plessner, *Die Stufen des Organischen und der Mensch. Einleitung in die philosophische Anthropologie*, vol. 4 (Frankfurt: Gruyter, 1981), 115.

6. Scheler, *Man's Place in Nature*, 61.

7. Michael Landmann, *Fundamental-Anthropologie* (Bonn: Bouvier, 1979), 78.

8. Plessner, *Die Stufen des Organischen und der Mensch*, 360.

9. Demmer Kamper, *Geschichte und menschliche Natur: Die Tragweite der gegenwärtigen Anthropologiekritik* (Munich: Hanser, 1973), 26, 45.

ness distinguishing the human existence from a mere instinctive conduct of life. Not least, these formulas were able to express that man is a spiritual-physical unity that can maintain a reflexive relationship to himself, since he has not simply to take over this unity but actively must give shape to it. Even the most different schools agreed that it was this anthropological difference that also formed the mysterious origin of all cultural achievements. Michael Landmann, for instance, stated: "Both the ability of cultural achieving and the ability of cultural receiving enter a gap by which, in contrast to the animals, the human being seemingly is characterized due to the non-specialization of its organs and the reduction of its instincts."[10] Plessner, once again, brought it to the point: "The eccentric form of life and the need for supplementation are the very same fact.... In this neediness or nakedness lies the motive for every specific human (i.e. pursuing the unreal and working with artificial means) activity, lies the ultimate ground for the tool and what it serves for: culture."[11]

So it is the eccentricity of human life to which we owe every cultural achievement. Thereby we also understand why we had to recall the founding period of philosophical anthropology. After the revolutionary progress and gradual separation of the humanities and the natural sciences in the nineteenth century, the need for an integral view of the human being was more urgent than ever. Philosophical anthropology solved this problem by conceptualizing the human being as a unity of body and soul that, at the same time, was characterized by a mysterious anthropological difference, that is, the undeniable doubling of that which is predetermined in man (*Vorgegebenheit*) and that which man must realize by his own free will (*Aufgegebenheit*). According to the decisive statement of the

10. Landmann, *Fundamental-Anthropologie*, 78.
11. Plessner, *Die Stufen des Organischen und der Mensch*, 383.

young philosophical discipline, it is precisely this difference that is at the origin of every cultural achievement.

The Anthropology of Sports

What conclusions may be drawn from these preliminary anthropological considerations? At least the following assumptions. Whoever seeks for the origin of sport has to revisit the distant past where the emergence of the anthropological difference can be discovered: that is, the very point when man changed from a natural entity to a cultural being. Against this background, it is important to discern that even in the animal kingdom we can find the concept of play as a social activity that includes the demonstration of physical power, speed, endurance, skillfulness, and so forth, often revealing a competitive element. It was the Dutch historian Johan Huizinga who pointed out the remarkable fact that even the animal's playing is not entirely determined by its biological function but, to some extent, shows an exemption from nature.[12] Therefore, it is when the human being becomes aware for the first time of his self and becomes a cultural being that he finds himself, at the same time, to be a playing being.

Due to the aforementioned anthropological difference, man's playing nature is not only pre-given but also something to be determined by himself. Therefore, he must give a cultural shape to it. And that means he has to give it form via rules. Just as poetry subordinates the ordinary rhythm of language to a meter, or as natural sounds, dictated by bar and melody, turn out to be music, the wild and archaic play gradually must be subjected to a firm set of rules. In the beginning, these rules were of precultural origin. For instance, the natural cycle of the year provides many an

---

12. See Johan Huizinga, *Homo Ludens: A Study of the Play Element in Culture* (Boston: Beacon Press, 1971), 17.

opportunity for ceremonies lending a peculiar meaning to games. In addition to these seasonal changes, primarily indicated by the equinox and the summer and winter solstices, cultural events (for example, the beginning and ending of the hunting season or the times of sowing and harvesting) also become a welcome occasion for rule-governed games.[13]

Apart from these external rules primarily determined by the sequence of natural and cultural events human games, playing becomes increasingly shaped by laws of its own, that is, by artificial rules of the game. Where such games are characterized by competitive elements and the performance of physical power, speed, endurance, and skillfulness one might speak of the origin of the first sport rules (even though we have to keep in mind that the history of sports is characterized by a great many discontinuities, so that each comparison between earlier and contemporary manifestations, to some extent, doesn't work).[14] After all, at this point, we can state that in an immemorial past man finds himself already as a playing being. The metaphor of finding oneself indicates, as has been said, the bridging of the anthropological gap or difference since the human being has to deal creatively with his or her nature. This requirement is met in that the human being culturally shapes its nature and subjects it to rules. In the beginning, these rules are orientated by natural processes. But, not much later, they appear to be a crucial challenge to the culture-achieving potential of the human being and so become an expression of the tremendousness of man's creative will.

13. See Carl Diem, *Olympiaden 1964: Eine Geschichte des Sports* (Stuttgart: Cotta Verlag, 1994).

14. See John Carter and Arnd Krüger, eds., *Ritual and Record: Sports, Records, and Quantifications in Pre-Modern Societies* (New York: Greenwood Press, 1990).

Rule-Competence in the Human Person

We should linger for a moment on the astonishing capacity of the human being to set rules for himself and to guide his behavior by these rules. However, we are dealing with the question as to how sport can serve the human being. The assumption to be developed here holds that it is the human rule-competence that provides appropriate criteria to assess whether or not a certain function of sports serves the human person.

To illustrate the problem of the human rule-competence we make use of a literary example. In 1948, the German writer Erich Kästner published a collection of witty, thought-provoking poems and short stories entitled *Der tägliche Kram*.[15] One of the prose texts narrates the meeting of two opponents in the context of an international wrestling competition. What Kästner actually portrays, however, can hardly be classified as belonging to the Olympic discipline of wrestling. It is rather a rabid scuffle. Be that as it may, much to the pleasure of the audience, almost every action that causes pain is permitted. "To their hearts' content, the rivals may grasp and grab, pinch and squeeze, beat, strangle, tear, bend, stretch and crush whichever part of the opponent's body they can reach with their fingers, their fists, their hands, their arms, their legs or their—very useful as battering ram—heads." In view of this extremely extended interpretation of the notion "freestyle," Kästner shows himself to be surprised, with some justification, that although the rivals apparently may do almost everything, they may not to pull each other's hair. The referee tolerates every seemingly brutal act with impunity. "But as soon as one of the fighters undertakes to tug the other's shock of hair, he steps in whistling an-

15. Erich Kästner, *Der tägliche Kram: Chansons und Prosa 1945–1948*, in *Werke*, vol. 2, ed. Hermann Kurzke (Frankfurt: Deutscher Taschenbuch Verlag, 1998), 157–59.

grily and so the offender immediately lets go the curls of his rival, whose stomach he now, once again, may hammer with his fists undisturbed and whose head he may pull off anew."

This remarkable contradiction between permitted brutality and forbidden banality prompts Kästner to make an interesting interjection about the origin and the meaning of rules. "Rules of the game," he writes, "have their secrets, not only in sports. In some cases, one is inclined to suspect, that behind those rules there is nothing but the sniggering arbitrariness of the rule's founder. Horrible acts are permitted and trifles are forbidden. The rules of the game are observed, and the founder, even after his demise, laughs up his sleeve." What Kästner presents here as a mere assumption, on closer inspection, turns out to be a provocative statement. The rules of sports, so he may be interpreted as insinuating, can be seen as an expression of malicious arbitrariness inconsiderately permitting or forbidding whatever it wants. Why some things apply in sport and others don't continues to be a dark secret evading every rational justification.

This insinuation alone would make the story worth mentioning. But there is still another reason. In the following, Kästner portrays the fight and the surprising victory of the unfancied challenger. After having described every gory detail with undisguised joy, Kästner ends up with a "satirical epilogue." In this he introduces an old lady who, after the performance is finished and the arena already is emptying, utters her annoyance about the fight she has seen. Of course, she is asked why she attended such a brutality at all when apparently possessed of such weak nerves. "'Oh,' she moaned, 'I was just wrong about the date. My ticket was for tomorrow!' 'What will be given here tomorrow?' She looked at us like a timid deer. Then she whispered: 'a philharmonic concert.'"

Without much effort from this final episode another interesting assertion can be drawn. Sport is valuable only for those who like it.

Others go to a philharmonic concert. Or, to put it more generally, sport as such is not valuable; its actual value depends on a more or less arbitrary value ascription.

With Kästner's challenging statements our initial problem receives a clearer profile. If the value of sport actually depends on a contingent attribution and its rules turn out to be an expression of pure arbitrariness, then the question still remains whether sports serve the human person. Much less do we get to know how it can do that. However, we are not as unprepared as before to solve these problems. After all, our anthropological considerations have taught us something about the human rule-competence, and that is exactly what we now should put the focus on.

For to do that, of course, we need not necessarily burden ourselves with a longwinded philosophical reflection on human freedom.[16] Rather we can recognize that the anthropological difference and the rule-competence stemming from it obviously indicate an astonishing human faculty. Since if the human being is at once pre-given and to be determined, then he or she cannot entirely be determined by its psycho-physical nature (i.e.. by the pre-given). In other words, the human being always maintains a certain distance or space with regard to his psycho-physical nature. Nothing else than this does the notion "anthropological gap" seek to express. By recognizing that he is called to realize himself and is not in complete submission to internal and external conditions that he acknowledges—at least in a formal sense—as unconditioned, the human person is unconditionally free to give a cultural shape to his or her psycho-physical preconditions. At this point it is important to note that the understanding of freedom must not be confused with indifferent arbitrariness. It is rather a moral demand. Hence, the aforementioned rule-competence can be recognized as a call

16. See Christoph Hübenthal, *Grundlegung der christlichen Sozialethik: Versuch eines freiheitsanalytisch-handlungsreflexiven Ansatzes* (Münster: Aschendorff, 2006).

or vocation to cultivate human nature. That is also the reason why freedom, as it has been said, in a formal sense is unconditioned, but in a substantive sense shows itself as to be conditioned, because it can be realized only by evoking cultural expressions or by symbolically expressing itself through cultural action.

Even these considerations, however, make not definitely clear which criteria should guide the cultivation of human nature, the symbolical acting, or the promulgation of rules. Yet, now we are sufficiently equipped to answer this question. If, in the recognition of freedom, the human being experiences himself as unconditionally called, then it must be this unconditionedness inside himself as well as—and this is decisive—the unconditionedness inside every other human being that orientates the culture-accomplishing use of freedom. In other words, wherever the human being recognizes her own freedom as well as the freedom of every other human being, she executes her freedom in an appropriate and adequate way. An authentically human exercise of freedom, therefore, manifests itself in actions granting every person approximately the same amount of opportunities to carry out their freedom. This means, concretely speaking, that each human person's psychophysical integrity is to be recognized, maintained, and promoted in such a way that she is enabled to make the same human use of her freedom as every other person.

Now, in order to thoroughly spell out the moral principles, norms, and rules that warrant the recognition and promotion of freedom, we would have to move from anthropology to ethics. Of course, this cannot be done here. Nevertheless it must be clear that each action intended to make visible the recognition of freedom must be an action oriented by moral standards. At this point, it also becomes clear how all this relates to our subject matter of "sports at the service of the human person." In fact, Kästner is wrong when he suggests that the rules of sports arise from irrational and malicious arbitrariness. At any rate, they must not. If they do, then sports are decisively not at the service of the human person and have to be firmly rejected as immoral. In the same way, Kästner is wrong when he declares that the value of sports emerges from an arbitrary valuation. On the contrary, sports can be seen as a genuine human value, at least when they are subjected to moral standards and therefore adequately express the recognition and promotion of human freedom.[17]

By that, we can formulate a first provisional answer to our initial question: sport is at the service of the human person when it becomes a cultural achievement—an achievement by which the human person gives to her natural preconditions a cultural shape and in doing so responds to the unconditional call within herself. This shaping process must be governed by rules and, in turn, realizes itself in rules that can be seen as a manifestation of the symbolic recognition of freedom by freedom itself. The relevant criterion of recognition is the morality of rules as well as the morality of the actions guided by those rules. Each single function, allegedly justifying the service character of sports, has to be oriented by moral standards, too. If we want to know what morality concretely means, we have to make use of genuine ethical considerations.[18]

The Aesthetics of Sports

With the preceding remarks our initial question has found an initial, and hopefully satisfying, answer. Being honest with ourselves, however, we must confess that, so far, we have overlooked

17. On freedom in sports, see Jörg Splett, "Der Mensch zwischen Freiheit und Zwang aus der Sicht der philosophischen Anthropologie," in *Sport zwischen Freiheit und Zwang,* Christliche Perspektiven im Sport 5, ed. Paul Jakobi and H. E. Rösch (Mainz: Matthias-Grünewald-Verlag, 1981), 118–33.

18. See Ommo Grupe and Dietmar Mieth, eds., *Lexikon der Ethik im Sport,* 99 (Schorndorf: Hofmann, 1998); Claudia Pawlenka, ed., *Sportethik: Regeln—Fairness—Doping* (Paderborn: Mentis, 2004).

a decisive—perhaps the essential—feature of sports. In particular our sport-anthropological sketch would be rather insufficient if we did not take into consideration the firsthand experiences of both those who participate in sports and those who watch at it.

Recently the Stanford University literary scholar Ulrich Gumbrecht has been criticizing the leading hermeneutic paradigm of the cultural sciences. Each scholarly analysis of cultural achievements, so he complains, aims purely at understanding their meaning. Such efforts, however, would entirely overlook the fact that there are also "presence" effects that are, at least, of similar importance for all kinds of cultural experience.[19] Presence, according to Gumbrecht, is to be understood as the immediate and intensive perception of substantiality and physical nearness on this side of all meaning. Such perception should be given much more attention when it comes to the scientific analysis and explanation of cultural achievements. The contemporary dominance of the meaning culture, should therefore, according to Gumbrecht, be supplemented by a growing sensibility for the presence culture.[20]

How is this controversy in cultural sciences related to our subject matter? In fact, we would not need to deal with the debate on meaning versus presence if recently Gumbrecht had not been making the attempt to exemplify his ideas about presence in relation to the cultural product "sports." The result of his endeavor is a marvelous book entitled *In Praise of Athletic Beauty*,[21] in which he submits a fascinating aesthetics of sports. Right in the beginning, he gives a clear account of what presence in sports could be about.

19. See Hans Ulrich Gumbrecht, *Production of Presence: What Meaning Cannot Convey* (Stanford, Calif.: Stanford University Press, 2003).

20. Of course, Gumbrecht is not interested in simply playing off presence against meaning. In an illuminating interpretation of Heidegger's essay on the work of art he shows that even a hermeneutic approach is to presuppose an oscillation between presence and meaning.

21. Hans Ulrich Gumbrecht, *In Praise of Athletic Beauty* (Cambridge, Mass.: Harvard University Press, 2006).

Imagine, your hero has the possession of the ball, followed and attacked by his competitors. A fraction of a second, before his opponent can put the screws on him, he plays a long ball. Suddenly you feel as if the world is moving in slow motion; and even though the ball flies past your place in the stadium, it is impossible to foresee where it will touch the ground. With the concentrated passion of a compulsive gambler seeding all his money on one and only number, you are afraid that a player of the opposing team will intercept it. But, while the ball describes an unlikely curve and slowly drops, suddenly—without you having realized it—a player of your own team appears right at the place where the ball will touch the field. Both, the motion of the ball and the motion of the player you just noticed, converge in a form already disappearing at that moment it emerges. The player of your team takes the ball by a hair's breadth; nevertheless he succeeds, outplays the opposing defense, and runs in a direction that no one (including yourself) has ever expected. For a moment, you think to encounter his fiery eyes. Between both moments, the short gaze of the player and your own perception, the world returns to its normal speed, and you can breathe again, so deep, that your breast hurts, and you feel relieved, proud, and confident in the face of the beautiful move you have experienced just now and which will never happen again in real time. The stadium booms—there is no other word for it—from 50,000 voices, including your own, a mighty accompaniment for the wave of enthusiasm and intensive experience that sweeps you along. Hours later, on the way from the stadium to your car, walking through the cool air of an autumn evening and being more exhausted than on any other evening of the week, you remember that moment of the game as to be a moment of entire happiness. Once again, but this time without any exertion, the beautiful move widens your breast and makes your heart move faster. In your memory the moment comes to life again and, while you wish to hold it tied, you feel a little itch in your legs as if you were to follow your hero on the playing field.[22]

One can hardly give a more vivid description of the deep emotions a sports event is able to evoke. It is a description of immedia-

_____

22. Ibid., 9–10.

cy, without any reflection on meaning or meaninglessness interfering with it. This is exactly what Gumbrecht means by "presence." Furthermore, the quotation indicates that presence effects can cause lasting impressions, a reminiscence, so to say, that gives rise to a timeless presence. But, of course, a mere description of sports events doesn't suffice for Gumbrecht. In the course of the book, he develops a typology of different sportive fascinations "due to which we can grasp and praise just that what makes out our joy in watching sports."[23] Additionally, one should mention that not only reception-aesthetical categories are at stake here, but also a production-aesthetical typology referring to presence effects charming those who do sports on their own.

In particular, Gumbrecht names six aspects that describe the beauty of sports: (1) to present beautiful bodies; (2) to face death; (3) to show charm and elegance; (4) to extend the potentialities of the body; (5) to realize preexisting forms; (6) to produce epiphanies of the form.[24] Some of these fascinations speak for themselves; others perhaps need further explanation, but this is not the time to do so. What is decisive though is that at the end of the book, Gumbrecht tells us what the presence of sportive beauty touches off in himself. To praise sporting achievements, he says, is an opportunity "to express gratitude for my life as well as for the loving of my life. Praise of sport originates just from this impulse of gratitude—even though it has to remain intransitive."[25] The intensive presence of sportive experiences can, and on that point we can only agree with him, evoke a feeling of comprehensive gratitude for the beauty of sports and, by that, for the beauty of life as such.[26] But why must this gratitude remain intransitive?

---

23. Ibid., 100.   24. Ibid., 101–29.
25. Ibid., 169.

26. In fact, Gumbrecht's argumentation is slightly more complicated than presented here. Before he deals with the topic of gratitude, he describes the breakdown

Why can't it have an addressee? Gumbrecht is quite aware of the fact that this question bears religious implications. Gratitude for the many happy moments in one's life and for life as such is either directed toward a divine addressee or remains intransitive, since the place of the addressee stays vacant and empty.[27] For personal reasons, Gumbrecht doesn't want to give a positive answer to this question. But what he himself believes or does not believe is not of immediate interest here. Important, however, is the observation that the presence effects of sport can raise the question about who is the addressee of gratitude itself. And that is what Gumbrecht brilliantly has worked out.[28]

Was it necessary, we can finally ask, that our sport-anthropological considerations took such a long way round the aesthetics of sports and its presence effects to show that the human being is confronted with religious questions in sports? The answer is no. In the previous sections we dealt with the anthropological difference and the fact that the human being is pre-given and at the same time a vocation to be realized. This implies the call to culturally shape one's psycho-physical nature in accordance with moral rules. Sports, as we have seen, are an excellent field to respond to this call. In this case, however, sports are settled right into a context that Gumbrecht, not without a critical undertone, calls "meaning culture." Sports, therefore, not only evoke presence effects, but also participate in the cultural production of meaning.

---

of many athletes after their career. Then he toys with the idea of thanking them for his intense experiences. But eventually he rejects this idea since he can indicate neither what he exactly is grateful for nor who the addressee of his gratitude is (see 151).

27. See the chapter "Gedanken zur Dankbarkeit" in Dieter Henrich, *Bewußtes Leben. Untersuchungen zum Verhältnis von Subjektivität und Metaphysik* (Stuttgart: Reclam, 999), 152–93.

28. This is in contrast with Martin Seel, who thinks that in sports the modern world celebrates "the mysteries of contingency"; see the chapter "Die Zelebration des Unvermögens. Aspekte einer Ästhetik des Sports," in Martin Seel, *Ethisch-ästhetische Studien* (Frankfurt: Suhrkamp, 1996), 188–200.

Astonishingly, here, too, an irrevocable openness for religious questions can be detected. If we try, in sports as well as elsewhere, to act in accordance with moral rules and thereby create cultural meaning we anticipate an ultimate meaning, even though we must acknowledge that we will never be able to produce it on our own.[29] As in the case of gratitude, we have two options. Either we say, notwithstanding our necessary pursuit for ultimate meaning, that this striving simply vanishes into thin air, or we believe that we are permitted to symbolically represent the ultimate meaning since it is irrevocably given to us. If we believe the latter, we can reasonably move from the anthropological perspective to a Christian vision of sport since Christianity looks at everything on the assumption that in Jesus Christ himself the ultimate meaning is revealed.

Even though these thoughts have focused on anthropology alone, it was explicitly intended in order to prepare the ground for a Christian vision of sport. As we now can summarize, sport eventually serves the human being by creating a feeling of comprehensive gratitude and a cognition of the need for ultimate meaning. This is what sports actually can evoke in every human being. It cannot, however, answer the questions whether there is an addressee of gratitude and whether the ultimate meaning is really given.

29. See Christoph Hübenthal, *Grundlegung der christlichen Sozialethik*, part 1.

Part 2   Theological Aspects

This section explores some theological foundations of a Christian vision for sport. Since Catholic theology is composed by systematic reflection on Scripture, tradition, ecumenical councils, pontifical teachings and so on, this section asks how Christianity may relate to the sporting phenomenon, whether through safeguarding it from possible deviations by offering discernment criteria or through its capacity of elevating these activities by placing them within the broader horizon of eternity.

In chapter 4, Father Koch offers a view of sport in the light of Scripture and the writings of Church Fathers. Here the claim is made that the Bible does not offer a direct justification of sport because it never intended to do so, but rather in a metaphoric way borrows statements and imagery from the sporting activity of its epoch to illustrate other values and truths pertaining to the biblical authors' historical context. Therefore, neither a Christian commendation of sport nor a theology of sport can be developed from these specific references in Scripture. However, Koch believes that the Bible does address what it means to be human in general and that this has direct implications for such cultural activities as sport. For this end, a survey study of these theological elements was examined, beginning with its grounding in sacred Scripture and in the early Church Fathers.

Following upon this is an in-depth study of the teachings about sport of three pontiffs: Pius XII, John Paul II, and Benedict XVI. We see in chapter 5 how Pius XII rigorously defended the Church's concern for sport, stressing that it is the entire person for whom the Church's care is addressed and not just the soul. So, "care" of the body—yes; but "cult" of the body—no! Pius XII sees the Church's engagement in the world of sport as a help to safeguard its true values, to enrich physical culture with all that tends to raise the spiritual value of man, and to elevate it by directing sport toward a noble exaltation of the dignity, vigor, and fullness of life that are most compatible with Christianity.

Chapter 6 builds on these themes with the "sporting pope," John Paul II, who has left numerous speeches from the occasions of his frequent private audiences with professional sports teams, as he sought to respond to what he considered almost a "sign of the time" by reaching out to the world of sport through contact with its leaders: professional athletes. Attentive to the demands and dangers of elite sport, John Paul II often makes reference to the primacy and dignity of the human person and the need for sport to always be at the service of the human person and never vice versa.

In chapter 7, Pope Benedict, as the then Cardinal Ratzinger, offers an interesting reflection on how the attraction and love of sport is a manifestation of our deeper longing for paradise. Here, he sees sport as a school of life where the person can practice self-mastery in order to exercise their freedom to its utmost potential, especially in team play but also off the field in other areas of life.

This theological approach is further complemented in chapter 8 by an approach to sport in light of the Second Vatican Council, with its emphasis on interpreting and responding to the "sign of the times," which includes the social dimension of sport as a world phenomenon. Here the author offers a spiritual and sociotheological perspective on sport. His argument begins with an examination of this sign, which he reads inductively as a cultural phenomenon, and deduces four applications from the observations of this phenomenon: bodily experience, aesthetic experience, moral experience, and religious experience. In the second part of this chapter, some spiritual foundations for a Christian view of sport are considered: competition as an aspect of justice and peace; the body as an integral part of the human person; creation's desire to celebrate its vitality; and so on.

Alois Koch, S.J.

4 Biblical and Patristic Foundations for Sport

The theme I am addressing—that of offering a Christian understanding of sport according to its foundations in Scripture and in the writings of the Church Fathers—reminds me of the old theses of dogmatic theology with which I was made familiar through my studies as a seminarian. In these, arguments were usually based on—apart from the actual "theological reason"—the testimony of Holy Scriptures, tradition, and the Church's teachings. These points were, of course, proper to a thesis, as well as to the "adversary's" argument. But it is difficult for our present topic because the subject of these considerations does not appear in a similar way in holy Scriptures and in the early Christian tradition. Modern sport, with which we are dealing, has, at best, only outward similarities to the agonism and athletics of Greece and Rome. It has other roots. It is also to be taken into account that neither Scriptures nor the early Christian writers explicitly and thematically dealt with the contemporary concept of physical exercises—apart from Tertullian and Novatian. But even these are referring mostly to sport as a spectacle among other "spectacles"—and not simply focusing on athletics.

A second remark refers to the method of my considerations. In the first part, I will deal with the attempts to provide a Christian foundation of today's sport. As a first step, I will consider the biblical statements about the physical nature of man and especially its use of images and metaphors from the world of ancient athletics in St. Paul's writings. In a second step, I will deal with some distinctive statements of the Church Fathers on man's physical nature, on physical exercises, and on the athletics of their time. Lastly, I will offer some foundational guidelines drawn from the above reflections that may help us better recognize and interpret the precarious developments of sport today.

The Search for Scriptural References to Sport

Biblical References to Man's Physical Nature

With the exception of two episodes in Maccabees,[1] Scripture does not deal with the phenomenon of the contemporary physical exercise of its time. This is why one who wishes to substantiate the sporting engagements of today from a Christian perspective should make reference to biblical statements on man's physical nature in general. But even here, these statements are usually taken out of their context, as one does not pay attention to the fact that they might serve for other truths.

That applies to the often-quoted passages from the two accounts of Creation in the book of Genesis, where man's "body" too was created by God, and "God saw everything that he had made, and said: It was very good."[2] The creation of man is not about, although this is often still assumed, a "double creation" (of body and soul), but about the creation of a person as a complete being who owes his or her entire existence to God: this one and whole human being is a creature of God and the "image of God."[3]

1. 1 Mc 1:13 and 2 Mc 4:7.   2. Gn 1:31.
3. Gn 1:27.

The Bible is primarily concerned with the fundamental relation of man to his Creator, and not with his body being in juxtaposition with his soul (*Geistseele*). Man is a being related to God. When the human person is considered as being in the "image of God," what is being stated is that his or her totality is in the "image of God" and not only his or her spiritual nature. When God breathes into them the divine "breath" and they become a "living being," this does not refer to the creation of an immortal soul. Rather, "breath" signifies that man is a living being. Hence the words "soul" and "body" are not used to denote components; they are only taken as different viewpoints under which the one and complete human person is considered.

This same argument applies all the more to the time and again quoted passages from the New Testament that are often taken out of their context. St. Paul's text from the First Letter to the Corinthians,[4] "Glorify God in your body!" to which reference is often made, is not intended as referring to sporting activity, but is directed against views in Corinth that regarded sexual licentiousness as morally illicit for Christians. Nonetheless, these verses of St. Paul are frequently quoted by theologians and pontiffs with reference to sports. I will cite two examples. Pope Pius XII says in his message of greeting to the Catholic athletes participating at the Olympic Games in Melbourne in 1956:

When at that time the Greek athletes began the celebration of Olympia with a ritual act, today, at the beginning of today's Olympic Games, it is far more meaningful to turn to the one and true God in order to dedicate to Him your young strength and to recognize his entitlement over our bodies and our lives: "For do you not know that your body is a temple of the Holy Spirit, ... and that you do not belong to yourselves? ... Thus, glorify God in your body!"[5]

4. 1 Cor 6:19.
5. Pius XII, "Paterni voti ed auspice per le olimpiadi di Melbourne" (October 24,

Pope John Paul II also quotes this statement of St. Paul in the First Letter to the Corinthians when he says:

In the first place, sport is making good use of the body, an effort to reaching optimum physical condition, which brings marked consequences of psychological well-being. From our Christian faith we know that, through baptism, the human person, in his or her totality and integrity of soul and body, becomes a temple of the Holy Spirit: "Do you not know that your body is a temple of the Holy Spirit within you, which you have from God? You are not your own, you were bought with a price (that is, with the blood of Christ the Redeemer). So glorify God in your body."[6]

As for the Apostle to the Gentiles, he is expressing something else with this statement. In the context of his letter, he is writing against Gnosticism with its body-despising attitude that is present in the Church in Corinth. What concerns him is that they are not regarding the body as an important reality, but rather considering it as a sphere that is irrelevant to moral behavior. (In this sense, a Gnostic might consider it licit to have intercourse with a prostitute!) For St. Paul, it is also not about escaping the slavery of the "flesh," that is, man's lower urges. Rather, for him, it is about respecting one's totality, that is, all the dimensions of one's life, devoting all of oneself to the service of God.

Hence it becomes also clear that the limitation of St. Paul's text to mere physical nature, in the sense of man's physical reality, is untenable and does not do justice to St. Paul's comprehensive view. For man belongs in his totality to God. So too, salvation in Christ—which is to be commemorated by the faithful—embraces all dimensions of the person's existence.

Consequently, referencing texts of the Old and New Testament

1956), in *Discorsi e Radiomessaggi di Sua Santità Pio XII*, vol. 18 (Vatican: Tipografia Poliglotta Vaticana, 1956), 890–92.

6. John Paul II, "International Jubilee of Sport: Homily at Olympic Stadium" (April 12, 1984), *L'Osservatore Romano*, English ed., no. 17, April 24, 1984, 4–5.

as reasons for the value of sport and physical exercises proves dubious and not tenable according to a thorough exegesis. It is also obvious how one who is seeking scriptural passages in order to theologically justify their own understanding of physical exercises and the Church's commitment to the world of sport can easily take these passages out of their proper context.

However, these preliminary conclusions are not implying that the Scriptures do not offer a view of man's physical reality that is far from any contempt and debasement. Precisely because the Old and New Testament conception of man does not know any metaphysical dualism, that is, man's separation into body and soul and hence into two unequal halves, the physical dimension is wholly integrated into man's being in the Bible. Consequently, the positive meaning and value of athletic and physical exercise are not to be derived from certain biblical statements about man's physical nature; rather, they are rooted in the very nature of the one and complete person who is the agent of all of his or her actions—even play and sport.

It was once said that play and sport are "expressive actions" of the one and whole man, activities "out of the impetus of being alive."[7] In play and sport this unity of body and soul within the one being, man, is actually expressed in a specific way. There is in no way a need to refer back to passages in the Bible in order to endorse or practice as a Christian the physical exercises, play, and sport. Christians—as people who know they are God's creatures—answer physical exercises in the affirmative because of the fact that they are human beings.

---

7. Corona Bamberg, "Von Wert und Würde menschlicher Muße," *Geist und Leben* 57 (1984): 17.

Sport Metaphors in St. Paul

When Christians write about modern sport, with all of its fascination and its problems, references to the images and metaphors of the ancient agonism used in St. Paul's letters are rarely missing. St. Paul is presented as one who is "familiar" with the sport of his time from his own experience and is considered as someone who had a positive view of this sport. For example, one Christian author notes: "As one who had been raised in a Hellenic culture, St. Paul referred repeatedly to examples from the sporting life to make comparison to the religious life and set so a wonderful example for the world of the value of sportsmanship."[8] Or, as another author states: "In St. Paul we find a Biblical authority who proves in numerous passages his own precise knowledge of the events in the stadium and gymnasium.... From a summary view Paul's texts, especially the First Letter to the Corinthians, there can be gained a comprehensive picture of sport from the view of the New Testament."[9]

Also in the speeches of the popes their comments about the sport metaphors in St. Paul are in a similar vein. Pope Pius XII, commenting on the First Letter to the Corinthians, the so-called sport epistle, stated: "These words illumine the concept of sport with a mystical radiance."[10] And John Paul II says in a homily:

Here we see that the Apostle of the Gentiles, in order to bring the message of Christ to all peoples, drew from all the concepts, images, terminologies, modes of expression, and philosophical and literary references not only

8. Rudolf Weiler, *Sportethik: Aufrufe zu Gesinnung und Bekenntnis* (Graz: Austria Medien Serv., 1996), 23.
9. Willi Schwank, "Christentum und Sport," in *Lexikon der Ethik im Sport*, ed. Ommo Grupe and Dietmar Mieth (Schorndorf: Hofmann, 1998), 85.
10. Pius XII, "The Sporting Ideal"" (May 20, 1945), in *A Catholic Perspective: Physical Exercise and Sport*, ed. Robert Feeney (Marysville, Wash.: Aquinas Press, 1995), 34.

of the Jewish tradition but also of Hellenic culture. And he did not hesitate to include sport among the human values which he used as points of support and reference for dialogue with the people of his time. Thus he recognized the fundamental validity of sport, considering it not just as a term of comparison to illustrate a higher ethical and aesthetic ideal, but also in its intrinsic reality as a factor in the formation of man and as a part of his culture and his civilization.[11]

Even some exegetes, commenting on these athletic metaphors, refer time and again to Corinth as place of the Isthmic Games and conclude that "the reader knew such competitions from the Pan-Hellenic Isthmic Games held in their city."[12] Characteristic of this is also Uta Poplutz's statement: "One can assume that the Apostle, who grew up in the Diaspora, was acquainted with the agonism practiced in his time."[13]

In light of this, the first thing to be said is that the images and metaphors used by St. Paul are not the "invention" of the Apostle. They draw upon a contemporary literary style, which was particularly used first by the Greek sophists, and later by the Cynic and Stoic philosophers. These are the so-called diatribes. Precisely at the time in which St. Paul's letters originate, the practice of virtue and the efforts to live a moral life were frequently compared with the struggles and sacrifices present in athletic competition. These comparisons are to be found far more explicitly and in greater detail in Seneca and the Alexandrian Jew Philon than with St. Paul.

Hence Poplutz's point that St. Paul had surely gotten to know the local athletic competitions from his native town, Tarsus, and also during the Pharisee training in Jerusalem,[14] cannot be proven. The thesis that the Isthmic Games had been "the concrete exam-

11. John Paul II, "International Jubilee of Sport," 4–5.
12. Jacob Kremer, *Der Erste Brief an die Korinther* (Regensburg, Germany: Pustet, 1997), 196.
13. Uta Poplutz, *Athlet des Evangeliums* (Freiburg: Herder, 2004), 264.
14. Ibid., 409.

ple, the familiar background for the metaphorical use" in chapter 1 of the First Letter to the Corinthians[15] can also not be proven from this, as familiarity with the Cynic-Stoic diatribes could be a quite sufficient reason for the use of these agonistic metaphors.

There is an important criterion that is usually not dealt with, but that was of decisive importance for the early Christian authors and probably also for St. Paul, even if it is not mentioned in his comparisons. It is about the fact that Hellenic agonism was closely connected with the pagan religion. The award ceremony with the presentation of the victory wreath, made of a tree dedicated to a god (in Olympia the wreath was made with branches from a sacred olive tree) was a ritual act; the award of the wreath meant the veneration of the god. This is the reason why it was unacceptable for the early Christians to attend and support such rituals, as the testimonies of the early Christian authors show.

In this context, there is also another fact that needs to be taken into account: the refusal to participate in Greek agonistic events would be most natural for strictly observant Jews, and in particular for Pharisees. So, when Poplutz points out that "the Greek physical culture seemed suspicious to pious Jews,"[16] the reason was not that a Jew was rejecting "physical exercises" per se. No. Rather, he was manifesting his concern about the danger of betraying his Jewish religion through these practices. As for St. Paul, he says in the Acts of the Apostles: "I am a Jew, born in Tarsus in Cilicia, but brought up in this city (Jerusalem). At the feet of Gamaliel I was educated strictly in our ancestral law and was zealous for God."[17] And in Caesarea, St. Paul admits before Agrippa and Festus: "All (Jews) have known about me from the start, if they are willing to testify, that I have lived my life as a Pharisee, the strictest party of our religion."[18] Hence it is hardly feasible that St. Paul—be it as

---

15. Ibid., 288.
17. Acts 22:3.

16. Ibid., 410, see footnote.
18. Acts 26:4.

participant or as spectator—had gotten his knowledge from direct contact with these agonistic events that were affiliated with the pagan cult.

The most detailed metaphor in St. Paul's writings is the well-known passage in chapter 9 of the First Letter to the Corinthians. Two points are necessary to mention here. The first is that the athletes' "abstinence from everything" means that their entire lifestyle was subjected to strict regulation: training after the tetrad system implied a strict diet, sleep, and (apparently) sexual abstinence.[19] The contemporary criticism of these athletic practices proves that these were not undisputed. Philostratus and Lucian of Samosata clearly dissociate themselves from these practices, and there are also passages in Seneca's letters that tear the athletes' way of life to pieces: "I also debar from the liberal studies wrestling and all knowledge that is compounded of oil and mud.... For what 'liberal' element is there in these ravenous takers of emetics, whose bodies are fed to fatness while their minds are thin and dull?"[20] When Seneca mentions the *enkrateia*, that is, the athletes' "regulated way of life," he is addressing only this sense: to regulate one's entire life as philosopher; to work by his whole conduct of life toward the aim to be achieved; to free oneself from the passions that oppose reason; to bring the sensual impulses and longings under the control of the mind. But St. Paul and the Christians use the word *enkrateia* in a different sense than the Stoic philosopher. For the Christian it refers to that way of life in accordance to the will of God and in his service.

The second point worth noting refers to verse 27a. Poplutz translates it so: "I strike my body [*hypopiazo mou to soma*]." Hence the

19. Cf. Julius Jüthner, "Die athletischen Leibesübungen der Griechen," in *Einzelne sportarten. Lauf, Sprung und Wurfbewerbe*, vol. 2, ed. Friedrich Brein (Vienna: Hermann Böhlaus, 1968), 195.

20. Lucius Annaeus Seneca, *Moral Epistles,* trans. Richard M. Gummere, Loeb Classical Library vol. 2 of 3 (Cambridge, Mass.: Harvard University Press, 1920), 403.

aim of the buffeting is the *soma*. Yet, with this expression here, as also in other places, St. Paul does not mean the body ("brother donkey"), nor the physical nature of man. The term *soma* is identical with the term *sarx,* or flesh, and implies not only the person's one and whole physical nature, but also that in the person which is lacking orientation toward God, that is, the sinful attitude: the turning away from God as man's salvation. The expression "to live according to the flesh" is synonymous with sin for St. Paul. Hence when he directs the punches to the *soma*, his doing does not mean the "beating up of the body," but that he is hitting the weakest, most sensitive point, for *hypopiazein* literally means to punch right below the eyes, and this implies the egocentric attitude, forgetfulness of God, and sin. Hence one may translate verse 27a in this way: "I direct all my efforts against that which is only human, that which is godless in me." For St. Paul this mentality is identical with *enkrateia,* the orientation of one's whole way of life toward the service of God.

From these explanations, it logically follows that one cannot read into the comparisons and images from the ancient agonism that Paul uses an evaluation or approval of the athletics of his time. Therefore, we should not uphold these comparisons as "a beautiful example of the world of values of sport";[21] nor should we claim from this that St. Paul included "sport among the human values" and regarded it "in its intrinsic reality as a factor in the formation of man and as a part of his culture and his civilization,"[22] as this cannot be proved from the mere use of these metaphors.

Rather, St. Paul wants to clarify the trouble and effort that the service of the Gospel requires of him as an apostle, and also of every Christian. Hence the comparisons illustrate the moral effort to which the Christian commits himself at baptism. The Christian life is inconceivable without this striving, just as the very determined

21. Weiler, *Sportethik,* 23.
22. John Paul II, "International Jubilee of Sport," 4.

way of life is required of the athlete if he wants to gain the victory in the contest.

References to Sport in the Church Fathers

After the treatment of these agon metaphors in the Bible, we will now deal with this theme in the Church Fathers. I will consider four points: (1) the view of man's physical nature in the Church Fathers; (2) the approval of physical exercises; (3) the refusal and condemnation of contemporary athletics; (4) and lastly, the images and metaphors from athletics in the writings of many Church Fathers.

The View of Man's Physical Nature

In early Christianity, the biblical view of creation and man comes into contact, or confrontation, with the views of Greek philosophy, in particular with the philosophy of Plato and Stoicism. The uninhibited view of the body and the physical nature characteristic of the Bible is replaced by a certain suspicion about man's physical nature. Nearly all representatives of early Christianity succumbed to this "epochal obligation" in their way of thinking, and consequently sought to even confirm their disdain of physical nature in Scripture. Thus, it should not surprise us when we find opinions that oppose each other. I quote here only a few of these texts that may be considered typical for these opposing views.

For example, Basil of Caesarea writes:

Whoever does not want to bury himself in the mud of sensual desire must despise the body in general.... Plato says the same as St. Paul, who warns against caring for the body and arousing its desires (Rom. 13, 14).... One is to punish ... the body and to hold it down with the impetuosity of an animal; and one is to calm the chaotic stirrings which it arouses in the soul with the scourge of reason, for one must not let sensuality take its course.[23]

23. Basil the Great, "On the Use of Pagan Authors," in *The Fathers, Historians and Writers of the Church: Literally Translated* (Dublin: W. B. Kelly, 1846), 445.

Such statements are also found in Ambrose of Milan. In his commentary on St. Luke's Gospel the human body is called in a Platonic way "the garment of our soul";[24] in the body "our soul is, as it were, locked up like in a prison."[25] Hence the demand is made that "the soul must not let itself be bent down by the aberrations of the flesh."[26] In the funeral oration for his deceased brother Satyrus, Ambrose says the soul longs "to escape from this prison of the body";[27] the soul is to learn "to free itself from the physical desires; . . . because the law of the flesh fights against the law of the spirit and hands the soul over to the law of aberration."[28]

However, these body-derogatory statements—which are in striking conflict with the doctrine of the goodness of creation—are not the only ones to be found in the Church Fathers. Take, for instance, as characteristic of the opposite view, Tertullian's positive appreciation of the body with his reference to the Incarnation in the terms of "caro cardo saluti," that is, "the flesh is the very condition on which salvation hinges."[29] Saint Cyril of Jerusalem summarizes the Christian teaching about man's physical nature created by God in this way: "Suffer none of those who say that this body is no work of God: for they who believe that the body is independent of God, and that the soul dwells in it as in a strange vessel, readily abuse it to fornication. And yet what fault have they found in this wonderful body? For

24. Ambrose of Milan, "Expositio Evangelii Secumdum Lucam" (bk. v. 107), in *Santus Ambrosius Mediolanensis*, (1815–1875), J. P. Migne, Patrologia Latina 15, 1665.

25. Ibid. (bk. vii. 48), 1779.

26. Ibid. (bk. vii. 91), 1722.

27. Ambrose of Milan, "Second Funeral Discourse," in *Funeral Orations by Gregory Nazianzein and Ambrose*, translated by John Sullivan and Martin McGuire (New York: Fathers of the Church, 1953), 205.

28. Ibid., 205.

29. Tertullian, *Latin Christianity: Its Founder Tertullian*, vol. 3 of *Ante-Nicene Fathers*, ed. Alexander Roberts and James Donaldson (Peabody: Hendrickson Publishers, 1995), 551 [n.b.: this particular translation was by Peter Holmes]. The Ante-Nicene Christian Library was originally published in Edinburgh between 1867 and 1873 by T&T Clark and edited by Rev. Alexander Roberts and James Donaldson.

what is lacking in comeliness? And what in its structure is not full of skill?"[30]

Particularly in St. John Chrysostom we find expressions that are far from any depreciation of man's physical nature. Thus we read in a homily on St. Paul's Letter to the Romans: "The nature of the flesh is not evil. For Christ accepted no other flesh than the original and changed nothing in its nature when he got ready for the fight with it. He left it in its natural condition and got it the laurel of victory over sin. And after the victory he let it rise from the dead and made it immortal." In the same homily he comments on Romans 8:8 ("Those who are in the flesh cannot please God.") in this way:

What then? Are we, to cut our bodies in pieces to please God, and to make our escape from the flesh? And would you have us be homicides, and so lead us to virtue? You see what inconsistencies are gendered by taking the words literally. For by the flesh in this passage, he does not mean the body, or the essence of the body, but that life which is fleshly and worldly, and uses self-indulgence and extravagance to the full, so making the entire man flesh.... But this is not the complaint, the being compassed about with the flesh, for this is so by nature, but the having chosen a carnal life. Wherefore also Paul says, "But they that are in the flesh cannot please God."[31]

By the way, in this text of Chrysostom appears the fundamental difference between the Antiochian school of exegesis and that of Alexandria whose exponent was Origen and whose Platonic convictions exerted a large influence on Basil and Ambrose.

30. Cyril of Jerusalem, "Catechetical Lecture IV," in *Cyril of Jerusalem, Gregory Nazianzen*, vol.7 of *Nicene and Post-Nicene Fathers: Series II*, ed. Alexander Roberts and James Donaldson (Peabody: Hendrickson Publishers, 1995), 24 [revised translation by Edwin Gifford].

31. John Chrysostom, *Saint Chrysostom's Homilies on the Acts of the Apostles and the Epistle to the Romans*, vol. 11 of *Nicene and Post-Nicene Fathers of the Christian Church*, edited by Alexander Roberts and James Donaldson (Peabody: Hendrickson Publishers, 1995), 434–35 [n.b.: this particular translation was by J. B. Morris and W. H. Simcox].

The Approval of Physical Exercises

Although the early Christian writers were influenced by the philosophical thinking of the time, that does not, however, mean a refusal of bodily care and physical exercise. The matters of everyday life continue to be practiced after conversion to Christianity. A Christian simply sought to omit or replace the pagan customs, which—by their close connection of paganism to the daily life of classical antiquity—often influenced even religiously neutral occupations.

This become apparent, for example, with regard to the attendance of the baths. Clement of Alexandria writes in *The Instructor:* "There are four reasons for the bath: for cleanliness, or heat, or health, or lastly, for pleasure. Bathing for pleasure is to be omitted. For unblushing pleasure must be cut out by the roots; and the bath is to be taken by women for cleanliness and health, by men for health alone."[32] It is known about Tertullian that he regularly visited the baths, except at the time of the Saturnalia.[33] Gregory of Nyssa counts the use of baths among the natural comforts in everyday life. John Chrysostom sees the punishment of the closing of the baths in Antioch by Emperor Theodosius as a draconian measure,[34] and the historian Palladius speaks about the saint being denied the comfort of a bath during his deportation.

Also, exercise and gymnasiums are fully accepted by Clement of Alexandria:

32. Clement of Alexandria, *Clement of Alexandria,* vol. 2 of *Ante-Nicene Fathers,* ed. Alexander Roberts and James Donaldson (Peabody: Hendrickson Publishers, 1995), 283 [n.b.: this particular translation is credited to D. Spencer].
33. Cf. Tertullian, *Latin Christianity,* 49.
34. John Chrysostom, "18th Homily on the Statues," in *Saint Chrysostom's Homilies on the Priesthood, Ascetic Treatises, and the Statues,* vol. 9 of *Nicene and Post-Nicene Fathers of the Christian Church,* ed. Alexander Roberts and James Donaldson (Peabody: Hendrickson Publishers, 1995), 463–64.

The gymnasium is sufficient for boys, even if a bath is within reach. And even for men to prefer gymnastic exercises by far to the baths, is perchance not bad, since they are in some respects conducive to the health of young men, and produce exertion—emulation to aim at not only a healthy habit of body, but courageousness of soul.... Nor are women to be deprived of bodily exercise. But they are not to be encouraged to engage in wrestling or running.... In the case of men, let some strip and engage in wrestling; let some play at the small ball in the sun, especially the game they call Pheninda.... Wrestling ... is to be practiced not for the sake of vain contest.... Everywhere one is to be moderate.[35]

But the reasons given for body care and physical exercises clearly show the influence of Stoicism. The experience of pleasure in any activity is as far as possible to be ruled out. Reason alone is to determine man's action, not pleasure or joy in the gymnastic exercise or in bathing. This kind of reasoning regarding the value of physical exercises will mold the Christians' view up until today.

Criticism of the Athletic Events of Their Time

The early Christian writers' devastating criticism of the athletic competitions of their time is clearly distinguished from the favorable attitude toward bodily care and physical exercises. Above all wrestling, boxing, and Pankration (a combination of wrestling and boxing) cast a shadow over the public arenas. Out of the many negative statements two authors should be mentioned: Tertullian and John Chrysostom, since in them the main points of this criticism are mentioned in a special way.

In Tertullian's treatise on *The Shows* the decisive argument against attending public spectacles is their proximity to and combination with the pagan cult. Christians have in their baptismal vows rejected in principle the pagan idols and the *pompa diaboli*.

---

35. Clement of Alexandria, *Clement of Alexandria*, 283.

In this connection he expressly mentions also the Olympic, Nemeic, and Isthmic Games, in which the entire milieu is "besmirched" with idolatry. "What wonder, then,—observes Tertullian—if idolatry pollutes the combat-parade with profane crowns, with sacerdotal chiefs, with attendants belonging to the various colleges, last of all with the blood of its sacrifices?"[36]

We can add to this not only wrestling but also the different races and throwing and jumping exercises that he considers not acceptable for a Christian, in particular because of the strict diet—also criticized by his contemporaries: "You will never give your approval to those foolish racing and throwing feats, and yet more foolish leapings; you will never find pleasure in injurious or useless exhibitions of strength; certainly you will not regard with approval those efforts after an artificial body which aim at surpassing the Creator's work, ... and you will abhor these people who have been fattened for the sake of Greek leisure." Finally he points to the brutality of the athletic exercises: "You will be unable to deny that what happens in the arena is unworthy of your sight: the punches, the kicks, the blows into the face, the impudent behavior of the fighters' hands and all the disfigurements of the human face, which is the image of God."[37] It is said further: "And will the boxer go unpunished? Are we to suppose that he received these caestus-scars, and the thick skin of his fists, and these growths upon his ears, at his creation! Or that God too, gave him eyes for no other end than that they might be knocked out in fighting!"[38]

Hence Tertullian emphatically rejects the athletic exercises. Yet, above all, he rejects the dietary practices of the athletes. In this point he knows his criticism is in agreement particularly with the Stoic philosophers who called the "fattening" of the athletes by "forcible diet" degrading and inhumane. Thus Philostratus, in his

36. Tertullian, *Latin Christianity*, 84.   37. Ibid., 87.
38. Ibid., 89.

work *On Gymnastics,* ridicules the athletes by caricaturing them of being "crammed full like Libyan and Egyptian flour bags."[39]

It is surprising that also for John Chrysostom, who wrote near the end of the fourth century, idolatry was the crucial point of criticism against the athletic competitions of his time—surprising also for that same reason that we assume the Olympic Games had in 393 found an end by the prohibition by Emperor Theodosius. The great preacher knew not the Olympic Games of Olympia, but the games that took place in the exclusive residential district of Antioch, namely up to AD 520. Because of the combination of these games with the cult of Apollo these contests taking place in Daphne were not acceptable for Chrysostom. He mentions, for instance, the festive pomp of the procession where the triumph of the devil is celebrated and where the demons dance.[40] Since a Christian is not allowed to enter a pagan temple, how much more is it wrong for him to go to a satanic celebration. Besides the Olympic contests, Chrysostom also considered the horse races in the hippodromes as "other satanic spectacles."[41]

The Use of Athletic Images and Metaphors

In the early Christian literature we meet from the outset time and again images and comparisons from the contemporary agonism and athletic competitions. They occur frequently in Basil of Caesarea and Ambrose of Milan. But in the use of the agon metaphors, John Chrysostom is unsurpassed. In his writings the sequence of the individual contests, for instance with the Olympic

---

39. Flavius Philostratus, "On Gymnastics," in *Sources for the History of Greek Athletics,* trans. R. S. Robinson (Ann Arbor: Cushing-Malloy, 1955), 229.

40. Cf. Alois Koch, *Johannes Chrysostom und seine Kenntnisse der antiken Agonistik,* (Hindesheim: Weidmann, 2007), 15–22.

41. John Chrysostom, in *Saint Chrysostom's Homilies on Corinthians I and II,* vol. 12 of *Nicene and Post-Nicene Fathers of the Christian Church,* ed. Alexander Roberts and James Donaldson (Peabody: Hendrickson Publishers, 1995), 138.

Games, can be proven without any gaps. For this reason I restrict myself to him and will offer only a few distinctive examples.

In his seventy-first homily on the Gospel of St. Matthew, St. Chrysostom refers to the importance of almsgiving:

For tell me, who has the skill of almsgiving? Obviously God, who is teaching us this virtue and practises it without limit. Now, if you are learning to be a wrestler, to whom do you look? Or to whom do you display your doings in the wrestling school, to the seller of herbs, and of fish, or to the trainer? ... If you are learning to box, will you not look in like manner to him who knows how to teach this? ... Isn't it foolishness to pay attention in all other arts only to the master and in the art of doing good to do the just the opposite?[42]

With reference to a verse from the Letter to the Galatians ("Carry each other's burden! In this way you will fulfill the law of Christ": Gal 6:2) is said:

Do you not see that the athletes stand in the middle of the arena at the Olympic contests; at midday they are as in a furnace on the battlefield with their naked body enduring the beating sunbeams; like iron statutes they fight with the sun, with dust and sultriness, in order to wreathe their head with the branches of laurel [*phylloi daphnes*]. Not such a laurel victory wreath is prepared for you, but the victory wreath of justice as reward for listening.[43]

In the twelfth homily on the Letter to the Philippians we read that the Christians are to follow the example of the athletes' way of life:

42. John Chrysostom, *Saint Chrysostom's Homilies on the Gospel of Saint Matthew*, vol. 10 of *Nicene and Post-Nicene Fathers of the Christian Church*, ed. Alexander Roberts and James Donaldson (Peabody: Hendrickson Publishers, 1995), 434 [n.b.: translated by George Prevost and revised by M. B. Riddle].

43. John Chrysostom, *Saint Chrysostom's Homilies on the Gospel of St. John, Hebrews*, vol. 14 of *Nicene and Post-Nicene Fathers of the Christian Church*, ed. Alexander Roberts and James Donaldson (Peabody: Hendrickson Publishers, 1995), 505.

Do you see how the runners depend in their way of life on certain regulations? How they do not allow themselves anything by which their strength could be weakened? How they daily exercise in the gymnasium under the supervision of a coach and under adherence to these regulations? You too copy this! … For an incomparably higher victory prize is your prospect. Great is the number of those who want to stop you (in the race)…. There are a lot of things that threaten to weaken your strength. Try to give your feet strength and stamina. (…) Let us attain for them the ease of motion, so that the weight of our body does not impair the nimbleness of our feet. Accustom your feet to a steady tread, for there are many slippery places, and if you fall down you will lose thereby importantly. Even if you should fall, stand up quickly for you can still achieve the victory. Never dare to run on slippery soil so that you will not fall down. "Run always on a firm course! Raise your head and eyes!"—so the coaches also shout to the runners. This is because strength must be held in balance. But if you bend your head downward, you may fall down and become exhausted. Direct your view upward where the victory prize is. Already the mere sight of the prizes increases one's eagerness. The anxious expectation lets you not feel the strains and lets the far distance appear short.[44]

Some General Conclusions Regarding a Christian View of Sport

After the explanations about the biblical and patristic "foundations," I wish to offer some suggestions or insights relating to the criteria of assessment of modern sport from a Christian view. These guidelines (or "guardrails") could indicate, as it were, the "room to move" within certain boundaries; hence they could take on the function of what the theologians call the *norma negativa*.

The effort to justify today's sport from the biblical writings is understandable, but in my opinion it is a waste of effort. Since

44. John Chrysostom, *Saint Chrysostom's Homilies on Galatians, Ephesians, Philippians,* vol. 13 of *Nicene and Post-Nicene Fathers of the Christian Church,* ed. Alexander Roberts and James Donaldson (Peabody: Hendrickson Publishers, 1995), 239.

there are not and cannot be direct points of reference, one refers back to biblical statements on the physical nature of man in general. Since they are usually used in a context, that is, to state other truths (than the value of sport), these aforementioned biblical quotations do not lead to the desired result, that of proving that sport was recommendable for Christians and morally valuable. Such an expectation proves to be an illusion. But that does not mean that the biblical writings do not offer a fundamental view to us about what is intended in all human behavior in the end. Man is related in his whole existence as a physical being to the absolute God. The Bible speaks of the person being created in the "image of God." This relation to God is constitutive for the human person. In fact, according to the Christian view, our "desire to be like God apart from God"—which is tantamount to claiming to not have need of a transcendental Absolute—is the cause of our hopelessness (*Heillosigkeit*). On the other hand, the health of our entire being (*Heilsein*), for which we Christians use the term "salvation," and the basic words of which are "mercy," "love," and "grace," cannot be achieved by man alone. Here we meet the fundamental difference between the Christian message and the conception that our secular society, and concomitantly modern sport, has of itself.

The criterion of assessment for today's sport results from these considerations: Does sport remain "open" to this salvific meaning that comes from above? Or is it enclosed in a manmade "secular religion" that tends toward the "cult" of man himself?

From the agon images and metaphors in St. Paul's writings, any assessment or approval of the athletics of his time cannot be derived. It is improbable, and in my opinion impossible, that St. Paul ever gave his approval for instance of boxing, which was a "life-or-death struggle."[45] All the more one cannot conclude from

45. Cf. Michael Poliakoff, *Combat Sports in the Ancient World* (New Haven, Conn.: Yale University Press, 1995).

the use of these comparisons a fundamental valuation of modern sport. The Apostle Paul wants only to illustrate the trouble and effort that the service to the Gospel requires of him as an apostle, but also of each Christian. Just as a life of privation is demanded of the athlete if he wants to achieve victory, so too, through baptism, the Christian commits himself to an appropriate effort.

As far as the views of the early Christian writers are concerned, it is to be made perfectly clear that they—due to the influence of the philosophical thinking of their time— express human nature in terms that are representative of anthropologic dualism, hence implying a lower valuation if not also a contempt of the body. But the doctrine about the goodness of God's creation, not to mention the positive references to the Incarnation, moderates these body-devaluing statements of many Church Fathers. Thus, in spite of these certainly dualist positions, bodily care and physical exercises are endorsed by early Christian authors. Yet one traces the justification of this positive attitude in the reasonableness of those actions and not in motives of pleasure or fun; only the motives of cleanliness and health are considered reasonable and therefore determining. This rational justification of physical exercises, which found its expression up to our time in moral-theology manuals, in lectures, and the like, needs to be corrected or supplemented. Health should not be the primary motivation for people to engage in sport, but rather, pleasure and joy in this physical movement. It is in the very moment of play where these motivations are manifested and best expressed. Physical play is an activity that stems out of an internal need, from the impetus of being alive.[46]

Nonetheless, different forms of athletics such as wrestling and boxing are decisively shunned by early Christian authors because of their cruelty—and brutality—and also because of the dietary practices associated with them. But the decisive argument against

---

46. Cf. Bamberg "Von Wert und Würde menschlicher Muße."

the athletic competition of their time was its link with idolatry. This applies not only to the Olympic Games but also to all the contests. They are regarded as meetings of demons, as gatherings that are dedicated to the devil. By his baptismal promises, the Christian has rejected these activities, the so-called *pompa diaboli*.

Here we should not be afraid of extending this critique to the Olympic idea. From its founder Pierre de Coubertin but also in the conception of his followers, the Olympic Games are conceived as cultic celebrations for the idolization of man and his achievement. Does this not also apply to other areas of modern sport? Can such a "sport" (especially the top-level sport), which has nothing or hardly something to do with educational and ethical values, still be reformed? Is it even still worthy to be reformed? How and to what extent should the Church cooperate with this degenerated sport, or even commit itself to it? Should we not agree with Eugen König's assessment that the top-level sport has become "in its internal structure an a-moral, nihilistic sport," "a sport that proves to be completely immune and resistant to all ... ethical measures"?[47]

As for the often detailed images and comparisons from ancient agonism that can be found in the writings of the early Christian authors, the same criteria applies here as it does for St. Paul's writings: no assessment or approval of their contemporary athletics may be read into them. With all the more reason, this applies to modern sport, particularly since this metaphoric language is accompanied by the decisive rejection of some of these athletic practices. In their homilies and writings, the images and comparisons based in examples from the well-known and popular athletic competitions serve principally as a way to admonish the listeners and to encourage them in the living of their Christian life.

47. Eugen König, "Ethik und Zweckrationalität des technologischen Sports," in *Sportethik: Regeln—Fairness—Doping,* ed. Claudia Pawlenka (Paderborn: Mentis, 2004), 203.

As a result of my statements on the biblical and patristic foundations for a Christian view of sport, it should be perfectly clear that I see only three main conclusions that can help as criteria in assessing modern sport. First of all, without the acknowledgement of man's relation to the transcendental God, sport becomes a "substitute religion," a type of "cult of man." In fact, the claim that sport in and of itself can be a "system that communicates sense" to people of today is to be firmly rejected. Secondly, the lingering negativity toward the body is be corrected. The nondualistic view of man as presented in the Old and New Testaments depicts play and consequently sport as an "expression" of the one, holistic human person, and is an expression of his being alive. Lastly, all approaches to sport, and particularly any practices within sport, that are directed against life, health, and the integral development of the person, are to be exposed as inhuman and to be categorically rejected.

Kevin Lixey, L.C.

5 Sport in the Magisterium of Pius XII

Before beginning our discussion on Pius XII, we should note that preceding pontiffs were certainly not hostile to sport. Pius X received Olympic founder Pierre de Coubertin in 1905. Coubertin came to Rome on a twofold mission: to ensure that the fourth Olympiad of 1908 would be held in Rome, and secondly, "to persuade the Vatican to raise the sort of 'interdict' laid on sports education in many clerical circles."[1] He said that his first point was not achieved, but his second was! Coubertin writes:

Unlike most heads of religious establishments, Pope Pius X and Cardinal Merry del Val, Secretary of State, were not at all prejudiced against sport.... His Holiness, interested in the idea of a Roman Olympiad, spoke very favorably of it. The following season a festival of gymnastics was held during a pilgrimage of French, Belgian, and other Catholic guilds, which the Pope presided over in the famous courtyard of St Damasus; a very sympathetic spectacle.[2]

Also, Pius XI was a former mountain climber who had ascended to the heights of Mt. Rosa and gave five brief discourses on sport: the

1. Norbert Müller, *Olympism: Selected Writings of Pierre de Coubertin* (Lausanne: I.O.C., 2000), 410.
2. Ibid.

"Achille Ratti Climbing Club" in England still bears his name as a witness to his sporting achievements.

However, even though Pius X and Pius XI received sporting associations in the papal courtyard, it was Pius XII who was considered a "friend of sport."[3] During his pontificate—one of the longest in history (1939–58)—he pronounced over twenty interventions that regarded the theme of sport. Some were brief, but there were three substantial discourses that gave much shape and substance to a Catholic vision of sport and physical recreation-education; namely: a speech given in Rome on the Feast of Pentecost, May 20, 1945, to a large gathering of Catholic youth sport associations; a speech given on November 8, 1952, on the occasion of the Italian Congress of Physical Education in Rome; a speech pronounced on October 9, 1955, to members of the Centro Sportivo Italiano gathered in Rome for the occasion of their tenth anniversary.

My approach to this study of sport in Pius XII is that of considering five central themes within these discourses: the Church's concern for sport; a Christian vision of the body and the person; the educational and formative aspects of sport; some precautions; and lastly, the connection between sport and the spiritual life.[4]

Pius XII Justifies the Church's Concern for Sport

Major characteristics of the social climate in postwar Europe at the time of Pius XII's pontificate were growth, reconstruction, and urbanization as well as the challenge of secularization. In Italy in particular, there was the problem of fascism, which caused frictions especially between Church associations such as Catholic Action and the dominating regime of the state. In fact, the Holy

3. Robert Feeney, *A Catholic Perspective: Physical Exercise and Sports* (Marysville, Wash.: Aquinas Press, 1995), 19.

4. For a further study of themes in Pius XII, cf. Luis Alberto Duque Salas, "El Valor Humano y Cristiano del deporte según el Magisterio Pontificio: de Pio XII a Juan Pablo II" (Ph.D. dissertation, Pontificium Athenaeum Sanctae Crucis, 1997).

Father had to discourage children and parents from participating in certain organizations, which, under the influence of this regime, were educating children in aggression. Sport was one of those particular fields that acutely experienced the threat of secularization. Catholic sporting associations that had sprung up at the turn of the century were in crisis because of the dominance of anti-Catholic regimes and other non-Catholic associations that were competing for the youth as well.

With his motivation of a zeal for youth, one of Pius XII's first objectives regarding the theme of sport was to overcome existing prejudices about the Church's involvement with sport itself. In 1942, during a discourse in which he commented on the second part of the Apostles' Creed to a group of priests and pilgrims, Pius XII noted:

> We live in an era marked by a "physical culture," which accuses the Church of giving too little importance to this. An unfounded accusation! The Church has never condemned the natural, healthy, and useful aspects that physical exercise offers. In fact, it can even improve (when it is not impeded) successful results in the education and discipline of youth. It also affirms and puts into practice the principle that the things of the body must be subordinated to the spirit, and provides a dyke against the assaulting waves of the cult of the flesh, that has no soul or conscience.[5]

This is his defense of physical culture, but what does he say about sport itself? At Pentecost in 1945, Pius XII received a large gathering of youth from the newly formed Centro Sportivo Italiano (CSI) together with members of the Italian Olympic Committee (CONI) in the courtyard of St. Damasus. He used this occasion to give a substantial discourse on the contribution that sport can make to the betterment of youth. We will soon touch upon many

5. Pius XII, "La verità della seconda parte del simbolo apostolico" [The truths of the second part of the Apostles' Creed] (February 17, 1942), in *Discorsi e Radiomessaggi di Pio XII*, vol. 3 (Vatican: Tipografia Poliglotta Vaticana), 371.

aspects of this discourse. I would now like to consider his opening argument in favor of sport, which he supports with St. Paul's
phrase: "In eating, in drinking," wrote the Apostle of the Gentiles
to the Corinthians, "in all that you do, do everything as for God's
glory" (1 Cor 10:31). Pius XII notes: "St. Paul here is speaking of
physical activity. In the phrase 'in all that you do,' therefore, may
well be understood the care of the body, 'sport'! He often speaks
of sport explicitly, in fact: of races, of fights, and not in a spirit of
criticism or condemnation, but as one acquainted with them, and
ennobling them with his Christian conception."[6]

These words of St. Paul provide the basis for Pius XII's approach
to sport. If St. Paul spoke of sports not in a spirit of criticism or condemnation, but as one acquainted with them, and ennobling them
with his Christian conception, then we must do the same. Pius XII
urged Christians to ennoble sport with a Christian conception of it
and to take interest in it. He concludes: "In the final analysis, what
is sport if not a form of education for the body? This education is
closely related to morality. How then could the Church not care
about it? And in fact, the Church has always shown for the body a
care and respect which materialism, with its idolatrous cult, has
never manifested."[7]

So, "care" of the body—yes; but "cult" of the body—no! According to Pius XII, the Church must be engaged in the world of sport in
order to safeguard its true values, enlighten it, and elevate youth
through its education components. As we read: "Strive earnestly
now to put this into practice, conscious that in the field of physical
culture the Christian concept needs to receive nothing from outside, but has much to give. No less than others, you, too, can ac-

6. Pius XII, "The Sporting Ideal" (May 20, 1945), in Robert Feeney, *A Catholic
Perspective: Physical Exercise and Sports* (Marysville, Wash.: Aquinas Press, 1995),
27–28.
    7. Ibid., 28.

cept and adopt that which in the various sporting meetings is truly good. But in what concerns the place which sport should have in human life, for the individual, for the family and the community, the Catholic ideal is a safeguard and enlightenment. The experience of the past decades has been most instructive in this sense: it has proved that only the Christian attitude toward sport can effectively combat false concepts and pernicious tendencies, and prevent their evil influence. In compensation, it enriches physical culture with all which tends to raise the spiritual value of man. What is more, it directs sport towards a noble exaltation of the dignity, vigor, and efficiency of life fully and strongly Christian. When he remains faithful to the tenets of his faith, the apostolate of the sportsman consists in this."[8]

The pope's address was very well received by the CSI, whose president, Luigi Gedda, considered this event to be a sort of "baptism" of sport on behalf of the Holy Father. Gedda remarked: "We have heard the praise of physical exercise, and especially of mountaineering from the Supreme spiritual authority, but never has your holiness sketched such a portrait so complete and so precise about the significance that sport assumes within a Christian perspective."[9]

Another occasion in which Pius XII defended the Church's interest in sport against certain prejudices came ten years later, when he explained why he had to make this argument in the first place. Referring to his previous meeting with the CSI, he observed:

It was necessary to explain that the Church could not overlook, as if something foreign to her, its concern for the body and physical activity, as if only the purely religious things, and the exclusively spiritual, were of her competence; it was necessary to explain that there exist natural and Chris-

8. Ibid., 33–34.

9. Alberto Greganti, ed., *Cent'anni di storia nella realtà dello sport Italiana*, vol. 2 (Roma: Centro Sportivo Italiano, 2006), 49.

tian virtues, without which sport would not be able to develop to the full, but would inevitably be trapped in a materialism, closed in on itself; it was necessary to explain that the Christian principles and norms applied to sport open it up to more lofty horizons, illuminated by heavenly light.[10]

Here there emerge three basic arguments of Pius XII's "apologia" in favor of the Church's concern for the world of sport: (1) both body and soul are included within the scope of the Church's care, and not just the soul; (b) the Christian virtues presuppose the human virtues and bring them to perfection; and (3) Christian principles can free sport from materialism and open it up to greater horizons.

One other significant moment in the promotion of the Church's interest in sport was the personal example that Pius XII gave in a discourse to the youth of Catholic Action. Breaking with certain protocols of formality then in place, Pius XII mentions the name of a famous Italian athlete in his speech to these youth! Notice also the sportive imagery of his speech directed precisely to young men:

The time for reflection and planning has passed. Now is the time for action. The difficult race that St. Paul spoke of is underway. Now is the hour of intense effort. Even a few seconds could be decisive to the victory. Admire your own Gino Bartali, member of Catholic Action: he has so many times won the much sought after jersey. You also, must compete in this greatest of championships, and in such a way that you will win a prize that is the most noble: Sic currite ut comprehendatis (1 Cor. 9:24).[11]

It was noted that when Pius XII pronounced the name "Bartali" there was a dizzy stir in the crowd as this was the first time it had ever happened. It seemed scandalous to those who never thought

10. Pius XII, "Le Virtù per una Cristiana Educazione Ginnica Atletica e Agonistica" [The virtues of a Christian education in gymnastics, athletics, and competition] (October 9, 1955), in Discorsi e Radiomessaggi di Pio XII, vol. 17 (Vatican: Tipografia Poliglotta Vaticana, 1955), 280–81.

11. Pius XII, "Agli uomini della Azione Cattolica" (September 7, 1947), in Discorsi e Radiomessaggi di Pio XII, vol. 9 (Vatican: Tipografia Poliglotta Vaticana, 1947), 214.

the word "sport" or the names of athletes would enter directly into the life of the Church.[12] Yet, as an apostle who was able to read the sign of the times, and sport being one of them, Pius XII used the example of this sports figure to motivate the youth of his day.

A Christian Appreciation of the Body and the Person

Once Pius XII had opened the door of the Church to the world of sport, he needed to also situate it into its proper context. As we have already seen, Christianity is seen as a factor that can and must ennoble sport. The first point to consider is that of the human body. How does Christianity ennoble a vision of the body and the human person? As early as 1942, in his commentary on the Apostles' Creed, Pius XII noted how the Christian belief in the resurrection gives new value to the body and our human actions on earth:

Each one will take up again their body and with their own eyes will contemplate Christ. It is good, that the body, our companion in the good and the bad of our life on earth, should also accompany the soul in the life of happiness or unhappiness in eternity.... In doing good, weren't both the body and the soul subject to fatigue and merit, effort and suffering? Therefore, it shall be that the body accompanies the soul into happiness.... And this is the most noble prize, the highest appreciation of the body.[13]

The human body is, in its own right, God's masterpiece in the order of visible creation, and Pius XII taught that the sciences should help us discover this. In his substantial discourse entitled "Sport and Gymnastics, in the Light of Conscience, Religion and Morality," given to participants of the Italian Congress of Physical Education in Rome in 1952, he eloquently points this out:

With every day that passes, these sciences [of the human body] give us new knowledge, and lead us from marvel to marvel, showing us the mar-

12. Cf. Greganti, *Cent'anni di storia nella realtà dello sport Italiana*, 47.
13. Pius XII, "La verità della seconda parte del simbolo apostolico," 370–71.

velous fabric of the body and the harmony of even its smallest parts. [...] From the aesthetic standpoint men of artistic genius in every age, both painters and sculptors, have themselves recognized the unutterable fascination of the beauty and living power which nature has bestowed on the human body. Religious and moral thought recognizes and accepts all this: but it goes even further. It teaches us to be mindful of the body's link with its first origin, and attributes to it a sacred character, of which the natural sciences and art have not, of themselves, any idea. The King of the universe, in one way or another, formed from the slime of the earth the marvelous work which is the human body. It was to be a worthy crown of creation. [...] Indeed, as the Apostle plainly says, the body belongs to the Lord; our bodies are "members of Christ." "Do you not know," he exclaims, "that your members are the temple of the Holy Spirit, who is in you, whom you have from God, and that you are not your own? ... Glorify God and bear Him in your body" (1 Cor 6:13–20).[14]

Pius XII noted that the Lord intended that the human body should flourish here below and enjoy immortality in the glory of heaven. He has linked it to spirit in the unity of the human nature, to give to the soul a taste of the enchantment of the works of God's hands, to help it to see the Creator of them both in his mirror, and so to know, adore, and love him. In fact, he reminds us that "it is not God who made the body mortal. It was sin!"[15]

Pius XII thus offers us a balanced realism about man as made in the imago Dei, but wounded by sin, which he takes up again in his discourse of 1952, where he comments on the passage from St. Paul's letter to the Romans: "I see another law in my members, warring against the law of my mind and making me prisoner of the law of sin that is in my members" (Rom 7:23). The pontiff soberly observes: "The daily drama woven into the life of man could not be more vividly described. From the day on which their full sub-

14. Pius XII, "Education and Sport" (November 8, 1952), in Feeney, *A Catholic Perspective*, 46–48.
15. Pius XII, "The Sporting Ideal," 28.

ordination to the spirit was lost through original sin, the instincts and powers of the body have gained a mastery, and, stifling the voice of reason, can prevail over the powers of the will in striving for good."[16]

In this sense, Pius XII sees sport as a double-edged sword. The person must be aware that their human nature is wounded by sin, and sport can also be an occasion for sin: "In the intensive use and exercise of the body, this fact must be taken into account. Just as there are gymnastics and sport which, by their austerity, help to keep the instincts in check, so, too, there are other forms of sport which reawaken them either by violent pressure or by sensual allurement."[17] Besides discovering the dignity of the body, another key premise or principle that emerges in Pius XII is this: sport must always be at the service of the human person and never an end in itself.

Sport as Formative and Educational

As mentioned, sport is not an end in itself, but must be directed to the overall good of the human person. Besides the immediate purpose of sport, which Pius XII sees as the education, development, and strengthening of the body in its constitution and power of movement, it can also serve as a means to achieve other ends: "as their more remote purpose, you have the use made, by the soul, of the body so prepared, for the development of the interior or exterior life of the person; as their still deeper purpose, that of contributing to its perfection; and lastly, there is the supreme purpose of man as man, the goal common to every form of human activity—that of bringing man closer to God."[18]

These aims flow from the idea of Pius XII, mentioned previ-

16. Pius XII, "Education and Sport," 49.
17. Ibid.
18. Ibid., 45–46.

ously, that Christianity can and must elevate sport to these greater horizons. So, how does sport achieve these remoter purposes? Let us begin with this idea, forwarded on more than one occasion, of sport as serving "to rest the mind and prepare it for new work, to sharpen the senses in order to acquire greater intensity and penetration in the intellectual faculties, to exercise the muscles and become accustomed to effort in order to temper the character and form a will as hard and elastic as steel."[19]

In order to further expound on this point, Pius XII comments on a passage from St. Paul:

And let no one reprove St. Paul his bold expression: "I buffet my own body and make it my slave" (1 Cor. 9:27). For in that same passage, Paul is basing himself on the example of the keen athletes! You are well aware from personal experience that sport, undertaken with conscious moderation, fortifies the body, gives it health, makes it fresh and strong, but to achieve this work of education, it subjects the body to a rigorous discipline which dominates it and really makes it a slave: training in stamina, resistance to pain, a severe habit of continence and temperance, are all indispensable conditions to carry off the victory. Sport is an effective antidote to softness and easy living. It awakens the sense of order, and forms the man in self-examination and mastery of self, in despising danger, without either boasting or cowardice.[20]

Pius XII sees willpower and self-mastery as distinct from mere physical strength, as it requires a conscious effort of the will and not mere passion. As he notes:

So you see already how it goes far beyond mere physical strength, and leads man to moral strength and greatness. This is what Cicero with incomparable lucidity of style expressed when he wrote: "Exercendum ... corpus et ita afficiendum est, ut obeodire consilio rationique possit in exsequendis negotiis et in labore tolerando." The body should be so treat-

19. Pius XII, "The Sporting Ideal," 31.
20. Ibid., 29.

ed and trained as to be able to obey the counsel of wisdom and reason, whether it be a matter of work to be done or trials to be borne.[21]

In a brief discourse given to representatives of the Central Sports School—an intercollegiate program in the United States—Pius XII keenly reaffirmed this point:

> Sport, properly directed, develops character, makes a man courageous, a generous loser, and a gracious victor; it refines the senses, gives us intellectual penetration, steels the will to endurance. It is not merely a physical development then. Sport, rightly understood, is an occupation of the whole man.[22]

As Pius XII noted previously, it is necessary to explain that there exist natural and Christian virtues, and that these have a reciprocal relationship. The Christian virtues help sport to develop to the full and prevent it from being closed in on itself.[23] Yet, the natural virtues also help in the formation of the Christian. This is a key point that is valid for all spheres of education: first the man, then the saint. In other words, the natural virtues form a pedestal upon which the theological virtues can rest. As Pius XII explained to the CSI in 1945: "Sport is the school of loyalty, of courage, of fortitude, of resolution and universal brotherhood: all natural virtues, these, but which form for the supernatural virtues a sound foundation, and prepare man to carry without weakness the weight of the greatest responsibilities."[24]

And the human virtues—as learned and acquired from the

---

21. Ibid., 30.

22. Pius XII, "Speech to the Central Sports School of the U.S Armed Forces" (July 29, 1945), original text in English in *Discorsi e Radiomessaggi di Pio XII*, vol. 7 (Vatican: Tipografia Poliglotta Vaticana, 1945), 129.

23. Regarding sport's educational dimension, Cardinal Eduardo Pironio notes the influence that Pius XII had on subsequent pontiffs. Cf. Eduardo Pironio, "Lo Sport nei documenti pontifici," in *Lo Sport nei Documenti Pontifici*, ed. G. Gandolfo and Luisa Vassallo (Brescia, Italy: La Scuola, 1994), 254.

24. Pius XII, "The Sporting Ideal," 30.

practice of sport—can in turn be put at the service of one's faith. We will take this up in greater detail at a later point, but allow me to quote once again his address of 1945, in which he speaks about the link between discipline that comes from the human virtues and martyrdom:

Have you ever noticed the considerable number of soldiers among the martyrs whom the Church venerates? Their body and character formed by the training inherent to the profession of arms, they were at least the equal of their comrades in their country's service, in strength, in courage; but they proved themselves to be incomparably superior to them by their readiness to fight and sacrifice themselves in the loyal service of Christ and of his Church. Animated by the same faith and by the same spirit, may you, too, be disposed to put everything in second place after your duties as Christians.[25]

Some Principles and Precautions for the Practice of Sport

Pius XII saw the Catholic ideal as a safeguard for sport. As mentioned above, he noted that the experience of the past decades has proved that only the Christian attitude toward sport can effectively combat false concepts and pernicious tendencies, and prevent their evil influence. The "Friend of Sport" took the occasion in 1952 of the Italian Congress of Physical Education, appropriately titled "Sport and Gymnastics, in the light of Conscience, Religion and Morality," to point out how the Christian perspective sheds light and can prevent possible deviations in sport.

When you turn, instead, to the religious and moral aspect the principle of finality, already mentioned, gives you the key to the solution of the problems which can arise in the forum of your conscience. In the consideration of ordinary activity, it is enough for you to bear in mind that every human action (or omission) falls under the prescriptions of the natural law, of

25. Ibid., 60.

the positive precepts of God, and of the competent human authority: a threefold law that is really only one—the Divine Will manifested in various ways. To the rich young man of the Gospel Our Lord briefly replied: "If thou wilt enter into life, keep the Commandments." And to the further question, "Which?" the Redeemer referred him to the well-known prescriptions of the Decalogue. The same can be said here. Do you wish to act rightly in gymnastics and sport? Then keep the Commandments.[26]

So as not to remain in the abstract, he made some concrete applications to the world of sport:

Give to God in the first place the honor that is due to Him, and above all keep the Lord's day holy, since sport does not excuse us from the discharge of our religious duties. "I am the Lord thy God," Almighty God declares in the Decalogue, "thou shall not have false gods before Me" (Exod 20:2–3), that is to say, not even our own body, in the physical exercises of sport, this would be a return to paganism. In like manner the Fourth Commandment, which bids us preserve the harmony that the Creator intended to reign in the bosom of the family, recalls fidelity to family obligations, which should take precedence over the so-called demands of sport and the things that pertain to it.[27]

As for the so-called extreme sports so in vogue today, the pontiff recalled: "The divine Commandments also demand the safeguarding of one's own life and the lives of others, as well as the health of one's own body and that of others, neither of which is it permissible, without good reason, to expose to serious danger in gymnastics and sport."[28] Pius XII distinguished between sport that is a "desperate gamble" and that which may involve certain risks. He states:

How distant it is, too, from that prideful madness which cannot resist ruining the health and strength of the athlete in unhealthy exaggeration

26. Pius XII, "Education and Sport," 54.
27. Ibid.
28. Ibid., 55.

simply in order to carry off the honors in some boxing bout or competition at high speeds and which at times does not hesitate to expose his life to danger. Sport which is worthy of the name makes man courageous in the face of danger, but does not authorize his undergoing a grave risk without proportionate cause. This would be morally illicit.[29]

Here Pius XII refers to a distinction made before by Pius XI between true danger and remote danger. "When I say 'true danger' I mean a state of affairs which either by its very nature, or due to the dispositions of the person subject to it, cannot presumably be faced without some evil resulting."[30] Pius XII notes that when his predecessor, Achille Ratti, climbed Mount Rosa, "He did not have the least intention of attempting what is called a 'desperate gamble'! True mountaineering is not a sport for breaknecks, but is all a question of prudence, and a little courage, strength, fortitude, and love for nature and her most hidden treasures."[31]

Regarding the sixth and ninth commandments and sport, Pius XII also observed:

Even from the aesthetic standpoint, in the pleasure derived from beauty and the admiration of rhythm in dance and gymnastics, instinct can subtly put its poison into the mind. There is, moreover, in sport and gymnastics, and in rhythm and dance, a certain nudism which is neither necessary nor proper. Not without reason did an impartial observer remark, some decades ago: "What is of interest to the masses in this regard is not the beauty of the nude, but the nudity of the beauty." The religious and moral sense places its veto on that kind of gymnastics and sport.[32]

To the media, Pius XII gave five fundamental principles for the governance of sport: (1) sport, being the care of the body, must not

29. Pius XII, "The Sporting Ideal," 31.

30. Giovanni Bobba and Fratesco Mauro, eds., *Scritti Alpinistici del Sac. Dott. Achille Ratti* (Milano: Bertieri-Vanzetti, 1923), 59.

31. Pius XII, "The Sporting Ideal," 31.

32. Pius XII, "Education and Sport," 49.

degenerate into the cult of matter, becoming an end in itself; (2) it is at the service of the whole man, and therefore it must not only not obstruct man's intellectual and moral formation, but must promote, aid, and second it; (3) sport, in relation to professional activity, be it intellectual or manual, should provide a relief which enables man to return to work with new strength of will and nerves relaxed; (4) sport should not compromise the intimacy between husband and wife, nor the holy joys of family life; (5) on Sunday, first place must be given to God. The Church does not forbid sports on Sunday. It looks upon it kindly, provided that Sunday remains the Lord's Day, the day of repose of body and soul.[33]

Sport and the Spiritual Life

Lastly, how does sport relate to the supreme purpose of the human person, the goal common to every form of human activity—that of bringing man closer to God? Our point of departure will be a brief address that Pius XII gave to a group of alpinists, titled "The Lessons of the Mountain," in which he noted that these lessons are spiritual uplifting, lessons more of moral than physical strength. After commenting on how contact with nature—with its pristine beauty, its fresh air, its silence and grandeur—refreshes one's soul and gives the alpinist a more lofty vision of creation, he eloquently observes:

Still higher! The confused, discordant noises of useless argument, or the futile nonsense of earth, the conflicts of self-love and mean interests, die out on the mountain, lost in the majestic silence which is no while disturbed by the soft murmurs or solemn rumbles of nature. And when the echo of thunder, or falls, or landslides rebounds from peak to peak, the heart, filled with emotion or anxiety, feels nonetheless more at ease in the midst of the purposeless and wicked chit-chat of man. Blessed is he

33. Pius XII "Fundamental Principles Governing Sporting Activities" (November 10, 1951), in Feeney, *A Catholic Perspective,* 42–43.

who can dominate the worldly bustle which surrounds him, and savor in silence and recollection the peace of God.[34]

Yet Pius XII noted that there is still something else, another force, that drives them on:

[Alpinists] are driven by a powerful interior impulse, by a mysterious passion to fight at any cost against difficulty and to overcome obstacles. This tendency, when it is not shackled but guided by reason (and not by thoughtless temerity) is an aspect of the virtue of fortitude, whose role it is, according to the Angelic Doctor, to make reason prevail over exhaustion caused by physical pain: "Dacit virtus fortitudinis, ut ratio non absorbeatur a corporalibus doloribus" (*Summa Theologica*, 2a2ae, q. 123, a.8).[35]

Thus sport can and should be at the service of God. In fact, as Pius XII noted: "But while the pagan subjected himself to the strict regime of sport to obtain a merely corruptible crown, the Christian subjects himself to the same yet with a nobler aim, for an immortal reward."[36] Noticing how often Paul used sporting images (in particular 1 Cor 9:24–27) to illustrate his apostolic life and the life of struggle of the Christian on earth, Pius XII observed:

These words illumine the concept of sport with a mystical radiance. But what matters to the Apostle is the superior reality of which sport is the image and symbol: unceasing work for Christ, the restraining and subjection of the body to the immortal soul, eternal life the prize of this struggle. For the Christian athlete and for you too, beloved sons, sport must not be the supreme ideal, the ultimate goal, but must serve and tend towards that goal.[37]

---

34. Pius XII, "Lessons of the Mountain" (September 26, 1948), in Feeney, *A Catholic Perspective*, 39.

35. Ibid., 40.   36. Pius XII, "The Sporting Ideal," 32.

37. Ibid., 34.

Conclusion

In this brief sketch of a Christian vision of sport in the writings of Pius XII, I have tried to underline some basic aspects. First, that it is the competence of the Church to be concerned with sporting activity, and not out of a curious interest, but for its important human and apostolic repercussions; that is, sport has a need of being ennobled by Christianity. Secondly, while avoiding the extremes of materialism, the body, though wounded by sin, is good, and with the presence of divine grace, becomes the temple of the Holy Spirit. As for the educational aspects of sporting activity, Pius XII highlighted the self-mastery and discipline that can be acquired through the practice of sport and the significance of the natural virtues as a basis of the supernatural virtues. Lastly, sport is seen by Pius XII as a symbol of the effort with which we must live our lives as Christians, always fixing our gaze on to the upward prize in Christ Jesus.

Along these lines, I wish to conclude with one last quote from Pius XII, which sums up this link between sport and the spiritual life.

If ... sport is for you not only an image, but also in some way the execution of your noblest duty, if, that is to say, in your sporting activity you render your body more docile and obedient to the soul and to your moral obligations, if, furthermore, by your example you contribute to modern sporting activity a form which better corresponds to the dignity of man and the commandments of God, then you are in one and the same activity putting into effect the symbol and the thing symbolized, as St. Paul explained it. And then one day you will be able to say with the great Apostle: "I have fought the good fight; I have finished the race; I have redeemed my pledge; I look forward to the prize that is waiting for me, the prize I have earned. The Lord, the judge whose award never goes amiss, will grant it to me when that day comes, to me, yes, and to all those who learned to welcome His coming" (2 Tim. 4:7–8).[38]

38. Ibid., 35.

Bishop Carlo Mazza

6 Sport in the Magisterium of John Paul II

Sport has always been a theme present within the agenda of the Church, as the many documents of the last century bear witness.[1] In a concise way, we can attribute the following characteristics to these pronouncements by the magisterium regarding sport: they have an exhortative character; they highlight the educational function that is accredited to sport while always safeguarding the dignity of life in the case of it being threatened by the practice of sport; they tend to underline sport's social-cultural aspect; and lastly, they provide an outline for a spirituality of sport.

Regarding this phenomenon of sport, the Church has sought to react without prejudice and has even manifested a sympathetic interest. Its concern has been that of offering a reflection within a pedagogical framework, sustained by the values of an ethical order that pertains to the threefold dimension of the good of the human person: the physical, psychological, and supernatural. Naturally, the Church has pointed out the benefits of sport, such as self-

1. See Commissione ecclesiale pastorale del tempo libero turismo e sport, *Sport e vita cristiana: nota pastorale 50* (Bologna: Edizione Dehoniane, 1995), 11–12.

discipline, "ascesis," and teamwork, while also indicating the risks and situations that can threaten the integrity and harmonious development of the human person. Most of the discourses addressing these issues have been directed typically to national and international sports institutions, to the directors and heads of the larger sports organizations, but not without failing to address directly, and on numerous occasions, professional athletes themselves because of their relevance as role models for generations of youth.

A preliminary analysis of these papal texts reveals no immediate or explicit intention to develop an organic formulation of the thought of the Church regarding sport in a systematic way. In fact, each pontifical intervention was made within a particular ecclesial context, and determined in great part by the specific characteristics of the audience, and often tied to a particular circumstance or the celebration of a particular event or activity within the Church or within society as a whole. Consequently, these exterior factors have determined the quality of these pontifical addresses, making it hard to speak of true and proper systematic magisterium in the technical sense, inasmuch as the intention of each of these discourses was conditioned on and tailored to the particular audience being addressed. However, this obviously does not take away from the supreme authority that is given to the one who pronounces these discourses.

Lastly, I would like to add an interesting fact. The quantity and quality of the discourses on sport on the part of the magisterium has intensified at certain transitory moments of history. I would like to recall two: that of the postwar period with Pius XII[2] and that of the so-called era of globalization or media revolution during the pontificate of John Paul II.[3] In both cases, the reflection on sport is

2. See chapter 5 of this volume on Pius XII.
3. See Carlo Mazza, "Sport as Viewed from the Church's Magisterium," in *The World of Sport Today: A Field of Christian Mission,* ed. Pontificium Consilium Pro Laicis (Vatican: LEV, 2006).

framed with a particular poignancy in respect to a critical analysis of the immediate culture and with stunning clarity with respect to the sphere of education and its ethical implications.

John Paul II: Athlete Pope and Pope of Athletes

The past century has experienced an explosion of sports consumption. Sport is the object of desire of millions of persons, of various profiles, becoming a prominent phenomenon of our times. The Church, on the strength of its missionary past, has never been disinterested in sport, and before its imposing emergence, the Church rises to face this challenge. Recently, a great interpreter of this phenomenon has been John Paul II. Many of us can recall unforgettable images and the significant titles given to him for his engagement in this field, such as the "Athlete Pope" or the "Pope of Athletes."

This twofold perspective needs to be taken into account in order to correctly evaluate the approach of John Paul II to sport. Within his person, part of his human identity has been shaped by sporting activity, which has left its mark upon him and is expressed by his affection for sport. On the other hand, the pontiff's reflections on sport give form to a thought that, while being in continuity with the magisterial tradition, produces a new characteristic, which consists in a rereading of previous magisterial teachings regarding sport from his personal experience as an athlete. In doing so, he creates a synthesis that combines his "practical" experience of sport with his philosophical and theological reflections on the same.

This synthesis was seen in a concrete way in the concluding ceremony of the Jubilee of Sport during the Great Jubilee of 2000. At a certain point during the event, the pontiff cast his pleasant gaze around the vast crowd that filled the Olympic stadium to its capacity: children were gathered at his feet; junior track athletes were nearby; while gathered around him were representatives of almost every sports discipline, from track and field members with disabilities to professional soccer players. His penetrating gaze embraced all both as pope and as athlete! This image not only captures a historic event, and an event so symbolic for Italian sport, but also illustrates in an elegant way the climate and the style of the message that this venerated pontiff wanted to give to the world of sport. He speaks to these athletes from within the world of sport itself: he is at home in this world and he speaks to them as one of them.

Rightly so, people speak of John Paul II as one who has been a sportsman from his youth, and thus he is even upheld as an excellent role model for younger athletes. However, highlighting only this does not do justice to the higher and enduring value therein. In fact, the "exemplary sportsmanship" of the pope is expressed above all in his service: in his "being for others"; in his unlimited dedication to humanity; in way of living that was always focused on the good of the human person and with an illuminating and a passionate intelligence of this reality that knows no discrimination; in the generous gift of self that knew no reserve and struck wonderment in all those who witnessed this, even the most skeptical observer.

Without a doubt, in such a symbolic context that unites the private and public life of the pope, sport takes on a broader meaning with regard to the full realization of the person. And this not only refers to amateur sport at the youth level, but also extends to professional sports. We can even say that it extends to those aspects of professional sport that tend to be transformed or manipulated into pure commerce, performance, or business. The modern-day metamorphosis of sport has not been condemned by John Paul II. However, he warns against it being denaturalized to the point that it becomes unrecognizable, thus losing its original identity as a beautiful and gratuitous gift.

In such a perspective the many discourses of the pontiff formulate an appeal for a significant co-responsibility on the part of those adults involved in sport structures at all levels. While pointing out the need for a new sport and the urgency for its renewal and genuine change, these discourses also reveal the weakness of these structures and their own incapacity for auto-reform. Nonetheless, the demanding requirements that such a renewal implies are made quite evident in the discourses of the pontiff. With great wisdom and long-term vision, John Paul II, the sportsman, does not offer a hypercritical analysis that is as heartless as it is sterile for being so far removed from reality. No! Rather, he perceives and reiterates a request that is implicit in the very sporting phenomenon itself, that is rooted in its dynamic progression and in the real emotions and "passions" of the athletes themselves.

It is not by accident that the pope made his appeal to "everyone, leaders, managers, sport enthusiasts and athletes," so that they might find "a new creative and motivating zeal through sports that know how, in a constructive spirit, to reconcile the complex demands made by the current cultural and social changes with the unchangeable requirements of the human being."[4] Marking the path to be followed with these words, he invites us to make an intellectual and moral leap that has the strength to guide sport in a new direction, rendering it a means of reconciliation between the demands placed upon it by the modern day and those perennial demands of the human person. In doing so, he thus bequeaths to sport a new function as a cultural mediator.

In such a way, to find a "new creative zeal" means investing one's best intellectual and practical resources in order to activate a cultural process that is realized by the effective use of good governance in sport. If this task is assumed by all in a harmonious

4. John Paul II, "Homily at the Mass for Sports Men and Women," 1.

way, and in view of this common project for the good of sport, this much needed movement should have as its final goal the "promotion of the unchangeable requirements of the human being" and the specific needs of each individual. In doing so the pontiff assigns to sport a particular role: that of using in a positive way its fascinating attraction in order to establish a means of mediation between the values—those of sport and of the human person—and cultural changes, thus establishing the necessary conditions for a quantitative leap with regard to the mission of sport in our modern epoch. Beyond all rhetorical emphasis, sport is considered by John Paul II as an important factor for safeguarding the human person inasmuch as it assumes this "reconciling" function within such an impervious cultural context.

The Modern Sports Phenomenon

This newness of sport is expressed on a broad scale, and goes hand in hand with the characteristics of modern culture, such as a cult of the body, the prevalence of technology, relativism, savage competition, dominant consumerism, and globalization. Sport does not spring up from nowhere; rather it develops in close collaboration with the various philosophies of man and in various meanings that are attributed to sport and leisure by civil society.[5]

With profound intelligence, John Paul II intuits the link between a subjective anthropology and the use of free time, acutely noting how such an individualistic and materialistic approach can threaten to empty man of his intrinsic meaning and worth. Thus, all aspects of modern sport need to be deciphered in order to bring to light the interpretive criteria that are capable of founding a new philosophy of sport made to the measure of man and with regard to ethical values that cannot be forsaken. By means of example,

5. See John Paul II, "Speech to Catholic Federation of Sports and Physical Education" (April 3, 1986), *L'Osservatore Romano*, English ed., no. 17, April 28, 1986, 5.

and in no way as an exhaustive list, I would like to briefly reflect on three of these criteria.

Sport as a "Sign of the Times"

Attributing to sport the Vatican II category of a "sign of the times" gives to it a value and a significance that is rich in meaning with regard to the advancement of the person, and of theological valence with respect to the economy of salvation, and particularly, with respect to the categories: creation, incarnation, redemption. The pope in fact explains that "in recent years it has continued to grow even more as one of the characteristic phenomena of the modern era, almost a 'sign of the times' capable of interpreting humanity's new needs and new expectations."[6] Here the emphasis is placed on sport as a mirror of our times that is capable of interpreting contemporary man's hopes and needs.

Consequently, sport becomes a carrier of meaning and thus transcends its simple function as mere physical exercise. It is now more in touch with the complex changes of contemporary society and reveals man's hidden hopes and aspirations. Sport as a "sign of the times" is capable of interpreting life and giving it new meaning in relation to the mystery of the human person. Consequently, the spiritual dimension of sport appears not as something added on to it from the outside, but rather, as an intrinsic quality that the athlete manifests in and through the aesthetically visible gestures of sport as they are perceived by the spectator.

The pope explains that "while it promotes physical fitness and strengthens character, sport must never distract those who practise and appreciate it from their spiritual duties. [...] The spiritual dimension must be cultivated and harmonized with various recreational activities, which include sport."[7] With extreme transparen-

6. John Paul II, "Homily at the Mass for Sports Men and Women," 1.
7. John Paul II, "Address to the International Convention: The Face and Soul of

cy, a twofold dimension appears: that which is at the service of the physical and psychological good of the human person, and that which is related to man's undeniable spiritual constitution. Both of these dimensions are considered as stable and integral to sporting activity. And—without pretending to make sport something greater than it is—the potential of these two dimensions is realized within the realm of sport and is connatural to it. While safeguarding the proper autonomy of these two functions, it can be held that the peculiar nature of sport is directed toward the integral whole of the person.

Sporting activity realizes its objectives in a harmonious way in a context that is fully human and rich in interior balance. And it is only in that perspective that sport can elevate the human person and generate social relations that are rich in human vitality, mental health, physical well-being, and joy-filled emotions pleasing to the entirety of the human person. In this sense, sport can be a sign of the times inasmuch as it can contribute toward the "perfection" of the human person.

The Global Dimension of Sport

The consideration of the global and cultural dimension of sport reveals something unprecedented that has relevant consequences not only for sport's social character but also for its aim and purpose. Beyond being a universal "language" sport can also convey, surprisingly enough, a universal "interpretation" of a sporting event that transcends the boundaries of race and language, constituting a sort of common denominator that brings together the entire human community. The pope recognizes that "sports have spread to every corner of the world, transcending differences between cultures and nations. Because of the global dimensions

Sport" (October 28, 2000), *L'Osservatore Romano*, English ed., no. 46, November 15, 2000, 9.

this activity has assumed, those involved in sports throughout the world have a great responsibility."[8]

These statements from the magisterium highlight an undisputed fact. Sports popularity has spread to every corner of the globe, transcending differences between cultures and nations, simply because it is a sign that is recognized and shared in and of itself as a part of the human patrimony, and because it is played with the same rules that have been universally accepted. From this flows the universal value of the sporting phenomenon and its extraordinary force of attraction. It is, therefore, a question of employing our intelligence in such a way as to look beyond the technical aspect of sport in order to see the many opportunities that arise around the sporting phenomenon and because of it.

Along these same lines and with a certain boldness, the Holy Father himself invited sportsmen "to make sports an opportunity for meeting and dialogue, over and above every barrier of language, race or culture. Sports, in fact, can make an effective contribution to peaceful understanding between peoples and to establishing the new civilization of love."[9]

As it can be easily seen, sport occurs within a spontaneous time and space dynamism. By means of its intrinsic transnational structure it provides occasions of encounter and exchange among the sports disciplines, among its local, national, and international representatives, that extend beyond the mere match or sporting competition. Consequently, sport becomes a catalyst in establishing social relations and knowing other peoples in ways that extend well beyond the playing field and locker room through initiatives of a cultural, fraternal, artistic, and spiritual dimension. Whether at the level of a sporting club or of a greater sports association, these become small steps toward the creation of a "civilization of

8. John Paul II, "Homily at the Mass for Sports Men and Women," 1.
9. Ibid.

justice, love and peace." As the pope notes: "competition between athletes is a universal language which immediately goes beyond the frontiers of nation, race or political persuasion."[10]

In addition, the actual condition of sport in the West manifests critical aspects to such a degree that they reveal that what is at stake is the very future of sport, evidencing a fight for its own survival. In such a context, this recalling of sport's universality, while diversely understood, tends to suggest the need for a sport in its most ideal form. Thus, the pontiff indicates the path to be followed with a renewed willingness and effort: a profound self-examination of the entire sport's system. This reference to sport's planetary dimension should also tend to reshape the way we approach it—a way that is more adapted to the needs of today's multiethnic and multicultural society that is still in the process of global and geopolitical globalization.

The Need for a Critical Analysis

As mentioned, sport is passing through a critical phase in its development, due to rapid cultural changes. More than a few observers claim that if sport intends to survive in its natural essence, it will be constrained to the point of almost disappearing in its actual form in order to find itself again. If this is so, it will require undergoing a critical self-analysis and a discerning process by which can be elaborated new aims of sport in line with this evolving reality in both its structure and its nature. Even in a summary analysis of the actual crisis of sport there emerge both positive and negative aspects, as in any other human activity. These aspects must be vigorously analyzed and then confronted with ethical criteria and with regard to its finality within the prospective of this "new sport."

10. Ibid.

This essential criterion comes to constitute, so to speak, "the soul of sport" and must seek to recall and to strengthen that which is the intrinsic meaning of sporting activity: a synthesis of the bodily, mental, and spiritual activity of the athlete, determined by the complex but undeniable psychosomatic unity of the human person. Regarding this, John Paul II vigorously affirmed: "It is important to identify and promote the many positive aspects of sport, but it is only right also to recognize the various transgressions to which it can succumb."[11] This suggests the need to give sport an ethical orientation, with the emphasis on recognizing the transgressions to which sport is vulnerable in order to remedy them in face of the often hidden complexities of the situation today.

At the same time, the pontiff does not hesitate to strongly encourage the need for a change of mentality and direction in order that "the educational and spiritual potential of sport must make believers and people of good will united and determined in challenging every distorted aspect that can intrude, recognizing it as a phenomenon opposed to the full development of the individual and to his enjoyment of life. Every care must be taken to protect the human body from any attack on its integrity, from any exploitation and from any idolatry."[12] In this way, there emerges the need for believer and nonbeliever to watch over sport and defend it from any aspect that deviates from its original nature and that would go against the natural transparency that sport enjoys.

However, this discourse aims at something still more ambitious. John Paul II is not afraid of assuming a pedagogical and almost didactic tone as he outlines in detail what the aims of this "new" sport should be. In fact, he explicitly urges all to strive together,

11. Ibid.
12. Ibid.

so that sport, without losing its true nature, can answer the needs of our time: sport that protects the weak and excludes no one, that frees young people from the snares of apathy and indifference, and arouses a healthy sense of competition in them; sport that is a factor of emancipation for poorer countries and helps to eradicate intolerance and build a more fraternal and united world; sport which contributes to the love of life, teaches sacrifice, respect and responsibility, leading to the full development of every human person.[13]

The profound intention of the Holy Father—as it is well articulated—is not to delineate who is responsible, but rather, to positively underline the undeniable potential of sport while, in order to indicate the sure path of conversion and of reform, stressing the increasing need for an attitude of discernment. It consists of three particular prerequisites: an unprejudiced reflection; a great openness of spirit; and a broad prospective. Only in this way will it be possible to construct a renewed ethical foundation for the sports system, where each subject, every organism, every society, find its place before its particular and concrete responsibility.

John Paul II situates the mission of the "rehabilitation" of sport principally in the area of discernment. This critical process of analysis must become a style of life for every sportsman and sportswoman. Discernment signifies distinguishing between good and evil; it means making a value judgment and finding its proper application in ethical action. Discernment is proper to every human action and therefore proper also to sport, where it consists in knowing how to take advantage of sports opportunities in order to serve the good of the human person, bettering its positive aspects and uprooting its negative tendencies, with a sound sports pedagogy and wise decisions.

13. Ibid.

Sport in the Service of the Overall Good of the Person

From the words of the venerable pontiff springs the conviction that sport will be valued to the extent that it can become a positive factor and dimension in participants becoming true men and true women of the twenty-first century. This perspective is not without its consequences, inasmuch as it qualifies sport as an identifying element of social, cultural, and anthropological value, and while distinguishing itself from other contemporary phenomena, it constitutes to a great extent that which could become a field of action where Christianity can recover from the advances of modernism. In fact, this claim that we are identifying with the term "new sport" earns for itself a more conscious placement among the different demands of personal and community existence, conferring upon itself a humanizing capacity with regard to an integral vision of that which contributes to the quality of life.

Precisely because sport is not everything for man, but simply one of man's activities, this presupposes a general life ethic and a dynamic and flexible structure capable of integrating into his life the most important and significant moments of human existence. Because of this, it is necessary that sport be lived and experienced with regard to its human and cultural aims, and according to the principles regarding the truth of man. That is to say, it must be lived with an intelligent and passionate spirit, with long-term ethical discipline, and with common sense—totally at the service of the person and aiding his ultimate fulfillment. For this reason, the Holy Father affirms that

sport is not merely the exercise of muscles, but it is the school of moral values and of training in courage, in perseverance, and in overcoming laziness and carelessness. Besides, it is an antidote for weakness, discouragement and dejection in defeat. There is no doubt that these values are of greatest interest for the formation of a personality which consider sports not an end in itself but as a means to total and harmonious physical, moral, and social development.[14]

In the perspective of John Paul II, the person is at the center of every sports activity. As such, the human person perfects himself in sport, and sport itself is perfected if it takes into consideration the primacy of the human person. If man's perfection is sought, not in an abstract way, but rather within a "complexity" that is real and personal, this avoids his being reduced to one more thing among things, and avoids his becoming denaturalized or falling prey to those who, without scruples and deprived of morals, will use him for their own sordid gain.

When sport maintains its high ideal, it will not get pulled down into that which is not proper to it. Consequently, safeguarding sport is a principle that is congruent with a "humanity in progress" and with reference to the spiritual nature of the person. In fact, the latter cannot be considered as something merely added on to the structure of the human person, but is intrinsic to it. Once more, sport accomplishes its end when it tends to be gratuitous, as a free gift of self in an altruistic or exemplary way.

The elevation of sport to the anthropological level where man reveals himself is the great inheritance bequeathed to us by John Paul II. This reaches its maximum social consensus in the degree to which sport is made to the measure of the expectations of the present moment, and is capable of overcoming the maladies that persistently cling to sport: that of violence, of racism, of doping, of hyper-commercialization of sport that degenerates into injustice, inequality, and profuse egoism. The lofty vision for sport in the writings of John Paul II is not only an invitation to review the authentic purpose of sport but also the key with which we should interpret it, which is in light of the human person, and within the

14. John Paul II, "Address to Italian Olympic Medal winners" (November 24, 1984) in *L'Osservatore Romano*, English ed., no. 50, December 3, 1984, 4.

new social and cultural horizons, and, lastly, in light of the unexpected spiritual awakening at the dawn of the third millennium of Christianity.

In this perspective, on the various occasions on which the pontiff has directed his attention to sport, he has expressed his sole and overriding concern for safeguarding the integrity of the human person. This is consistent with a line of thinking that gains its force and is deeply rooted in Christian anthropology and the social doctrine of the Church, above all, the principles of human dignity, subsidiary, and solidarity. With respect to the inalienable dignity and the integrity of the person, as a unity of body and soul, John Paul II demands that sport not only respect the identity and good of the person, but also acknowledge that in doing so it is allowing the human person to reach his or her utmost potential in accordance with the plan of God his Creator, through the free exercise of his conscience and with an ethical responsibility both to himself as an individual and to society as a whole.

John Paul II, while attentive to the latest findings and research in the human sciences, focuses on making a clarification that presupposes the acceptance of the primacy of the person when he explains that

sport, as you well know, is an activity that involves more than the movement of the body: it demands the use of intelligence and the disciplining of the will. It reveals, in other words, the wonderful structure of the human person created by God as a spiritual being, a unity of body and spirit. Athletic activity can help every man and woman to recall that moment when God the Creator gave origin to the human person, the masterpiece of his creative work.[15]

In synthesis, within the framework of the Church's magisterial teachings, where sport is considered a process of development

15. John Paul II, "Address to Participants of Athletic World Championships" (September 2, 1987), *L'Osservatore Romano*, English ed., no. 36, September 7, 1987, 5.

toward "perfection" that brings into play all of the human faculties, the person is upheld as the insurmountable and indisputable point of reference. In fact, as the Holy Father observes, sport "seeks to develop a person's psychic faculties, such as strength, stamina, skill—all working together toward a harmony of movement and action. Through sport we try to attain physical excellence.... However there is another dimension to sports activity. Sport is also an important moment for guaranteeing the balance and total well-being of the person."[16] In such a way, sport is directly and synthetically connected to the true identity of man: both in regard to how he was originally created and also with regard to the glory to which he has been destined.

Sport in a Redeemed Body

From his own sporting experience, John Paul II cannot but recognize how it perfects the body; consequently, he has intended to "cultivate" this intuition and manifest the potential that can be realized through sport. Awareness of being in a "living body" offers a privileged vantage point for providing an analysis of the rapport between sport and the body, in order to outline sport's anthropological value in reference to it. This rapport is seen not only in the moment of maximum performance, but also when it experiences its limit, which can also be a dramatic moment.

The ultimate question, however, is not that of identifying the "limits" of sport, but that of determining the structural limits of the body, something at once weak and sinful as well as powerful and glorious in light of its redemption. In this way, the body's potential, which is manifested in so many ways through the various sporting activities and in the very complex dynamic of sport itself, also confirms—in the light of revelation and the event of redemption—its misery and its need for liberation through grace.

16. Ibid.

In fact, if sport can be seen as a "metaphor of life," it is also accompanied by deviations that appear as cracks in a mirror. They reveal the pressing need for what some have called the "conversion of sport." Sport, which makes up a part of the "all" of that humanity that has been called to salvation in Jesus Christ, is itself in need of redemption. Based on the Pauline doctrine of the body, the pontiffs have often expressed a vigorous appeal for the athletes to be aware that they are "temples of the Holy Spirit," to "glorify God in their bodies" (see 1 Cor 6:13–20), and to exercise a prophetic witness through their good example, as a "true athlete of Christ."[17]

In the words of the Holy Father: "Christ is the more powerful man" (see Mk 1:7), who for our sake confronted and defeated the "opponent," Satan, by the power of the Holy Spirit, thus inaugurating the kingdom of God. He teaches us that, to enter into glory, we must undergo suffering (see Lk 24:26, 46).[18] Consequently, through the Incarnation, sport too is included in the saving work of redemption as the very action of a glorious and redeemed body; it is a manifestation of a new body that is part of the dawn of a new world, and therefore also, a "new sport."

This attention to the values of the corporeal dimension and the stress on its subsequent need for redemption does not hide the fact—on the contrary; it highlights it—that sport must play a dutiful role with regard to the fulfillment of the person. John Paul II summarizes in an excellent way the significance of sport in our age when he says:

Sport is the joy of life, a game, a celebration, and as such it must be properly used and perhaps, today, freed from excess technical perfection and professionalism, through a recovery of its free nature, its ability to strengthen bonds of friendship, to foster dialogue and openness to others, as an expression of the richness of being, much more valid and to

17. John Paul II, "Homily at the Mass for Sports Men and Women," 1.
18. Ibid., 2.

be prized than having, and hence far above the harsh laws of production and consumption and all other purely utilitarian and hedonistic considerations in life.

These ideas of the pontiff, as evident in his writings as they are explicit in his practice of sport, shed light on a Christian vision for sport as they seek to redefine sport as a "recreation" of one's life and a source of joyful social relations which can contribute to building a new humanity.

Conclusion

It is clear that this attempt to recapitulate John Paul II's "sportive reflections" is in no way exhaustive. Nonetheless, it seems that these brief remarks should be enough to delineate the salient points of a magisterial teaching that is original and closely connected with the epochal changes of his time; that is both sensitive to the new and appreciative of the old, according to the Gospel adage of the scribe who is attentive to combine both the old and the new.

In this perspective, the scope of the pontiff's teaching, while attentive to the various deviations of sport, is directed toward the anthropological and cultural phenomena of sport as they pertain to the human person. While describing sport's potential for good, he does not hesitate to point out at the same time its negative aspects, but always within an overall vision that is consistent with the providential designs of Creation and Redemption.

Ultimately, it is man's salvation, in its complex totality, that is so close to the heart of the great "athlete pope."

Bishop Josef Clemens

7 Sport in the Magisterium of Benedict XVI

Philosophical Foundations of the Sporting Phenomenon in Cardinal Ratzinger

More than thirty years ago, on June 1, 1978, at the start of the World Cup that was being held in Argentina (June 1–25, 1978) and was marked by bitter defeat for the Germans, the fifty-year-old Cardinal Joseph Ratzinger, already having been for one year archbishop of Munich-Freising, explained the nucleus of his thought on soccer and sport in general in an interview on the Bavarian Radio program *Zum Sonntag*.[1]

I would like to use as a leitmotif of this investigation this profound and original interview, in which the cardinal and theologian offers a brief philosophical analysis of the modern phenomenon of sport, and soccer in particular. This will help us to better under-

---

1. This interview was first published in German in the Archdiocese of Munich-Freising Bulletin *Ordinariats-Korrespondenz*, no. 19, June 3, 1978; note also its prompt publication in the Catholic journal *Deutsche Tagespost*, June 7, 1978. An English translation is found in Joseph Ratzinger, *Co-Workers of the Truth: Meditations for Everyday of the Year* (San Francisco: Ignatius Press, 1992), 262–63.

stand the typically brief but numerous comments that Pope Benedict XVI has made about sport throughout his pontificate.

It does not seem that Cardinal Ratzinger as head of Congregation for the Doctrine of the Faith (1981–2005) dealt with the phenomenon of soccer or sport in general, but he did include this interview in an anthology of texts published in 1985, and also as pope he permitted it to be included in a publication printed in 2005.[2] All of this indicates the perennial value of these fundamental reflections on the phenomenon of modern sport.

The Attraction of the Sports Phenomenon

The first aspect that I would like to bring our attention to is that the cardinal speaks of soccer as "a 'global event,' that irrespective of boundaries, links humanity around the world in one and the same state of tension: in its hopes, its fears, its emotions and joys."[3] This observation, made thirty years ago, is all the more valid today given the enormous expansion of soccer's popularity around the world!

No other event on the planet is capable of involving so many people in a similar way as a professional sporting event, and especially soccer. According to Cardinal Ratzinger, "this tells us that some primeval human instinct is at play here" and raises the question as to the source of the spell that this game exerts.

Pope Benedict XVI will show his appreciation for this universal dimension of the sporting phenomenon with its potential to peacefully unite diverse nations and races of the earth.

---

2. Cf. Joseph Kardinal Ratzinger, *Suchen, was droben ist. Meditationen das Jahr hindurch* (Freiburg: Herder Press, 1985), 107–11; Benedikt XVI/Joseph Ratzinger, *Gottes Glanz in unserer Zeit. Meditationen zum Kirchenjahr* (Freiburg: Herder Press, 2005), 188–90; *Mitarbeiter der Wahrheit, Gedanken für jeden,* vol. 1, ed. Irene Grassl, 3rd ed. (Würzburg: Naumann Press, 1992), 266.

3. Ratzinger, *Co-Workers of the Truth,* 262–63.

Sport as "Play"

The pessimist will respond to the question of why sport is a universal phenomenon by saying that it is the same as the case in ancient Rome, where *panem et circenses* (bread and the circus games) constituted "the only meaning in life for a decadent society, which does not know any higher aspiration."[4] But even if we accept this explanation, the question would still remain: "Why is this game so fascinating that it ranks on an equal with bread?" To answer this, we might look again to the past and see that the cry for bread and games was in reality the expression of "a longing for the paradisal life—an escape from the wearisome enslavement of daily life."

In this context, the cardinal reveals the profound sense of play as an activity that is totally free, without limits or constrictions, and both engages and fulfills all the energy of man. Consequently, play could be interpreted as a sort of effort to return to paradise: as an escape from the "wearisome enslavement of daily life" (*aus dem versklavten Ernst des Alltags*) for the free seriousness (*freien Ernst*) of something that should not be so, and therefore it is beautiful. In this way, sport, in a certain sense, overcomes (*überschreitet*) daily life.

Besides this capacity to overcome ordinary life, play possesses—as we can see in children—another characteristic: that of being a school of life. Play symbolizes life itself and anticipates it in a way that is characterized by a freeform manner.

Sport as a "School of Life"

According to this very original reflection of Cardinal Ratzinger, the fascination for soccer consists in the fact that it unites these

---

4. The expression "panem et circenses" was coined by the Roman poet Decimus Iunius Iuvenalis (cir. 55–127) in his work *Satire* (10, 81). The original meaning referred to the horse races held in the *circenses*, or hippodrome.

two following aspects in a persuasive manner. First of all, it "compels man to exercise self-discipline," so that he may gain control over himself, and through this control, self-mastery. In turn, this self-mastery leads to freedom. Sport can also teach a disciplined cooperation with others (*diszipliniertes Miteinander*). In team play, one learns to insert one's individuality into the service of the entire group. Sport unites people in a common goal: the success and failure of each one lies in the success and failure of everyone.

Sport can also teach fair play, as the rules of the game, which all mutually obey, bind and unite the competitors together. The freedom of play—when play is according to the rules—becomes serious competition that is resolved only into the freedom of a finished game.

In watching a game, the spectator identifies himself with the game and the players. In this way, he feels himself a part of both the team play and the competition, participating in the players' seriousness and in their freedom of action. The players become a symbol of his own life; and that works vice versa. The players know that the spectators are seeing themselves represented in them, being affirmed by them.

Threats to and Deviations from Sporting Activities

At the end of this interview, rich and dense in content, Cardinal Ratzinger discussed the temptations and dangers that threaten the world of sport. The goodness of the game can easily be spoiled by commercialism, which casts the grim pall of money over everything, and changes sport into an industry that can produce an unreal world of horrifying dimensions.

But this illusory world will not thrive when sport is based on positive values: as a training for life (*Vorübung*) and as a stepping out of (*Überschreitung*) our daily life in the direction of our lost Paradise. Both cases, however, require finding a discipline for freedom in order to train oneself to follow the rules of teamwork (*Mit-einander*), of competition (*Gegeneinander*), and of self-discipline (*Auskommen mit sich selbst*).

After considering all of this, we can conclude that through sport something new about learning how to live can be gained. This is because sport makes some fundamentals of life visible: man does not live by bread alone. Yes, the material world is only the preliminary stage (*Vorstufe*) for the truly human, the world of freedom. But that freedom is based on rules, on the discipline of teamwork (*Miteinander*) and fair competition (*Gegeneinander*), independent of outward success or arbitrariness, and is thereby truly free. Sport as life—if we look at it more profoundly, the phenomenon of a football-crazy world can give us more than sheer entertainment.

Observations of Pope Benedict XVI Regarding Sport

We can now consider some observations that Pope Benedict XVI has made regarding sporting activity in a general way that have as their presupposition and foundation these reflections made thirty years earlier.

In addition to the numerous remarks about sport that the Holy Father has made in his greetings to pilgrims at the end of the Wednesday general audiences and his Angelus messages, there are two speeches that he has delivered during two special audiences: one to the Austrian National Ski Team (October 6, 2007)[5] and the other to the participants of the World Swimming Championship (August 1, 2009).[6] As both speeches were addressed to the athletes

5. Cf. Benedict XVI, "Ansprache an Die Österreichische Alpine Skinational-mannschaft" [Speech to the Austrian National Ski Team] (October 6, 2007), in *Inseg-namenti di Benedetto XVI*, vol. 3 (Vatican: LEV, 2007/2), 422–23.

6. Cf. Benedict XVI, "A Spectacle of Humanity and Tenacity That Teaches Important Lessons for Life: Speech to the Participants of the World Swimming Championship" (August 1, 2009), *L'Osservatore Romano*, weekly English ed., no. 31, August 5, 2009, 12.

themselves who were received by him, they offered the Holy Father the occasion to deal with the theme of sport more amply. To facilitate our analysis, I will subdivide his reflections into five points.

Virtues and Values Inherent in Sporting Activity

For considering the values inherent in sporting activity, the Holy Father's speech to the Austrian ski team offers us an excellent program. Pope Benedict XVI observes that sports can help to foster basic virtues and values and offers an exemplary list: "perseverance, determination, spirit of sacrifice, internal and external discipline, attention to others, team work, solidarity, justice, courtesy, and the recognition of one's own limits, and still others. These same virtues also come into play in a significant way in daily life and need to be continually exercised and practiced."[7]

While receiving the participants of the World Swimming Championship in August of 2009 in Rome, the Holy Father underlined again the potential values that are inherent to sporting efforts, this time enumerating a list from a complementary perspective:

---

7. Cf. Benedict XVI, "Ansprache an Die Österreichische Alpine Skinationalmannschaft," 422–23. Cf. also "Wednesday General Audience of October 5, 2005," in *Insegnamenti di Benedetto XVI*, vol. 1 (Vatican: LEV, 2005), 636, where the Holy Father addressed these words to the Festa dello sportivo participants: "This manifestation raises up in you a great love for those values, such as a healthy practice of sport, that contribute to the construction of a society where mutual and fraternal acceptance reign"; see also his greeting to representatives of the Venarotta Calcio Association: "Dear Friends, you are messengers not only of the serene joy of play, but also that which comes from partaking in fraternity and solidarity," in *Insegnamenti di Benedetto XVI*, vol. 2 (Vatican: LEV, 2006/2), 624; cf. greeting to participants in the third Festa dello sportivo: "Dear young people, . . . may you always know how to unite sport, friendship, and the spiritual life," as found in *Insegnamenti di Benedetto XVI*, vol. 3 (Vatican: LEV, 2007/2), 426; cf. "Wednesday General Audience: Greeting to the Athletes of the European Taekwondo" (April 9, 2008), in *Insegnamenti di Benedetto XVI*, vol. 4 (Vatican: LEV, 2008/1), 546, where the Holy Father encouraged them to "promote respect for one another and fairness through the practice of this sports discipline."

With your competitions you offer the world a fascinating spectacle of discipline and humanity, of artistic beauty and tenacious determination. You show what goals the vitality of youth can achieve when young people submit to the effort of a demanding training and are willing to accept numerous sacrifices and deprivations. All this is also an important lesson for life for your peers.... Sports, practiced with enthusiasm and an acute ethical sense, especially for youth become a training ground of healthy competition and physical improvement, a school of formation in the human and spiritual values, a privileged means for personal growth and contact with society.[8]

Athletes as Role Models

Speaking to these top-level Austrian skiers, the Holy Father touched upon the fact that they are role models for the young people especially. "In fact, you, dear athletes, shoulder the responsibility—not less significant—of bearing witness to these attitudes and convictions and of incarnating them beyond your sporting activity into the fabric of the family, culture, and religion. In doing so, you will be of great help for others, especially the youth, who are immersed in rapidly developing society where there is a widespread loss of values and growing disorientation."[9]

And also in the above-quoted speech to champion swimmers, he affirmed similarly: "Dear athletes, you are models for your peers, and your example can be crucial to them in building their future positively. So be champions in sports and in life!"[10]

The Holy Father reminds these athletes that their "role as a champion" goes beyond the confines of their sport because their

8. Benedict XVI, "A Spectacle of Humanity and Tenacity," 12.

9. Benedict XVI, "Ansprache an Die Österreichische Alpine Skinationalmannschaft," 422–23.

10. Benedict XVI, "A Spectacle of Humanity and Tenacity," 12. At the end of his speech, he repeated a similar message in German: "Dear Friends, as sports competitors you offer performances of a very high-standard and are an example for many young people."

sporting activity becomes for many youth a model of a life of achievement and success. This brings with it a great responsibility because it can be a determining factor in someone's entire life project. In a time when exemplary personalities whom the youth respect are lacking, the champion athlete indirectly becomes an "educator" as the young people look to them for guidance. Because of this, sporting ideals must permeate not only sport but life itself in order to be authentic and credible.

These considerations cause us to examine more closely a very important aspect for the pontiff: the educational potential of sport and how it can contribute in confronting the growing "educational emergency" that is witnessed more and more in our time.[11]

Sport as a Response to the Educational Emergency

In a Wednesday general audience on January 9, 2008, the Holy Father greeted the directors and athletes of the level D Italian soccer league with these words: "May the game of soccer always be more of a means of teaching the values of honesty, solidarity and fraternity, especially among the younger generations."[12]

11. Cf. Benedict XVI, "Letter to the Diocese of Rome on the Urgent Task of Educating Young People" (January 21, 2008), *L'Osservatore Romano*, weekly English ed., no. 6, February 6, 2008, 10: "Educating, however, has never been an easy task and today it seems to be becoming ever more difficult.... It then becomes difficult to pass on from one generation to the next something that is valid and certain, rules of conduct, credible objectives around which to build life itself.... In fact, none of these difficulties is insurmountable. They are, as it were, the other side of the coin of that great and precious gift which is our freedom, with the responsibility that rightly goes with it.... Not even the greatest values of the past can be simply inherited; they must be claimed by us and renewed through an often anguishing personal option"; cf. also "Address to the General Assembly of the Italian Bishops Conference" (May 29, 2008), *L'Osservatore Romano*, weekly English ed., no. 23, June 4, 2008, 5: "When, in fact, in a society and in a culture marked by a pervasive relativism and not rarely by aggressiveness, fundamental certainties, the values and the hopes that give life meaning seem to weaken, the temptation is easily spread among parents as well as teachers to renounce their own duty, and even preceded by the risk of not clearly understanding their own role and mission."

12. Cf. Benedict XVI, "Wednesday General Audience of January 9, 2008," in *Insegnamenti di Benedetto XVI*, vol. 4 (Vatican: LEV, 2008/1), 48.

I would like to recall another quote from the Holy Father that was directed to soccer students at a training club that forms part of the young scholastic sector of the Italian Soccer Federation (FIGC). At the end of the Sunday Angelus, Pope Benedict XVI made this appeal: "May sport be a gymnasium of true preparation for life."[13]

On the occasion of the Pontifical Council for the Laity's most recent sport seminar ("Sport, Education, Faith: Towards a New Season for Catholic Sport Associations," November 6–7, 2009), the Holy Father strongly accentuated in his message the educative value of sporting activity: "Sports have considerable educational potential in the context of youth and, for this reason, great importance not only in the use of leisure time but also in the formation of the person."[14]

In the actual educational emergency, provoked by a unilateral and exaggerated demand for personal freedom, sport can assume an important role as a means to educate many young people. Sport can demonstrate—by means of its rules and team effort—that there is an undeniable need for discipline and a shared responsibility.

In this regard, the Holy Father, in his letter to the diocese of Rome on the theme of education, stated: "If no standard of behavior and rule of life is applied even in small daily matters, the character is not formed and the person will not be ready to face

13. Cf. Benedict XVI, "Angelus Greeting of December 18, 2005," in *Insegnamenti di Benedetto XVI*, vol. 1 (Vatican: LEV, 2005), 1004; cf. "Greeting to Professional Soccer Referees at Wednesday General Audience, January 25, 2006," in *Insegnamenti di Benedetto XVI*, vol. 2 (Vatican: LEV, 2006/1), 105: "Dear friends, to a necessary technical and athletic preparation add an adequate human and spiritual formation that will make you ever more mature and responsible persons."

14. Cf. Benedict XVI, "Message to the President of the Pontifical Council for the Laity," 5; cf. also his "Address to Civil and Political Authorities in Prague" (September 26, 2009), *L'Osservatore Romano*, Italian ed., no. 224, September 18–29, 2009, 5: "In sports, the creative arts and academic pursuit, young people welcome the opportunity to excel. Is it not equally true that when presented with high ideals they will also aspire to moral virtue and a life of compassion and goodness? I warmly encourage parents and community leaders who expect authorities to promote the values which integrate the intellectual, human and spiritual dimensions of a sound education worthy of the aspirations of our young."

the trials that will come in the future. The educational relationship, however, is first of all the encounter of two kinds of freedom, and successful education means teaching the correct use of freedom."[15]

Sport represents an appropriate field for finding the right balance between freedom and discipline, which is perhaps the most delicate point in the task of education today. Many young people consider sport as a positive phenomenon in their life and easily undergo the rigor and fatigue that it implies, as well as following its rules. Especially in the case of soccer, we see how teamwork groups together the freedom of each individual and the need of respecting the rules for the benefit of the common good.

As we have seen—in the context of this formative process—the Holy Father counts much upon sports men and women to be "credible witnesses" of its virtue and values. In this sense, speaking to the General Assembly of the Italian Bishops' Conference (May 29, 2008), where the Holy Father made explicit reference to the parish recreational centers, he noted that "precisely the current educational emergency increases the demand for an education that truly is such: therefore, concretely speaking, educators who know how to be credible witnesses of these realities and of these values upon which it is possible to build both one's personal existence and a common and shared project of life."[16]

The Unifying and Pacifying Capacity of Sport

A fourth aspect to consider is sport's capacity to unite people of different countries and races in friendly competition, as is often attested with particular eloquence in the occasion of the Olympics or the World Cup.

At the end of a general audience on September 22, 2005, the

15. Cf. Benedict XVI, "Letter to the Diocese of Rome," 10.
16. Benedict XVI, "Address to Italian Bishop's Conference," 5.

Holy Father spoke these words to a delegation of UEFA and the Italian Soccer Federation present with a numerous group of children in attendance from sixteen countries: "Dear friends, ... may today's manifestation be an occasion for you to renew your efforts so that sport can contribute to building a society that is distinguished by reciprocal respect, fairness in behavior, and solidarity among all races and cultures."[17]

Once more, after praying the Sunday Angelus on February 12, 2006, a few days before the Winter Olympics in Turin, the pope expressed his desire that "this great sports competition be imbued with the Olympic values of fairness, joy and fraternal relations and in doing so, contribute to fostering peace among peoples."[18]

---

17. Benedict XVI, "Greeting, Wednesday General Audience" (September 21, 2005), in *Insegnamenti di Benedetto XVI*, vol. 1 (Vatican: LEV, 2005), 567.

18. Benedict XVI, "Angelus Greeting of February 12, 2006," in *Insegnamenti di Benedetto XVI*, vol. 2 (Vatican: LEV, 2006/1), 180; cf. also "Angelus Greeting of July 8, 2007," his words to the Interamnia World Cup handball participants who gathered from more than a hundred different countries, some of which are in conflict with each other: "Yet this peaceful gathering of athletes is an example of how sports can bring us together in the spirit of fellowship between peoples and cultures. Sports are indeed a sign that peace is possible." Cf. *Insegnamenti di Benedetto XVI*, vol. 3 (Vatican: LEV, 2007/2), 32; cf. "Wednesday General Audience of May 7, 2008," *Insegnamenti di Benedetto XVI*, vol. 4 (Vatican: LEV, 2008/1), his words to the directors and players of Inter: "I take this occasion to underline once more the importance of the moral values of sport in educating the new generations" and his greeting to an Austrian delegation from Österreichischer Fußballbund: "I also greet the delegation from the Austrian soccer federation. Today is a day for soccer, as we also are happy to have present with us, one of the top Italian soccer teams, Inter. May the Holy Spirit help you as Christians to give witness to others in doing good," in *Insegnamenti di Benedetto XVI*, vol. 4 (Vatican: LEV, 2008/1), 732–34. Also significant are Pope Benedict XVI's words at the conclusion of the "Wednesday General Audience of August 1, 2007," after Iraq's soccer victory in the Asian Cup final. The Iraqi team, which was made up of players from various religious confessions and ethnic backgrounds, played with a black band on their arms as a sign of mourning for those killed in a bombing days before. In the 71st minute of play, a header goal off a corner kick by team captain Younis Mahmoud gave Iraq an unexpected lead. When the final whistle blew, Iraqi players and fans exulted in joy at winning. The Holy Father commented on their victory with these words: "I would like to record some good news about Iraq which has sparked an explosion of popular joy throughout the Country. I am referring to the victory of the Iraqi football team, which won

Also in his greeting to the participants in the twenty-ninth edition of the Summer Olympics in Beijing, the Holy Father placed the accentuation on the pacifying dimension of sport: "I am following with deep interest this great sports event—the most important and anticipated in the world—and I warmly hope that it will offer the international community an effective example of coexistence among people of the most different provenances, with respect for their common dignity. May sports once again be a pledge of brotherhood and peace among peoples!"[19]

These considerations of the Holy Father remind that an excessive nationalism and racism are contrary to the ideals of sport ("Olympic values") as they destroy this unifying and pacifying capacity. Especially the Olympic Games and the other global sporting events can easily miss this opportunity and become the occasion, as has happened in the past, for a display of power and superiority of one nation's political system over another's. In these cases, sport is not an occasion for uniting, but is in opposition to the entire peoples as well as to the single individual.

The Holy Father does not only ask this from others, but he also directs this appeal in a particular way to groups within the Church, especially Catholic sport associations. Benedict XVI asks them to be active in promoting a balanced appreciation of sporting activity in conformance with the sporting ideal and a Christian vision of the human person.

---

the Asian Cup and for the first time has become the football champion of Asia. I was happily impressed by the enthusiasm that infected all the inhabitants, driving them out onto the streets to celebrate the event. Just as I have so often wept with the Iraqis, on this occasion I rejoice with them. This experience of joyful sharing shows a people's desire to have a normal, quiet life. I hope that the event may help in building in Iraq a future of authentic peace with the contribution of all, in freedom and reciprocal respect. Congratulations!" *L'Osservatore Romano,* weekly English ed., no.32/33, August 8/15, 2007, 4.

19. Benedict XVI, "Angelus, Greeting with Occasion of the Forthcoming Olympic Games in Beijing" (August 3, 2008), *L'Osservatore Romano,* weekly English ed., no. 32, August 6, 2008, 1.

The Contribution of the Church and
Catholic Athletes

The greatest asset the Church has to offer to the world of sport is its own insights regarding the overall phenomenon of sport, insights enriched by a vision of the human person rooted in Christian anthropology and also in the light of the faith.[20]

For the pope, sport is not simply the exercise of one's physical qualities but rather something that involves the entire person. Along these same lines, in his speech to the Austrian skiers already quoted above, he affirms:

Body, spirit and soul form a single unity and each component must be in harmony with the other. You know how necessary this interior harmony is in order to reach sporting goals at the highest levels. Consequently, even the most demanding sports must be rooted in a holistic view of the human person, recognizing his profound dignity and favouring an overall development and full maturity of the person. Otherwise, if sport is only focused on mere material performance, it will fall short of realizing its necessary social dimension. In the end, sporting activity must help one to recognize their own talents and capacities, their very efforts and their own very life as gifts that come from God. For this reason, sport should always have God our Creator as its ultimate point of reference. It is in this sense that the Apostle makes reference to sports competition in order to recall man's highest calling: "Do you not know that the runners in the stadium all run in the race, but only one wins the prize? Run so as to win. Every athlete

---

20. Benedict XVI, "Message to Cardinal Severino Poletto, Archbishop of Turin in Occasion of the Upcoming Winter Olympic Games" (November 29, 2005), *L'Osservatore Romano*, weekly English ed., no.6, February 8, 2006, 2: "For Christians, reference made to light points out the Incarnate Word, Light of the world that illumines man in all his dimensions, including sports. There is nothing human—except sin—that the Son of God by becoming man did not give worth to.... Among the various human activities is sport, itself awaiting to be illumined by God through Christ so that the values it expresses are purified and elevated both at the individual and collective level."

exercises discipline in every way. They do it to win a perishable crown, but we an imperishable one" (1 Cor 9:24–25).[21]

Speaking to the participants of the swimming championship, the Holy Father included in his speech a reflection on the transcendent dimension of the human person, bringing out the loftier aspects of our creaturely status and concluding with what could almost be considered a prayer of thanksgiving to God:

Watching these swimming championships and admiring the results achieved make it easy to understand the great potential with which God has endowed the human body and the interesting objectives of perfection it is able to achieve. One then thinks of the Psalmist's wonder who in contemplating the universe, praises the glory of God and the greatness of man: "when I behold your heavens," we read in Psalm 8, "the work of your fingers, the moon and the stars that you have set in place what is man that you are mindful of him, or the son of man that you care for him?" (vv. 3–4). Then, how can one fail to thank the Lord for having endowed the human body with such perfection; for having enriched it with a beauty and harmony that can be expressed in so many ways?[22]

With respect to the frequently referred to educational emergency, the Holy Father has pointed out those tasks that belong to the Church, especially to its pastors and the educational institutions and sport associations. It is significant that Pope Benedict XVI, during a meeting with the clergy of Rome, regarding the theme of the parish recreational center, had this to say:

Of course, an after-school centre where only games were played and refreshments provided would be absolutely superfluous. The point of an after-school catechetical and recreation centre must be cultural, human and Christian formation for a mature personality.... I would say that this is precisely the role of such a centre, that one not only finds possibilities

21. Benedict XVI, "Ansprache an Die Österreichische Alpine Skinationalmannschaft," 423.
22. Benedict XVI, "A Spectacle of Humanity and Tenacity," 12.

there for one's leisure time but above all for an integral human formation that completes the personality. Therefore, of course, the priest as an educator must himself have received a good training and must fit into today's culture, and be deeply cultured if he is to help young people to enter a culture inspired by faith. I would naturally add that in the end, the central point of orientation in every culture is God, God present in Christ.[23]

Along this very same line of thinking, in his message to our recent seminar of study (Vatican, November 6–7, 2009), he underlined this point:

Through sports, the ecclesial community contributes to the formation of youth, providing a suitable environment for their human and spiritual growth. In fact, when sports initiatives aim at the integral development of the person and are managed by qualified and competent personnel, they provide a useful opportunity for priests, religious and lay people to become true and proper educators and teachers of life for the young.

In our time, when an urgent need to educate the new generations is evident, it is therefore necessary for the Church to continue to support sports for youth, making the most of their positive aspects also at competitive levels, such as their capacity for stimulating competitiveness, courage, and tenacity in pursuing goals. However, it is necessary to avoid every trend that perverts the nature of sports by recourse to practices that can even damage the body, such as doping. As part of a coordinated, formative effort, Catholic directors, staff, and workers must consider themselves expert guides for youth, helping each of them to develop their athletic potential without obscuring those human qualities and Christian virtues that make for a fully mature person.[24]

While acknowledging that not all athletes share the same vision of the human person down to its last detail, the Church would

---

23. Benedict XVI, "Meeting with Clergy of Rome" (February 29, 2009), L'Osservatore Romano, weekly English ed., no. 10, March 11, 2009, 4.

24. Cf. Benedict XVI, "Message to the President of the Pontifical Council for the Laity," as cited in 14.

like to offer its assistance in furthering a more profound and integral vision of the sporting phenomenon, in order to avoid the error of valuing this beautiful, but penultimate, reality as the ultimate and supreme activity of man. This service could help to reduce the temptation to use inappropriate ways (unfair play, corruption) or means (doping) that contradict the very essence of the nature of sport.

Some might be surprised to find these words of the Holy Father regarding sport, as their first impression might be to consider Pope Benedict XVI distant from the world of sport, especially if we consider his lack of participation in sport during his youth.[25] However, as we have been able to see, already as the young archbishop of Munich he dedicated himself to this theme with a philosophically profound reflection, pointing out the potential of sport for the integral development of the person on the individual level and its capacities on the national and global levels.

Cardinal Ratzinger—and also as Pope Benedict XVI—inserting sporting activity into a broader anthropological context, sought to bring these debates out of a dead-end path of pure entertainment or sterile self-autonomy. I myself was surprised to find that the Holy Father, in the first two and a half years of his pontificate (2005–8) touched upon the theme of sport in various ways on no less than fifty occasions.[26]

Nor is it purely a coincidence that it is during the pontificate of Benedict XVI that a delegation of the Holy See participates in an Olympic Congress—that of Copenhagen last October 3–5, 2009, with a reflection on the theme of "Olympic values." For, as we recalled elsewhere, the Servant of God, John Paul II in the begin-

25. Cf. Joseph Ratzinger, *Milestones: Memoirs 1927–1977* (San Francisco: Ignatius Press, 1998), 25–26.
26. Cf. the index of themes as found in the seven volumes that have been published to date (2005–2008), of *Insegnamenti di Benedetto XVI*.

ning of the year 2004 instituted the section Church and Sport to ensure a more direct and systematic attention to the vast world of sport on the part of the Holy See. And as we have seen from the above reflections, during the pontificate of Pope Benedict XVI, the interest and concern of the Universal Church to the vast world of sport continues as it seeks to dialogue with the renowned sports institutions at the international level while fostering a renewal of pastoral work in and through sports at the local level.

Dietmar Mieth

8 A Christian Vision of Sport

This article makes neither a religious nor a moral criticism of sport (which is the traditional manner of tackling the matter) nor a song of praise about sport full of problematic directness (which would be the other traditional way of discussing the question). Instead it offers a spiritual and sociotheological perspective of sport.

Methodological Requirements for a Christian Vision of Sport

Updating the Signs of the Times in the Light of the Second Vatican Council

"Recognize the Signs of the Times" was the message that Pope John XXIII gave the council fathers. Not only was "aggiornamento" a keyword for the council, but it also was used in his encyclical *Pacem in Terris*[1] as a reference point for an analysis of the social, religious, and other changes of the present day. As such, it recognized a challenge and also pointed to a possible solution. (For example, the pope mentioned the awakening of young people and women as such "signs of the times.")

1. John XXIII, Encyclical Letter *Pacem et Terris*, 40th anniv. ed. (Vatican: LEV, 2003), 59.

Above all, the signs of the times were understood as a dialogical Moment: as the beginning of a dialogue "with the world about the world." This concept was retained in the council documents and in the inaugural encyclical of Pope Paul VI, *Ecclesiam suam,* and finds its expression in the subtitle of *Guadium et Spes: The Pastoral Constitution on the Church in the Modern World.*[2] The chief thrust of the dialogue found in this text is that of a "discernment of spirits," that is, the reference to the signs of the times should be seen as having a double meaning: as a call for both integration and criticism.

The concept of "world" as used by Vatican Council II was a collective term for all secular social powers. It applied particularly to the modern industrial and scientific world. However, the world of modern times, to which the council refers, is not the world of the postmodern, postindustrial era. In this respect the world of the council is not the same as the world of today, which is distinguished by economic globalization and the digital culture.

I believe we can discern an ethical meaning for the signs of the times if we distinguish between a simple diagnostic of time—the analytical meaning of the term—from that of time as a theological-eschatological concept.

The council document *Gaudium et Spes* has as its *Sitz im Leben* an ecclesial ethic. This is drafted as a theological ethic, since it is conceived not only in the light of reason but also in the light of the Gospel. Hence the ethical meaning of the signs of the times passes through space as a *locus theologicus* and becomes the place

2. See Paul VI, Encyclical Letter *Ecclesiam Suam* (Vatican: Tipografia Poliglotta Vaticana, 1964), and *Gaudium et Spes*, 922. I am under the impression that one decided to forfeit the concept of time for the benefit of the common use of the concept of world. Nonetheless the concept of world included in itself from the very beginning the concept of "a sign of the times" through stressing the concept of "today." See also Dietmar Mieth, "Das Weltverhältnis des christlichen Glaubens am Beispiel der theologischen Ethik," in *Fundamente der Theologischen Ethik. Bilanz und Neuansätze,* ed. Adrian Holderegger (Freiburg: Herder, 1996).

of theological thought. This presupposes that the concept of the signs of the times cannot be primarily defined theologically, even though it is secondarily receipted from a theological perspective. For this reason, I suggest studying the meaning of this concept alongside the entire theology of Pope John XXIII. In this way we will be confronted with a series of problems but also with a series of solutions.

If time is the place of perception, of memory, of language, and of thought, then we are placed in a perspective that is an ongoing process. We see developments and changes of circumstance and of necessity, the imperfection of successions, the displacement of clusters of actions and of the so-called paradigms. All this takes place within human history, that is, within a time in which the human being takes his destiny in his own hands, and also his responsibility for it. The glance at the concept of "the times" is to be distinguished from the existential glance upon a time transgressing the unchangeable being, which has to be distinguished from accidental changes. This is why the methods that help us approach scientifically historical time are simultaneously targeted at changes and at continuities in these changes. Continuity is not a substantial equality even though it contains an axis of consistency. Changes are not simple modifications but have a beginning that can be reconstructed and deconstructed. This happens certainly from a modifiable perspective, possibly from an intention disposed to modification and maintenance at the same time. To examine temporal processes means to partake of them, to strengthen or to weaken their implicit intentionality. At the same time it is necessary for this examination to contemplate the synchronicity of the immediate present, which allows the examiner to view the present moment in its deviation from past times and possible future times.

Intentionality in the contemplation of historical time becomes apparent through the fact that historically understood time is "spoken about" time. History speaks about historical events.[3] The form of storytelling enforces intentionality. But since any form-giving is at the same time fiction and invention we have to provide an account for it. A great part of the responsibility of people consists in providing this account, which is influenced by its dependency on time. Our attempt to understand time situates our actions and implements them in this intentionality in which we form our time. This forming is not objective from a historical perspective but is possible to achieve in a trans-subjective way, as the conditions of the emergence of a form that gives identity to time is subordinated to a discourse. For example, since the period of "poststructuralism" we talk about "deconstructionism."

When we speak about the "signs" of the times, we understand the grammatical construction as a genitive case; that is, we do not mean the signs for the time, but the signs that are given by the time, the signs that emerge from the time. We assume that the time that is condensed in the present but that contains in itself the past and the future represents itself at the height of its perception, its memory, its language, and its thought and produces by this differentiation interpretational clusters. The represented sign points at the designated sign that appears in it. Signs are not entities; they are not compact objects, but they are nodal points of factual and linguistic agreements on common, trans-subjective experiences. For instance, when we talk about globalization, although our descriptions and our evaluations of this phenomenon vary, the phenomenon as such becomes a point of reference of an intentional experience of time in a discourse. The reference to the "terrestrial globe" contained in the concept related to spatial fullness and a shortening of distances in time penetrates the reference that the

3. See Arthur Danto, *Narration and Knowledge* (New York: Columbia University Press, 1985), 347ff.

Pastoral Constitution on the Church in the Modern World makes about the world as a secular and social *mundus*.

This distinction is easily found in theological ethics if one analyzes how Alfons Auer understands the concept of a "world ethos" in comparison to Hans Küng. For Auer the concept alludes to the secular, social *mundus*, whereas Hans Küng understands the concept as "global ethics" since he views it from another temporal perspective: the postmodern time in which religions have made an asynchronous comeback, perhaps because of the historical consequences of World War II.

We said that time represents itself through its own signs and opens by them potentials of interpretation. We pretend as if time were an actor who represents himself, an actor on whose development (through the passing of time) we depend. In reality actions create the scenarios for the human actors, and these human actors are responsible for them. Accordingly we could separate ethics from what is being predicted, so that it imposes itself on the basis of the passing of time. This process of separation exists very clearly in the modern media, which comment on everything. It is easy to show that the journalistic commentaries see the intentionality of time in what is being achieved, in what finds a euphoric confirmation or in what leads to apocalyptic fears.

And here we must begin formulating our theological issue. According to theological ecclesiology we must distinguish between various signs. First there are those that mark the presence of God in history and that comprise the Church as a sign starting with the symbolic acts of Jesus and ending with sacramental theology. Other signs must be understood from the point of view of a theology of creation by integrating history into the theology of creation and not the theology of salvation. An immediacy to salvation history can be avoided here, but a certain redemptive significance in a general sense cannot be denied. This is expressed in a special way through the concept of *kairos*. This concept, which is related to the present time, points to the future.

The stress on the significance of salvation should not surpass the autonomy of the reference to creation in any theological and ethical analysis. The understanding of the significance of salvation is a second step going from ethical responsibility to the theological hope, which strengthens this motivational responsibility.

If we wish to analyze the signs of the times from the point of view of creational theology we must begin with the teaching of *vestigia Dei,* or the traces of God. These signs left by God as entries in the *liber creaturarum* (opposed to the *liber revelationis*) are to be distinguished from the *imago Dei* concept that can be considered as a teaching on the *imago Dei* in the context of theology of creation and as a teaching on the *similitudo Dei* in the context of a theology of salvation. The theological concepts of *vestigia* and *imago* were prevalent in the Middle Ages and especially in Albert the Great's pupils of natural philosophy. At the same time, these contain a moment of deconstruction of the empirical knowledge on nature through the categories of creative *ratio* and the *intellectus agens* of Dietrich von Freiberg.[4]

The council commissions did not take over these references because there was a competition between the nonhistorical and the historical contemplation of nature in Neo-scholasticism. Nevertheless the mentioning of the natural, humanistic, and social sciences and their autonomous perception as depicted by the council Document *Gaudium et Spes* is a clear hint as to how one can perceive the signs of the times also in the external forum and integrate them from the perspective of a theology of creation. The council does not teach that we are faced with an unrelated autonomy of moral knowledge, but with the autonomy of many types of

4. Cf. Kurt Flasch's *Meister Eckhart. Die Geburt der "Deutschen Mystik" aus dem Geist der arabischen Philosophie* (Munich: Beck, 2006).

knowledge, which are relevant for an ethical responsibility. Recognition of the signs of the times (as, for instance, the challenges of a conciliar process) requires a double task—the challenge and the reflection, which can be found at the intersection of autonomous and creational knowledge.

The council fathers were influenced not only by the teaching on the *vestigia Dei* but also by the teaching of the logoi, which demands and sets the foundations for a deep theological reflection. These teachings are also understood as signs and summarized in an analogy. While they, as signs, refer to the signified objects, similarity and dissimilarity are thought of together. An understanding of the signs of the times as a conceptual interpretational framework demands at the same time an appropriate interpretation. In this way one carefully avoids the dominance of the sign on the signified object, as this could be interpreted by anxious people as a dominance of the spirit of the time over the truth.

One has to refer to the analogy of history as understood by Johann Sebastian Drey in his theory on society and the Kingdom of God. He stresses the change of forms of power and domination.[5] To interpret this change theologically and from the perspective of its own time presupposes that one has to separate its unmistakable characteristics.

One could also speak about an analogy of morality because the signs of a development from the *Sittlichkeit* (in a Hegelian sense) can be determined as conceptual interpretational clusters, which need integration in a theological horizon. This is where we could mention the priority of justice (John Rawls) or, on an everyday basis, elements of a certain "political correctness." In this context Wilhelm Korff has developed the teaching on the "normative pow-

5. See my chapter, "Das Reich Gottes bei Johann Sebastian Drey und die Begründung einer Katholischen Soziallehre," in *Theologie als Instanz der Moderne*, ed. Michael Kessler and Ottmar Fuchs (Tübingen: Francke, 2005).

er of ethically-lived convictions," which are to be distinguished from the normative power of the factual.[6]

One can certainly depict elements of a theologically integrated semiology, which have led to a fundamentally new understanding of ethics with the help of the impulses given by Vatican Council II. These are mentioned in the work of Klaus Demmer. It is probably sufficient to mention just one element. In the first chapter of his work *Gottes Anspruch denken. Die Gottesfrage in der Moraltheologie* he analyzes "the ethical cognition in the horizon of the idea of God" and mentions among other things "the cognitional challenge of temporality."[7] He writes: "Moral theology has the pretense to be an experience of time cognitionally surmounted" and adds: "this attitude sets clear limits to a deductive thinker."[8] Because of this Demmer speaks about a "spiritually affected temporality." By mentioning this he surpasses what I attempted to describe with the concept "a creational Paradigm." There is a difference between my point of view and that of Demmer, who is influenced by *Zeit und Ewigkeit* and constantly remains in the absolute. Yet, that which we can understand should not be ignored. This is why, in my writings on "Morality and Experience," I chose an inductive perspective for the interpretation of reality as based on experience. Without wishing to be absolute in my choice I offered reality in preference to experience. This perspective tries to understand the conceptual interpretational model of the signs of the times from their genesis and tries to reconstruct its genesis by analyzing the "normative powers" that define it.

Let us now turn away from this general analysis of the potential of the teaching on the signs of the times and attempt to find

6. See Wilhelm Korff, *Norm und Sittlichkeit* (Mainz: Grünewald, 1975); See also Dietmar Mieth, *Moral und Erfahrung*, vol. 1, 4th ed. (Freiburg: Herder, 1999), 136–53.

7. See Klaus Demmer, *Gottes Anspruch denken: Die Gottesfrage in der Moraltheologie* (Freiburg: Herder, 1995), 19–33;26.

8. Ibid., 26–27.

its contemporary meaning for the phenomenon of sport—and first and foremost, sport as a cultural phenomenon.

Inductive Elements of an Examination of Sport Using the Example of Cultural Studies

Sport Is a Cultural Phenomenon

Sport is a cultural phenomenon, and this has a double meaning with regard to culture: culture provokes, predetermines, and specifies human action. It can serve the goal of living a good and fulfilled life. The same can be said about the culture of sport; culture contains conventions and models that we can and must question. The horizon of questioning is not tied to culture but is conscious of its own relativity. This is also valid for sport in as far as it can be viewed with critical sympathy, a mixture of engagement and distance.

Bodily Experience

Sport conveys bodily experience. This bodily experience is a cultural phenomenon that today is reflected in the culture of fitness. During the rediscovery of the modern Olympic idea the bodily experience was strongly related to competition between different nations and representing one's own country, while today it is simply to be found in individual self-determination. Bodily experience is indeed an individual generality (in the sense of Hegelian dialectics) because more than ever before today's individual displays general features that are consciously obtained. At the same time bodily experience has always had an aesthetic dimension.

Aesthetic Experience

Sensuality is always present in the aesthetic experience, but at the same time an interior sensuality is produced. (The recognition of the "inner senses" is part of the religious history of experience but also finds its place here.) In this way one achieves a repeat or a doubling of the semi-sensual feeling of pleasure. For example the feeling of taste can be also repeated on the level of reflexive pleasure. (See the relationship between *sapere,* to taste, and *sapientia,* experience, wisdom.)

Martin Seel and Marcus Düwell make a distinction between experience that is contemplative and aesthetic (viewed from a distance) and experience that is co-responsive (everyday) and imaginative (stirring the imagination). The aesthetic experience needs a reflexive moment, which does not disassociate itself from the senses.

Moral Experience

Moral experience is my experience as a moral self.[9] When moral contrasts change, moral experience appears in the mode of an experience of contrasts. When I have moral goals, moral experience appears in the mode of the experience of the senses. When I have to make an unavoidable moral analysis, moral experience appears in the mode of motivational experience.

If experience is inspired, mediated, passed down by the culture of sport, then what we said about aesthetic experience is also valid for the ethical and the religious experience (See my examples taken from the significance of cult).

Culture communicates aesthetic and moral experience. The meanings of storytelling and narrative ethics are based on that. Through such things as exemplary figures, narrative ethics represent a *pars pro toto* because the communication of culture also includes imagery phenomena. The ethical relevance passes through a culture of the form. This connection can be exemplified by two model cases in sport: the analogy of sporting events to liturgical

9. See Mieth, *Moral und Erfahrung.*

events and the presentation of such ideals as exemplary sportsmanship, fairness, and the discussion on social justice (since John Rawls).

Religious Experience

"Experientia facit theologum," said Martin Luther. Experience is a theologically controversial category. Karl Barth writes in the introduction to his *Kirchliche Dogmatik* against the theoreticians of religious experience because they try to explain revelation through religious experience.[10] Revelation should surpass experience. This is seen in a completely different way by, for example, Karl Rahner. He sees in the "super-natural existential" a religious potential of experience relevant in anthropology.

This "existential" has a long tradition: *scintilla animae,* synteresis, *apex mentis,* depth of the soul, and so on. This tradition belongs to the mystical tradition because religious experience and mysticism belong together.[11]

The types of religious experience can be drawn from the history of spirituality. They appear often as metaphors that lead to "teachings," that is, the teaching on love, on the bridal characteristics, on the wedding, the experience of nature and of creation (all creation is full of God and a book in itself—the *liber creaturarum*), the Word as experience (metaphorical interpretation of scripture), the experience of memory or the culture of remembrance (an example is "déjà vu"), alternate states, such as the experience of ecstasy or of rapture.

One can discuss religious experience in an interreligious way.

10. See Walter Haug and Dietmar Mieth, eds., *Religiöse Erfahrung: Historische Modelle in christlicher Tradition* (Munich: Fink, 1992).
11. See my article: "Mystik—theologiegeschichtlich" [Mysticism in the history of theology], in *Neues Handbuch theologischer Grundbegriffe*, vol. 3, ed. Peter Eicher, 135–45 (Munich: Koesel Verlag, 2005).

In this way one encounters limits that can be relevant for the personal religious experience.

Anthropological Integration via Philosophy
(Theology Seeking Reason)

Alfons Auer makes anthropology a crucial subject of his theology.[12] He does not ask whether one is dealing with philosophical anthropology or not. Yet, for him, the fundamental disposition of the human existence lies in his rationality, in his capacity for self-reflection. It belongs to the duty of a philosophic anthropology not only to answer questions about "where man comes from and where he is going,"[13] but also to bring together humanistic knowledge on the real status of mankind in general. This knowledge is grounded in the objective methods of the corresponding disciplines, such as, for instance, human biology, psychology, and the social sciences. Objective methods are not departmental methods. They do not concentrate on the whole but see the whole from a specific perspective, which gains its exactness from the limits set by the requirements of a constrained framework. If one dissolves these limits, then everything will be connected to everything. One will arrive at general contexts, which not only help in the understanding of connections but also can explain the reference framework itself. The open horizon and the characteristics of not being enclosed into a particular context are a sign of a philosophical reflection, which knows that its object, especially the unobjectifiable man, is worth investigating, but, at the same time, remains indescribable.

12. See Alfons Auer, *Autonome Moral und christlicher Glaube*, 2nd ed. (Düsseldorf: Schnell & Steiner, 1984); See also with my article: "Anthropologie und Ethik," in *Was ist der Mensch? Theologische Anthropologie im interdisziplinären Kontext*, ed. Michael Graf (Stuttgart: Metzler, 2004).

13. Max Scheler, *Man's Place in Nature*, trans. Hans Meyerhoff (Boston: Beacon Press, 1961), 3.

According to Auer, the fundamental quest for the essence of man cannot be ultimately answered as a philosophical question. The openness for the transcendental connection was always answered by him from a philosophical position. Yet, in ethics he distinguishes between the autonomy of rationality and the conviction of faith. He understands this distinction not as a separation but as a possibility for a reciprocal learning process.[14] This distinction leads not to a separation but to a multiplication of perspectives, which enables the establishing of a reciprocal correction and a relationship that must always be newly created.

The Two Fundamental Triple Levels in the Methodology of Auer

According to Alfons Auer, philosophical anthropology has "the specific duty to reflect on the meaning of human existence and on the meaning of the world as being centred in the human personality."[15] The argumentation of his thesis is rooted in the fundamental meaning of the "Autonome Moral."[16] The retraction of a specific theological anthropology for the benefit of a philosophical anthropology as a sufficient normative authority, as an integrational background for ethical norms, constitutes one of the main ideas of Auer's "Autonome Moral."

Auer's three steps consist in humanistic grounding, anthropological integration, and ethical standardization.[17] We do not explicitly find any theological reflection in these three steps. The way in which these steps function (previously described in his book *Autonome Moral und christlicher Glaube*) is presented by Auer in his "one-world-ethic" (*Umweltethik*)[18] without any theological com-

14. Alfons Auer, *Zur Theologie der Ethik* (Freiburg: Herder, 1995).
15. Ibid., 44.
16. See ibid., 128–54.
17. I want to point out the moral-didactical significance of Auer that is found in the works of his former student Albert Biesinger.
18. See Alfons Auer, *Umweltethik Ein theologischer Beitrag zur ökologischen Diskussion* (Düsseldorf: Patmos, 1984).

ments. Theology does not lose its functions, but the functions of theology have to be related to the concrete ethical issues. The second level presented by Auer regards the critical, integrative, and stimulative functions of theology and also refers to the competence of ecclesial discourse and its authority.[19] The critical, integrative, and stimulative functions of theological statements are an integrative part of Auer's conception: the anthropological integration and the ethical standardization have to be thought upon in a second step from a theological perspective.

Philosophical anthropology had a special meaning for Auer before "the radical, metaphysical and religious decisions" already mentioned. The following statement of Auer is more decisive: "From his own existence man is faced with the inalienable demand of the predetermined reality.... If ethical views and behaviours infringe upon what is authentically humane (which was earlier called the essential structure of man) then they miss the sense of their existence and cause frustration."[20] In order to make the criterion of an essentialistic anthropology convincing, one needs a "primal trust in the development of history and in personal existence." By this statement he wants to say that it makes sense to live and to take responsibility for oneself and for others. He believes further that the world is ruled by a fundamental order that is made up of a complicated network of relations. He knows that reality and our lives are not ultimately illuminable, but he believes that all unavoidable irrationalities stand in the horizon of a rationality regarded as certain—for whatever reason.[21] This primal trust can be also called a trust in the meaningful par excellence. Certainly one cannot relate this trust in the meaningful to a particular reality. Moreover, it develops itself in the horizon of hope

19. Ibid., 185–97.
20. Auer, *Zur Theologie der Ethik*, 30.
21. Ibid., 32.

on the possibilities that exist in reality but have not yet become a possibility. "Reality is reliant on enabling a fruitful human and historical existence."[22]

Communicability of Language: The Example of Fairness

In this section I want to deal with the human phenomenon and its cultural significance after the so-called pragmatic linguistic turn. We are interested in the predetermination of our knowledge by language. We have also to consider the phenomenon of the secularization of language, of the appearance and disappearance of words in the language. We can demonstrate this by a list of virtue and vice but also through "political correctness." In the cultural phenomenon of sport we can observe a transformation of language through the use of sporting terms. The principle of fairness and the image of a competition that is not dominated only by commerce are special points of connection. The modern Olympic idea is not entirely unproblematic—because of its nationalist characteristics—but also in the era of capitalism it supports, at least partially, the idea of competition without commerce. And even today the two images—of competition and commerce—can still be differentiated despite their factual connection.

Levels of Ecumenism

In order to develop a method for analyzing a Christian vision of sport one must integrate it in an ecumenical project. If one talks about living an authentic Christian life while engaging in sport as it is postulated in documents of the Church and Sport section within the Vatican's Pontifical Council for Laity, then we must accomplish this ecumenically in cooperation with churches and church communities. Because the council document *Nostra Aetate*

22. Ibid., 33.

acknowledges that even the non-Christian religions have elements of truth, one should also search for cooperation in dialogue with them. This is possible, as I personally experienced it at a symposium of the Goethe-Institute in Istanbul.

There is a humanistic coalition around sporting activities, which is noticeable in relation to the campaign against doping, in programs for the protection of young people, and in partnership programs for the disabled. These levels of ecumenism correspond to the Christian social teaching. The vision of an "authentic Christian life" is also possible in cooperation between churches and church communities. The same can be said about integrating sport in a religious "praxis of surpassing contingency."[23] Sport ethics should be practiced with "all people of good will." In what follows I will analyze the first level of the single motifs of a Christian vision on sport.

Spiritual Grounds for a Christian View of Sport and for an Authentic Christian Life in Sport

The Transformation of Competition into Fairness

The first point to be considered here is that of competition and its transformation (demythologization, demilitarization, participation) into fairness, in the tradition of justice and peace.

Justice as Fairness?

Can justice be considered as fairness? In the Sermon on the Mount (see Mt 5, 6) Jesus taught that those who hunger and thirst for righteousness will be blessed; those who are persecuted for their righteousness will be also blessed. As one looks for the Kingdom of Heaven one should also look for righteousness (see Mt 6:33). Righ-

---

23. See Hermann Lübbe, "Religion Nach Der Aufklärungan," *Zeitschrift für philosophische Forschung* 33, no. 2, ed. Vittorio Klostermann (April–June 1979): 165–83.

teousness should go beyond the law (Mt 5:20) so that we can "fulfill all righteousness" (Mt 3:15). Love is greater than belief (1 Cor 13) but it is never said that it is greater than righteousness. Of course the Bible talks about a righteousness that justifies those who hunger after it and in whom Christ lives. In Hosea 10:12, we read: "Sow righteousness for yourselves, reap unfailing love. Break up the unploughed ground for yourselves for it is time to seek the Lord until he comes and showers deliverance upon you." And in the Letter to the Romans Paul says: "The Kingdom of God is righteousness, peace and joy" (Rom 14:17).

Can we understand today righteousness as fairness? By saying "justice is the virtue of social institutions" John Rawls refers to the capacity of social institutions to support justice. Virtue should be understood as a capability, as an epitome of ethical fairness.

How do we fulfill God's righteousness today? Through solidarity (con-solidarity and pro-solidarity), through reflection on the conditions of institutional justice (theory of justice), through the "option for the poor."

Peaceful Competition; Competition without Commerce

According to Norbert Müller, an expert in the founder of the modern Olympics, Baron Pierre de Coubertin owes the Olympic formula *citius, altius, fortius* to his friend, Dominican priest Henri Didon. Didon made this formula a symbol for catholic progress as he saw in sport the possibility of preparing individuals for the requirements of a fulfilled life and the chance for an ethical understanding between different people.

The Body and Its New Interpretation

The human body is the human person. Thus the distinction "human" and "body" is to be found on a conceptual and analytical level: the human being has a multiplicity of perspectives but remains the same person. The human body does not only partake in its totality and vitality in the rights of a human being, but it is the very subject of the human person. The human being as a body is at the same time "matter," since even spiritual processes are constituted as corporal phenomena.

Sport thematizes and experiments the body under two suppositions: on the one hand, the clause of nonavailability, or inviolability, and on the other, the methodical materialism. The body of the human person has a structure of meaning that lifts him above goals and finalities. This structure of sense consists in the fact that humans can only live with it and in it. Humans can set their own active goals within this finite body and can communicate only with their finite body. The capacities of humans are dependent on the structure of the body. This characteristic is brought out in the concept "body." The transcendence over goals and intentions does not withdraw itself through human self-control, which we philosophically call "freedom." Freedom cannot be separated from the body, but can be distinguished from the body in such a way that the human and his body are at the same time united with and separated from each other. The body is a paradox, since it represents at the same time unity and divergence.[24]

The structure of signification of the body can be strengthened or modified by religious concepts on humanity. In a Christian context the concepts can be modified with the help of symbolism, which radiates on the body through the belief in the resurrection of Christ and does not influence the motivational correlation of what is ethically correct, but influences the sensitivity for the acceptance of the body, irrespective of its threats. The human body exists in different stages; it is like a res extensa (Descartes), a "di-

24. See Alfred Gierer, Die Physik, das Leben und die Seele (Munich: Piper, 1985); see also the issue dedicated to "The Body and Religion," edited by Regina Ammicht Quinn and Elsa Tamez, of Concilium: International Journal for Theology 2 (2002).

visible" body. The body can also exist in a reductive form (as a disabled body).

Can the parts of the human body be objects that can be dealt with commercially? Or do the parts of the human body inherit the nonavailability and the nonequivalence that arises from human dignity?

Self-determined persons are in the position of reflecting on their corporality—to make an abstraction of it—in order to put themselves in a relationship with their body that they objectivize by transforming it into an object. The question is what aspects of corporality should be withdrawn from co-modification. The extent to which we understand self-determination plays an important role in this issue. Self-determination can contain defects, can create formal problems that may even require counseling, and can create drawbacks for others. Self-determination can come into conflict with the self-esteem or with the integrity of the body, whose objective protection is guaranteed by common human rights. When we are in a different situation we have problems of setting limits so that the disposer and the disposed (as body) can be viewed as one and the same person. The disposer should have the same rights as the disposed.

The more extensive influence there is on the body in today's sport, the more one talks about the power of using the body. The power of disposition becomes something like a competence of the powerful toward the powerless, toward the ones who are "manipulated" in a neutral way.[25] A recent book on the topic of body and power deals extensively with its commercialization.[26] Through the multitude of possibilities that humans possess (or for which they make themselves available) the exposure of the body grows, and

25. See Emily Martin, *Flexible Bodies: Tracking Immunity in American Culture from the Days of Polio to the Age of AIDS* (Boston: Beacon Press, 1994).
26. See Annette Barkhaus and Anne Fleig, eds., *Grenzverläufe, der Körper als Schnittstelle* (Munich: Fink, 2002).

with this grows the possibility of control over one's own body. Yes, the body can appear as a goal of several activities, as a project. It has always been like this but not to the extent to which it is today, when various ways to modify the body are partially created or partially strengthened by life sciences.[27]

The body seems to be a medium of its own self-control and own self-management. A multitude of services assist in developing this self-control and substitute the capacities of the body and damage its sovereignty. Identity is defined with the help of bodily measures and bodily limits, and new concepts of the self are created.[28] The body can be conventionalized either into a machine[29] or into a center of sensitivity that annuls and surpasses the "intellectualization."

The fact that there is a heteronomous use and a commercialization of the body in sport is not sufficient to justify a utilitarian ethic, because the factual is not the normative. Nevertheless one can show that the human being and the body can constitute a unity that may be differentiated in itself. One sees from general observations that the nonavailability and the ultimate end in itself of humans and the inviolability of the human body, which are summarized as deontological and ethical positions, counteract the commercialization and the co-modification of the body. On the other hand the fact that one can use mankind and make a profit out of it shows that it is possible to have an utilitarian ethic that can either annul or relativize the *prima vista* commandment or apply it in such a way that it does not violate the general criteria.

---

27. See Hille Haker, "The Perfect Body: Biomedical Utopias," *Concilium: International Journal for Theology* 2 (2002): 9–18.

28. See Hille Haker, "Selbstkonzepte aus feministisch-ethischer Sicht," *Freiburger Zeitschrift für Philosophie und Theologie* 116 (2002): 126–43.

29. See Jakob Tanner, "Be a Somebody with a Body—Die Körpermaschine der Arbeitsgesellschaft," in *Wieviel Körper braucht der Mensch?* ed. Gero von Randow (Hamburg: Koerber-Stiftung, 2001).

Understanding Creation as a Celebration of Life

Creation can be understood in two ways. First, as a *liber creaturarum* (see above under *"Religious Experience,"* where "All creation is full of God and a book in itself) inasmuch as it has a value to be read independently to the *liber revelationis*. Secondly, it can be considered as a *creatio continua*, that is to say, as an ongoing creation of permanent care and reception as seen in the thought starting with Meister Eckhart and on down to the process theology of John Cobbs.

Concrete Applications of Environmental Justice
and the Sustainability of Life

Does nature offer us "conviviality"?[30] The conflict between life—holiness of life, "dignity of creation"[31]—and freedom in the modern world could be envisioned as being resolved in the following ways. Sentiments and empathy for life could be resolved in mutual, creaturely status; respect toward life could be resolved in the principle of conviviality; sensitivity for suffering could be resolved by extended compassion; each person's rapport with their body could be resolved in biblical respect for the body; the setting of personal limits is resolved in humility; respect for biodiversity is resolved in "aesthetical enrichment"; sustainability could be seen as "openness to new generations"; and so forth.

Training Contains Moments of Transformation

A parallel exists between acquiring competence in sport and the Aristotelian-Thomistic concept of virtue as *habitus operativus bonus*. The Aristotelian and the ascetic tradition have some similarities. They both speak of "theological virtues" because religiosity

30. See Ivan Illich, *Tools for Conviviality* (New York: Harper & Row, 1973).
31. See Heike Baranzke, *Würde der Kreatur? Die Idee der Würde im Horizont der Bioethik Epistemata Philosophie* (Würzburg: Königshausen & Neumann, 2002).

can be also cultivated as a practice or an exercise. There is no learning of a practice without a relationship to a certain practical thing. Thereby we must distinguish between the temporary and the ultimate aims of mankind. Sport moves within the realm of temporary aims. Therefore analogies should recognize both the similarities and the dissimilarities between a monk and a sportsman. Certainly all training implies moments of effort and sustenance, but it also has moments of an opening toward new possibilities.

Perfectibility

Perfectibility can be considered as a spiritual image; *citius-altius-fortius, imperfecti, provecti, perfectio, purificatio, illuminatio, unio* are all metaphors of experience. "Be perfect [*teleios*] just as your heavenly Father is perfect" (Mt 5:48). This quest for the absolute form (the resurrected body) involves segments that are based on continuous actions that cannot be understood in a categorical sense but are defined in a transcendent way. It includes concepts of an ascetic and mystical disposition: *puritas cordis, tranquillitas mentis, humilitas.* It is the stuff of perfection and implies levels of perfection, progress of accomplishment or progress of receptivity (*potentia oboedentialis*).

From the studies of Norbert Müller, I will now quote a statement of the founder of the modern Olympics, Baron Coubertin, in which he speaks about the possibilities for the development in perfection through sport: "The sportsman does not seek to obtain a profit. He sets an aim for himself and for no-one else. He is not obliged to follow this same aim the next day in order to ensure his daily sustenance. Sportsmen cultivate their aims purely for the sake of achieving the aim; they set themselves limits or aspire to greater heights which they want to achieve."[32]

32. Norbert Müller, *Olympism: Selected Writings of Pierre de Coubertin* (Lausanne: I.O.C., 2000), 543.

In today's world we can speak in this way about "sport" only if we are referring to it as a leisure occupation. The professionalism of sport has pushed into the background the idea of "caring," which has been replaced by sport-medicine supervision. Sport and spirituality have similarities in their backgrounds despite the distinction between the temporary and final determination of man.

Exercise as a Means for Celebrating Vitality;
the Metaphor of the "Way"

Sport is a phenomenon of exercise. The statement "Germany exercises" is a motto that should lead to improved health. Exercise is also self-referential, as life is movement, and movement underlines our very vitality. This is experienced every day by the long-distance runner as well as by the person who goes for a walk. Moreover, every movement, evident even in dancing, contains meditative possibilities, rhythms. The ancient word for method, *meta-theodos,* is in fact "a teaching on the way." Movement and being "on the way" are interconnected. The continuing interest in exhausting pilgrimages underlines this connection. For instance, we can think of the pilgrimages to Santiago de Compostella in Spain, which are still popular today. The term "the way" is an auto-referential goal. "The way" also has a spiritual meaning. We see that in St. Bonaventure's teaching on the "triple way" (*De triplici via*).

The preparation for the journey, the accompanying insights along the way, and the experience of unity in all of this run parallel at the bodily and spiritual level. This can be asserted not only when one speaks about individual training but also when one talks about the solidarity movement, in which cultural and national borders become relative.

Sport cannot be compared with a private "way," even if this is as important as a pilgrimage, since sport that leads to peace among nations reminds us of the biblical images of exodus and the people of God in pilgrimage in an eschatological sense. Distance and connection between people find their expression in the Bible through the Tower of Babel and Pentecost.

Babel and Pentecost: Relationships between Persons

The Bible story about the construction of the Tower of Babel and God's decision to create many languages in place of one (Gen 11:7–8) does not deal with human hubris, that is, with the imposing height of the tower, but with the unification of culture in contradiction of God's instruction to fill the earth, that is, to diversify creation. This is why God separates different cultures through their languages. This separation is not suspended by the miracle of speaking in tongues at Pentecost, but is relativized by the possibility of experiencing unity in diversity. A Hymn of Adam of St. Victor comes to mind: "Harmonia diversorum, et in unum redactorum, dulcis est connexion." The connection needs to respect the dissimilarities. This can also be said about the unifying force among people that is postulated by sport.

Enthusiasm and Contingency

This function unites people and is easier to realize in the era of globalization because globally released economic power often produces enthusiasm and ecstasy instead of the required sobriety. Enthusiasm is positive if it is not controlled by ideological or nationalistic aims and if it does not overwhelm what mankind has learned through history. Human beings are finite, fallible, and vulnerable, and they remain so also in sport. The enthusiasm for extraordinary achievements should not lead to the expectation that we deal with a trans-human personality. In the so-called genetic doping we are already faced with trans-human dreams in which it is forgotten that it is the same finite, vulnerable, fallible humans who dream these things and that these characteristics remain whenever they wish to achieve something.

Discerning Spirits

This theme regards child protection, gender identity, doping, fan violence, trans-humanism, and limits for tolerance.

The philosopher Immanuel Kant believed that because the human being is not an angel his desires should be accompanied by his duty to do something. This statement may be translated into theological language in the following way: not everything is useful to the human being, and not everything leads to benefit the community *sympherein* (1 Cor 8). This is why we must make a discernment of the spirits that dominate the sport of our time by making reference to that which is really useful for the human person.

The Ten Commandments remain as a guide for us. (Cf. Exodus 20:2–21, as here they will be liberally translated): I am God, to whom you belong since I freed you from Egyptian slavery. Do not honor anyone except me. Make yourself no idols. Do not misuse my name by invoking me wrongly. Do not abandon my Commandments in the name of religion. I withdrew into a time of peace after I completed the work of Creation. You should also have a day of rest on the seventh day and leave all work aside and preserve the Creation. This day is holy. If children honor their parents and parents love their children, then the offspring will live a good life. The earth is the common heritage of all humankind. All share the responsibility to pass it on to future generations in a good state. Do not commit murder! Do not torture! Do not terrorize people! Do not misuse those in your power. Don't be aggressive and violent! Be faithful to your spouse! Do not break contracts! Take responsibility for your relationships! Do not steal and do not exploit others! Don't be corrupt and do not misuse your power. Do not make false accusations against others! Do not discriminate against people! Do not cheat! Seek the truth! Do not be envious and begrudge the possessions or the income of others! (Do not be envious if you are on a lower scale and do not have the things that others have; do not begrudge from a higher level because others also rise in life !)

There are two hermeneutical rules to keep in mind. These short phrases are subordinated in the Jewish tradition to the double command of "love God" and "love thy neighbor." We can understand them best with the help of one of the most important teachers of the Latin Church, St Augustine, who reminds us that Godly love is God's love toward people. One should obtain this love from God's heart. Only then will we have a heart for the poor and the disadvantaged and not make any difference between people who need our affection.

This is the hermeneutical method for the interpretation of the Ten Commandments in one's personal actions: the action should be filled with the spirit of the love for your neighbor. Those who obey the Commandments but do not have love do not fulfill their meaning (See 1 Cor 13).

The social hermeneutical key is justice. Jesus of Nazareth says: "Seek God's Kingdom and his Justice." Justice (and righteousness) come from God: every human being is a creature who was wanted by God, who is accepted by God and is created in his image. This concept goes beyond the structures of human society. A proper society can distinguish which rights and values should be granted to everyone and which disparities should be avoided.

Here are some practical rules for considering the challenges of the present time. Those who listen to God should not tolerate slavery because God freed us from slavery. In other words: people should not be instrumentalized against other people against their own will. Mankind finds its real significance in God and his purpose in themselves. This is important when we talk about the protection of athletes, but particularly for the protection of children and handicapped people.

God does not want religion to be misused. Religion and violence do not tolerate each other. Who uses the name of God in military disputes misuses his name. Not long ago soldiers would wear as a sign on their belt buckle "God is with us." Religious signs can be misused, as we often see in sports.

God wants human beings to be human. This is why he gave mankind not only the work of Creation but also the peace of Creation and in this way gives his Creation rest. This is why we must defend Sunday as a day of rest and not use the whole weekend for sport.

God does not want mankind to threaten or hurt each other. This is not compatible with his absolute and unconditional acceptance of every human being and, therefore, with his love. Who loves others created by God does not destroy life, does not damage love, and does not divide people into races and classes, into stages of development or into no-longer-fashionable models.

The Ten Commandments are an obligation for all and not a privilege for the pious. Paul says at the beginning of his Letters to the Romans that even the heathens know in their heart what is good and right. Meister Eckhart believes that sometimes it is better to listen to philosophers who are unbelievers because the morality of those who fear God is not always right. In this way the philosophers and those who fear God can learn from each other.

Teaching on Imperfection and Guilt

From a Christian point of view, the human being is neither his own master nor the master of his own history in the sense that he can control it. Hence we tackle the fundamental question of the perfection of mankind. However, as we have seen, that does not exclude perfection in an individual—in sport or in spirituality.

The aim of becoming perfect can be understood as an all-encompassing and fundamental program whose final form is multidirectionality. The creation of a new mankind would be the most complete form of the final product. This concept is connected to a total objectification of humankind through humankind. It presupposes a teleological worldview, which is either predetermined so that the human being can understand it or established by humans through a permanent surpassing of the limits set on them by nature or tradition (evolution?). A maxim erected at the entrance of the National Museum of the United States reads: "Man is called to create men."

One may also understand the aim of "perfecting oneself" as a particular "optimization" of a single characteristic (or possibility) of a human being. In this case we talk about individual programs or individual processes, in which progress is to be found in the elimination of a defect or in improvement of a capacity within the person. In such a case we could talk about surpassing limits without connecting these individual limits to a person who is perfectible (that is, in the sense of a process of developing individual capacities).

These two dimensions have an influence on the concept of "perfectibility." In the first case a debate developed on the fundamental question of whether a person can become entirely another person (*conditio humana*). This is where we should position the debate on the promise and warning of utopias. Here we find a competition between natural and social teleologies. The same competition can be found between teleologies and an anti-teleological culture of the "imperfect." We may include here the debate between different views on the world and on humankind in their relationship to the humanities or to the sciences. We must also mention the debate on whether a human person can be "objectivised" or on whether he should be "objectivised."[33]

In the second case the questions are more relative. One may ask oneself if progress in limiting or eliminating a defect or in the increase of a certain potentiality is not in fact connected to a po-

33. See Michel Foucault, "Afterword," in Hubert Dreyfus and Paul Rabinow, *Michel Foucault: Beyond Structuralism and Hermeneutics*, 208–64, 2nd ed. (Chicago: University of Chicago Press, 1982).

tential of risk and loss. One formulates a question in a scientific context and it is resolved in this context but, at the same time, the solution opens the door to another problem as soon as the horizon of the discussion is enlarged. New problems come about as one opens new fields through progress, through understanding and applicability, and also from not understanding and from jumping to ambivalent conclusions. Fundamental and relative matters can be described by the use of concepts such as "the perfect man" on the one hand and "the man who advances in particular spheres" on the other hand. Counter- and cross-concepts are also to be distinguished fundamentally or relatively.

Between these two fields there are similarities and intersections. Characteristic here is the issue of "surpassing limits": do we set ourselves new limits, or do we drop completely the concept of a limit?

The difference between current questions and the views of the religious world arises from the fact that—from a philosophical and theological perspective—one asks what is the source of the perfection of humankind, while modern society, and the sport culture that depends on it, asks in what way can a person be "optimized."

The imperfections of humankind include humans' capacity for making mistakes. In the sporting world dealing with fault and failure is an important form of human contact. It has an important role in a Christian counseling process. The imperfection of the human person hints at his transience, at the transience of his fame. The Apostle Paul showed us how the fame of man belongs to the space of the immediate, of transient goods. On the other hand he praises himself for being persecuted for his defense of the Cross. Some traces of this are to be found in sport when one has to deal with important defeats or when the eternal "number two" is more loved by the public than the "number one" (for instance in the cyclists' Tour de France).

The "Mystical" Dimension of Sport: The Moment of Tension as the High Point of the Parable

Our spiritual and theological analysis of a Christian vision of sport would be incomplete if we did not mention an experience that is possible in sport but that has deeper meanings. In order to describe this experience one often uses the image of drawing a bow to shoot an arrow. There is a point at which the bow is so tense that the arrow is forced to leave it to achieve its goal. We speak of this as the moment of greatest intensity. The power is not yet released. The bow is drawn further, the arm is tense, and the arrow does not leave its place. This image of greatest tension of the bow—before the arrow starts its arched flight and eventually falls to the earth—has often been described in lyrics by the poet Rainer Maria Rilke.

In the same way one finds in spiritual writings the concept of a "mystical" moment, that is, a moment in which one has the highest degree of disposition of receiving the eternal Word of God. The spiritual tradition calls this moment "potentia oboedentialis," in which one finds the potentiality of reception at its highest. At this moment one waits for a special experience—which never occurs because, as Meister Eckhart would say, we cannot control experience. Such experiences are given to us freely by the One who gives life.

Similar moments of the intensity of success or the achievement of an aim can be found in sport. They are intensively celebrated, or they demand an inner celebration. These signs are not auto-referential but point to something beyond them. For the immediate human existence sport is today the "most important minor concern in the world," offering endless possibilities for human happiness. These signs are better understood when one becomes aware of the imperfection of these moments of apex and one longs for an agglutination of the immediate with the definitive.

Part 3   Pastoral Aspects

This final section seeks to move this predominantly philosophical and theological discussion to the practical level: the pastoral dimension. These three chapters seek to give support both in theory and in praxis to the pastoral ministry of sport. The Church must be engaged proactively in this phenomenon in order that the Gospel may enlighten the work of those who dedicate numerous hours a week to this phenomenon. But how? The possibilities of pastoral initiative will vary as much as the sport disciplines vary and can stretch across various levels of play from children's to adult, amateur to professional. Nor should the Church's concern be limited to the players alone; it should overflow to coaches, parents, fans, owners, and others affiliated with these sporting events. Thus, the Christian mission within the field of sport is as vast as the multifaceted world of sport itself.

In chapter 9, the author claims that sport as a sign of the times requires our discernment. This discernment needs the help of other disciplines, while in itself it needs to be continually developed and updated, as the very sign it attempts to convey is itself subject to rapid change. This applies to those who engage in this activity at the amateur level as well as the professional level; it is just as true for traditional sports as for sports that have evolved and have become more individual-centered and continue to evolve, taking on more "extreme" forms. Because of this, the approach to sport on the part of the Church is also in a phase of continual development. It is not limited to simply encouraging a practice of sport that is in accordance with human and

Christian virtues. Rather, this new approach seeks to announce the Gospel of salvation from "within" this modern phenomenon of sport. The first claim is supported by a new trend in sociology that some call "body turn" as it focuses more predominantly on the body. Sociology permits theology to trace specific historical realities like the body (e.g., modes of movement, social practices, style, knowledge by skill, and religion), which anthropological reflection by itself leaves at the level of general remarks.

Chapter 10 presents the concrete experiences of an Olympic chaplain who for more than two decades has accompanied an ever-changing group of predominantly Catholic athletes who have made up the Austrian national Olympic team. Because elite sport offers a unique window of pastoral opportunity that has multiple resonances with the youth who look up to them, the sport chaplain should respond to this occasion to the best of his ability by knowing the culture of sport and the joys and struggles of the athlete in his effort to provide spiritual care for these sportspersons. The author squarely addresses the rampant problem of egoism in sport, because it is contrary to the Gospel's ethic of charity. Finally, the author concludes with practical suggestions and answers to particular issues related to the intersection of faith and the public sphere of sport.

Chapter 11 presents a synthesis of the reflections and points of action as elaborated in the document "Sport and Christian Ethos: a Joint Declaration," which was fruit of the work between the Catholics and Evangelicals involved in sport ministry in Germany. It is an invitation to reconsider the many opportunities for pastoral work in sport, namely, for the coach.

Stephan Goertz

9 Sport as a Sign of the Times
Pastoral Observations and Challenges

Sport as a Sign of the Times

The question that was posed to me—sport as a concrete pastoral challenge—turns out to be quite intractable. "The closer the look one takes at a word, the greater distance from which it looks back"—this aphorism by Karl Kraus proves also true when looking at the term "sport."[1] The topic appears amorphous. Hence, without specification of what exactly we are talking about when we talk about sport, instructive insights seem unachievable. The topic and the challenges deriving from it are multifaceted.

A second observation is to be made. In a number of recently published pastoral-theological encyclopedias and compendia the entry word "sport" is absent.[2] Also, the *Catechism of the Catho-*

---

1. Karl Kraus, *Pro Domo et Mundo* (Munich: Langen, 1912), 74.
2. See Leo Karrer, ed., *Handbuch der Praktischen Gemeindearbeit* (Freiburg: Herder, 1990); Herbert Haslinger, ed., *Handbuch Praktische Theologie*, vol. 2 (Mainz: Grünewald, 1999/2000); Norbert Mette and Folkert Rickers, eds., *Lexikon der Religionspädagogik* (Neukirchen-Vluyn: Neukirchener Verlag, 2001); Gottfried Bitter et al., eds., *Neues Handbuch religionspädagogischer Grundbegriffe*, 2nd ed. (Munich:

lic Church (1993) and the German Conference of Catholic Bishops' *Catechism for Adults* (1995) do not touch on the topic at length.[3] This is a surprising lack of consideration since, according to John Paul II, sport falls under the category of a "sign of the times"[4]—a category that otherwise marks the theological importance of historical and social developments. To carry out its tasks, the Church commits itself to "the duty of scrutinizing the signs of the times and of interpreting them in the light of the Gospel. Thus, in language intelligible to each generation, she can respond to the perennial questions which men ask about this present life and the life to come, and about the relationship of the one to the other."[5] Yet, as Cardinal Lehmann says in a comment on this key text,

[It] is easier to talk about this duty than to act accordingly. Two things were evident from the beginning. The "signs of the times" are not clear-cut; therefore it is difficult to interpret their true meaning. Secondly, it follows that a faithful response to the "signs of the times" must not mean that the Church simply adjusts herself to the situation as it is. Rather, discernment is needed to obtain clear criteria.[6]

Kösel, 2006). Among the journals in the field of pastoral theology, *Diakonia* has published an issue on sport: "Sport: Spiel und Kampf," in *Diakonia* 36, no. 4 (2005).

3. See no. 1882, 2187 and 2289 of *The Catechism of the Catholic Church*; it should be noted that although some popes—above all Pius XII and John Paul II—have commented on the topic of sport, sport has not been given a certain level of importance in Church teachings.

4. John Paul II, "Homily at the Mass for Sports Men and Women" (October 29, 2000), *L'Osservatore Romano*, English ed., no. 44, November 1, 2000: 1; see also Carlo Mazza, "Sport as Viewed from the Church's Magisterium," 69 in *The World of Sport Today: A Field of Christian Mission*, ed. Pontificium Consilium Pro Laicis (Vatican: LEV, 2006): 55–73; 69.

5. Vatican Council II, "Pastoral Constitution on the Church in the Modern World: Gaudium et Spes," n. 4, in *Vatican Council II: The Conciliar and Post Conciliar Documents*, vol. 1, ed. Austin Flannery, 1988 revised ed. (Dublin: Dominican Publications, 1988), 905.

6. Karl Lehmann, "Neue Zeichen der Zeit. Unterscheidungskriterien zur Diagnose der Kirche in der Gesellschaft und zum kirchlichen Handeln heute," Inaugural address to the plenary assembly of the Germans Bishops' Conference (September 19, 2005), as published in *Der Vorsitzende der Deutschen Bischofskonferenz 26* (Bonn: Sekretariat der Deutschen Bischofskonferenz, 2006), 6.

Two consequences follow from this: first, to interpret the identified signs of the times, theological reflection needs theoretical support from beyond its own realm; second, to reach a substantial appraisal, theological-ethical criteria need to be developed.[7] In the following, we shall mainly work on the first aspect.

We have noted that the lack of consideration given to sport in pastoral-theological research and the Church's teaching stands in great contrast to its enormous significance as a sign of the times. At the same time, we can observe a long and stable cooperation between the Church and institutions of sport on various levels in Germany (and not only there).[8] Also, in the field of ethics some substantial theoretical work has been done.[9]

What can explain this discrepancy between the neglect of the topic on the one hand and the repeatedly expressed appreciation for sports that usually is accompanied by critique of its negative concomitant phenomena on the other hand? Is sport—in the face of pressing issues such as health, relations within the family, labor, social inclusion, environment, and so on—somehow considered not important enough for Christian theology to tackle? Or is the neglect I have noted a product of theological contempt for

7. See Christoph Hübenthal, "Der menschliche und religiöse Sinn des Sports," *Diakonia* 36 (2005): 235–41.

8. See Franz Enz, *Sport im Aufgabenfeld der Kirche* (Munich: Barth, 1970); Paul Jakobi and Heinz-Egon Rösch, *Sport und Religion*, Schriftenreihe Christliche Perspektiven im Sport 8 (Mainz: Topos-Taschenbücher, 1986); "Sport und christliches Ethos: Gemeinsame Erklärung der Kirchen zum Sport," in *Arbeitshilfen des Sekretariats der Deutschen Bischofskonferenz*, no. 80 (Bonn: Sekretariat der Deutschen Bischofskonferenz, 1990). For a brief survey see: Manfred Paas and Klaus Peter Weinhold, "Kirche und Sport," in *Lexikon der Ethik im Sport*, ed. Ommo Grupe and Dietmar Mieth, 2nd ed. (Schorndorf, Germany: Hofmann, 1998), 289–92.

9. First and foremost some works of Dietmar Mieth should be mentioned, such as: "The Ethics of Sport," *Concilium: International Journal for Theology*, English ed., no. 205 (1989): 79–92; "Die Folgen des Fouls: Ethische Verantwortung im und für den Sport," *Herder Korrespondenz* 58 (2004): 397–402; "Towards an Ethic of Sport in Contemporary Culture," in *The World of Sport Today: A Field of Christian Mission*, 23–43.

the body that exercises, competes, and moves? What does theology think and know about the meaning of the body for the self-perception of individuals in our society?

A final observation: time and again, we hear that sport has a quasi-religious function for many people, even for society itself. If this is the case, we are facing a rather obvious practical-theological challenge that calls for discernment. Yet, here also differentiated assessment must precede appropriate formulation of the challenges.

"Body Turn": Sociological Approaches

The classification of sport as a sign of the times shall guide our remaining considerations. Drawing on the notion of a sign of the times, John Paul II asserts that analyzing the phenomenon of sport solely on an anthropological level does not suffice. A strictly anthropological analysis might seduce us into neglecting the concrete historical, social, and cultural contexts in which sport is practiced, and into talking about the general meaning sport has for the human being.[10] However, we have to take into account that people today engage in physical exercise differently from people in the past and that human bodily expression develops.[11] Neglecting the historical and social contexts of sport leads to very general remarks about the value sport has for the human person as well as about the mischief it contains. Moral appeals that are founded on the grounds of exclusively general anthropological reflection remain nonbinding and ineffective. By contrast, the notion of a sign of the times builds on the theological insight that the Gospel can be truly liberating only when the specific historical realities

10. See Roland Barthes, *Mythologies* (New York: Noonday Press, 1972).

11. See Bero Rigauer, "Die Erfindung des menschlichen Körpers in der Soziologie. Eine systemtheoretische Konzeption und Perspektive," in *Body Turn: Perspektiven der Soziologie des Körpers und des Sports*, ed. Robert Gugutzer (Bielefeld, Germany: Transkript Verlag, 2006), 65.

are answered. In delineating the specific historical realities with regard to sport, sociology can be useful, especially since sociology has discovered the body. This trend is what some sociologists refer to as a "body turn" that is currently taking place in their field.[12] In the wake of this "body turn," sport becomes at the center of attention. As one cannot think about sport without thinking about the body in motion, sport is a natural topic for the emerging sociology of the body.[13] As Markus Schroer puts it: "Theoretical questions about the body are at home in the realm of sport."[14] Theology can gain from this new sociological attention for the body. In order to develop a deeper understanding of sport both as a sign of the times and as a practical, pastoral challenge, I shall draw on some reflections sociology offers.

Sport-Systems as Modes of Movement

We have already indicated the danger inherent in talking about sports in general. The diversity of modes of body movement holds a key position when distinguishing various sports.[15] Sport embraces modes of bodily movement shaped by distinctive, rule-governed forms. These modes of bodily movement allow for (non-verbal) communication between the sportsman and the observer—in which the role of the observer can be taken up by the sportsman himself, by his teammates, by the referee, the coach, or the audience. A sport-system is shaped when bodily movements follow other bodily movements not in an arbitrary way but selectively,

---

12. See Robert Gugutzer, ed., *Body Turn: Perspektiven der Soziologie des Körpers und des Sports* (Bielefeld, Germany: Transkript Verlag, 2006), and Markus Schroer, ed., *Soziologie des Körpers* (Frankfurt: Suhrkamp, 2005).

13. See Robert Gugutzer, "Der body turn in der Soziologie. Eine programmatische Einführung," in *Body Turn*, 9–53.

14. Markus Schroer, "Zur Soziologie des Körpers," in *Soziologie des Körpers*, 7–47, 33.

15. See Bernd Schulze, "Körperbewegung als Formbildung. Ansätze einer systemtheoretischen Bewegungskonzeption" in: *Body Turn*, 81–93.

defined by "the objective of the tournament and by the means allowed by a set of rules."[16] Observers are able to follow the course of the bodily movements. Sport-systems emerge when interactive modes of movement are systematically observed as achievements and comparatively evaluated. These thoughts lead to another realm of theory that is closely linked to the name of Pierre Bourdieu.[17]

Sport as a Field of Social Practices

The late sociologist of culture Pierre Bourdieu was interested in the possible distinction stemming from the practice of various sports. His hypothesis states that the distinctions between social spaces are mirrored in the space of sporting practices.[18] Distinction and distance between social positions are not leveled but enforced by sporting practices. Bourdieu gives an example:

The most distinctive practices are those which ensure the most distanced relation to the adversary; they are also the most aestheticized.... Social distance can be easily retranslated into the logic of sport: golf everywhere establishes distance from non-players, through the reserved and harmoniously arranged space in which this sporting activity takes place, and distance from adversaries by the very logic of confrontation which excludes all direct contact, even by the intermediary of a ball.[19]

As modes of social distinction in pluralistic, differentiated societies do change, the interrelation between certain sporting practices and social positioning is changing. Sporting activities that

16. Ibid., 88.
17. See Pierre Bourdieu, *In Other Words. Essays Towards a Reflexive Sociology*, trans. Matthew Adamson (Stanford: Stanford University Press, 1990), 156–67; P. Bourdieu, "Sport and Social Class," *Social Science Information* (Paris) 17, no. 6 (1978): 810–40.
18. Pierre Bourdieu, *Distinction: A Social Critique of the Judgement of Taste*, trans. Richard Nice (Cambridge, Mass.: Harvard University Press, 1984).
19. Bourdieu, *In Other Words*, 157–58.

were yesterday hidden because they seemed to betray a low social position may tomorrow become a status symbol. A good example for this change of meaning and status in a sporting activity is surfing.[20] Even if possibilities of change are limited—it is most probable that a golfer won't suddenly start to engage in wrestling—we can observe certain flexibility in the social attractiveness of sporting activities.

However, according to Bourdieu another development shows even more dramatic consequences: "the yet sharper opposition between participation in sport and the mere consumption of sporting entertainments."[21] The importance given to the observer changes the function of sports—more precisely, of particular sporting activities and events. They turn into economically profitable spectacles with effects that seriously damage the reputation of sport. This problem also concerns values associated with active sports. The "aristocratic ideology of sport as disinterested, gratuitous activity"[22] is overruled by the mentioned transformation. According to Bourdieu, the permanent growth of audience that cannot claim any practical sporting competence leads to a change of interests. Technical virtuosity, the promptness of a movement, successful combinations, or the orchestration of a team strategy lose importance, whereas formal aspects such as results and victory gain attention. Professionalization of actors, as well as of the organization of sporting events, coincides with the coarsening of perception; thus the gap between sport as a spectacle produced for mass consumption on the one hand and sport as everyday praxis on the other hand grows, and laymen, reduced to the role of mere consumers, become more susceptible to instrumentalization by other

20. See "The Sport of Hawaiian Kings Attracts a Modern Aristocrat," *New York Times*, February 19, 2007, section D.
21. Bourdieu, "Sport and Social Class," 828.
22. Ibid.

interests. "It might be wondered ... whether some recent developments in sporting practices—such as doping, or the increased violence both on the pitch and in the bleachers—are not in part an effect of the evolution" we have just traced.[23] It does not come as a surprise that elite sport institutions establish constraints that hardly go along with moral standards such as fairness and health.

Sport as Style

Sport produces and reproduces distinctions. This observation can be elaborated by looking at the type of relation to the body that different sporting practices require. Sport, as one could phrase the core of the hypothesis, "does not have the same pivotal meaning for people of all cultures, but is exercised in accordance with a given culture, time, gender, age and educational status and hence in accordance with a particular social class and milieu."[24] General and long-term social developments express themselves in sporting practices. Therefore we can identify the creation of a unique style as a constitutive element in the formation of sporting communities. Sport becomes part of the task of forming an individual identity; the body becomes an instrument of identity-formation. As traditional sources of the formation of the body such as labor decline in importance, the individual becomes responsible for shaping her body on her own account. Sport is part of the myth of the self-reliant, creative subject that invents itself and authenticates its individuality. Yet, if the individual person wants to be part of a community, he or she has to stick to a specific style offered by the market of possibilities.

The logic of social modernization also helps to explain the universe of adrenaline or "extreme sports," which in a way constitutes an antipode to the growing abstractness and complexity of mod-

23. Ibid., 829.

24. Michael N. Ebertz, "Sport-Treiben als (Er)Lebensstil," *Religionsunterricht an höheren Schulen* 5 (1997): 291–99.

ern social life. In modern social life, the body has to subordinate itself to the requirements of the particular subsystems. This is not the case in adrenaline sport. "Human beings use their bodies to climb the mountain top, climbing the mountain of scientific truth is a cognitive endeavour."[25] Body and nature represent a palpable, distinct, and firm reality. In dealing with the body and nature, alternative ways of experience and acting can be tested. In contrast to the widespread social marginalization of experiences that are primarily bodily in nature, adrenaline sports disclose an entire world of meaningful, sensuous, bodily experience.

Moreover, sporting practices can be distinguished by social milieu. In accordance with social milieu, differences in orientations toward an active or passive engagement in sport can be noted. Further investigations could reveal correlations between age, gender, and educational status and the sort and frequency of particular sporting activities. As studies show, similar phenomena can be observed in different youth cultures.[26] Also in the lives and lifestyle of young people, sport fulfills different functions and is enmeshed in various patterns of orientation. Sport and the body may be in the center or at the margin of strategies of identity-formation. Special attention should be given to the ways in which sport facilitates the production and reproduction of gender roles.[27] Do sporting practices reinforce or demystify gender stereotypes? Do they hinder or facilitate liberating identity-formation?

25. Karl-Heinz Bette, "Risikokörper und Abenteuersport," in *Soziologie des Körpers*, ed. Markus Schroer (Frankfurt: Suhrkamp, 2005), 295–322, 306; see also: Karl-Heinz Bette, *X-treme. Zur Soziologie des Abenteuer- und Risikosports* (Bielefeld, Germany: Transcript, 2004).

26. See Anja Langness, "Jugendliche Lebenswelten: Familie, Schule, Freizeit," in *Jugend 2006*, ed. Shell Deutschland Holding (Frankfurt: Fischer, 2006), 49–102, 94ff.

27. See Marion Müller, "Geschlecht als Leistungsklasse. Der kleine Unterschied und seine großen Folgen am Beispiel der gender verifications im Leistungssport," *Zeitschrift für Soziologie* 35 (2006): 392–412.

Sport as Religion

It is quite tempting to attribute religious qualities to phenomena of sport,[28] as one has the impression that it is effortless to uncover religious motives, courses of action, and the formation of communities in sports. Looking at the pages of an internet blog named Playersprayers,[29] one can explore the often bizarre world of encounters between sport and religion. In Western Europe, there are two areas of sport above all to which religious functions are ascribed: the Olympic Games and soccer. Pierre Baron de Coubertin (1863–1937) certainly did show a strong sense of mission.[30] And the staging of the opening and closing ceremonies of the Olympic Games definitely reminds us of cultic rituals. When it comes to soccer, things seem equally clear. Just to hint at some observations: in the course of the Soccer World Cup held in 2006 in Germany, a book bound in black leather with a gilded edge and bookmark-ribbons was published entitled *Our Football*.[31] Referring to a player as a "football god" is a way fans express their highest admiration. Or think of the chanting (it is there in the football stadium—and not in churches—where men are singing!): it sounds not less ritualistic nor fervent than the ancient hymnals. The fans form a staunchly committed community, making pilgrimage from game to game, bearing all kinds of hassles without complaint. Those phenomena express more than the urge to merge with mass-

28. See Dietmar Mieth, "Jenseits aller Moral: Sport als Religion?" in *Ich habe meine eigene Religion: Sinnsuche jenseits der Kirchen*, ed. Hermann Kochanek (Düsseldorf: Benziger, 1999), 115–29; Elk Franke, "Der Sport—die Religion des 20. Jahrhunderts," in *Explicatio mundi. Aspekte theologischer Hermeneutik*, ed. Harald Schwaetzer and Henrieke Stahl-Schwaetzer (Regensburg: Roderer, 2000), 219–39; Alois Koch, "Sport als säkulare Religion," *Stimmen der Zeit* 220, no. 2 (2002): 90–102.

29. See http://playersprayers.blogg.de (accessed on March 8, 2007).

30. See Gunter Gebauer, ed., *Olympische Spiele—die andere Utopie der Moderne. Olympia zwischen Kult und Droge* (Frankfurt: Suhrkamp, 1996).

31. Eduard Augustin et al., *Fußball unser* (Berlin: Süddeutsche Zeitung Edition, 2006).

es of like-minded people. On the contrary—this claim will prove important for our further reflections: "A soccer-fan wants to sense himself: his body and his power."[32] In the stadium, new "dimensions of sensing oneself ... dimensions never thought of in everyday life" open up.[33] Through collective action, the profane world is transcended; an alternative ideal is created, embodied, performed. Being a member of a community that exceeds everyday life makes the individual feel special. In order to become a member of such a community, the individual—be it a soccer fan, skateboarder, or hip-hopper—first of all has to prove himself worthy by acting, performing, and moving accordingly. These new communities, these new "congregations of young men,"[34] as Gunter Gebauer calls them, "overwhelm their believers by vitality and intensity; in contrast to the distant solemnity of church service, they offer boisterous participation of the whole community."[35] Gebauer also warns the critics of these practices not to turn a blind eye to "the religious involvement, the commitment to certain values, the feeling of obligation and the voluntary dedication shown in and to these communities."[36] The churches themselves, as Gebauer views it, will not be able to gain from this new interest in religious dynamics. On the contrary, communities organized around sports or pop music represent potent competition for the churches.[37] Members of such freely chosen communities—be they permanent or temporary members—are in those moments of paramountly intense experiences part of a better world.

It has to be noted, though, that we are facing a type of transcendence that lacks a distinct transcendental reference point. The kind of significant meaning that embraces and influences life

---

32. Gunter Gebauer, "Bewegte Gemeinden. Über religiöse Gemeinschaften im Sport," *Merkur* 53 (1999): 936–52, 938.

33. Ibid.   34. Ibid., 937.

35. Ibid., 936.   36. Ibid., 937.

37. See ibid., 950.

as a whole is not put into practice here. Hence, we have to take a closer look at the religious function of sports. In doing so, we have to endorse our principle of differentiation: exactly which sporting activity are we talking about—soccer or table tennis? Who are the persons involved, how old are they, and what is their social background? These questions answered, we can state that certain social functions once designated as "religious" have ceased to be monopolized by the church's interpretations of them: social integration, transcending everyday life, relief from daily burdens, intensive self-awareness. Consider the example of social integration. Even if we have to realize that the Church no longer plays an important role in this, we can still raise the question whether social integration is in fact an objective of the proclamation of the kingdom of God.[38] To pose the question of God is not equivalent to the search for the possible functions religion may have for the individual person or for society. Even if religious aspects can be discovered in sport, we should not thereby conclude that the question of God is settled—and posing the question of God is what Christian faith is first and foremost about.

Sport as Practical Knowledge

Sport sets bodies in motion. Assuming that practical knowledge expresses itself in sporting movements of human bodies has consequences for the notion of the acting subject.[39] The body cannot be reduced to an organ carrying out the intellect's plans. Hence, we have to take into account the special expertise of the

38. To prevent misunderstanding, it should be noted that by talking about the socially integrating function of religion I do not address the sociomoral fabric of a society nor the churches' engagement in the integration process of people with special capabilities and needs or migrants.

39. See Hans Joas, *Die Kreativität des Handelns* (Frankfurt: Suhrkamp, 1992); Thomas Alkemeyer, "Bewegen als Kulturtechnik," *Neue Sammlung* 43 (2003): 347–57; Michael Meuser, "Körper-Handeln. Überlegungen zu einer praxeologischen Soziologie des Körpers," in *Body Turn*, 95–116.

body. Considering the expertise of the body and its practical sense is decisive for truly overcoming the often-criticized dualism of body and mind.

What do we mean by practical sense of the body? The notion of practical sense (*le sens practique*) was coined by Pierre Bourdieu[40] to express the insight that social structures do not just influence mental structures, but are literally embodied. Bourdieu also speaks of habitus when referring to something that is simultaneously internal and external. What is important to us—the values we follow, the feelings we have, the worldview we promote—all of these are deeply entwined with the distinctive way we move, with our distinctive posture and our distinctive gestures. Practical sense thus means that without prior consideration we are able to move with certainty, playfulness, and routine in a given situation. We are able to do so because we can build on an intelligence that has an "understanding with one's body."[41] This bodily understanding, this bodily intelligence, is most clearly apparent in sport: we watch the body taking over and performing a move with instinctive certainty. As Hans Joas, Michael Meuser, or Thomas Alkemeyer convincingly shows, bodily practices contain innovative potential. Once again, the example of sport points to the creation of new cultures of movement that shape the self and that, together with like minded others, develop preferences for certain movements; the self is being formed through body movements.

We do not understand social orders correctly if we view them only as cognitive constructs. In his widely noted study on boxing, Loic Wacquant demonstrates how practical competence is formed by bodily understanding.[42] To acquire the specific habitus of box-

40. See Pierre Bourdieu, *The Logic of Practice,* trans. Richard Nice (Stanford, Calif.: Stanford University Press, 1990).

41. Ibid., 166.

42. Loic Wacquant, *Body and Soul: Notebooks of an Apprentice Boxer* (New York: Oxford University Press, 2004).

ing, one has to actually participate in the practice of boxing. It is the body that understands and learns, that grasps and internalizes the logic of boxing. "Being an out-and-out bodily practice, boxing can be understood only through practicing it."[43] Thus, embodied knowledge is generated. The body's ability to act corrects the picture of human action as completely planned and goal-rational. Analyzing body movements in sport discloses the "creative and constructive potential of the socialized, cultured body that is necessary for reacting in unforeseen situations."[44]

Challenges

Drawing on the sociological propositions I have presented here, we can pinpoint three intertwined levels of challenges: the theoretical, the practical, and the religious.

Prior to asking about the place that Christian faith could occupy in today's world of sports, we have to comprehend the theoretical challenge posed by such an endeavor. In recognizing sport as a sign of the times, the Church's teaching answers this challenge. Hence, trying to scrutinize and understand sports has to be at the top of the agenda. Doping, violence, commercialization, and the like call certain sports phenomena into question. However, the reasons for such problematic developments lie not in sport itself. Rather, a number of social factors have to be taken into consideration.

Consulting sociological research, as I have suggested here, improves the chance of a deeper, more differentiated understanding of sports phenomena. Two aspects can be highlighted. Systems theory, inspired by the late sociologist Niklas Luhmann, helps us to understand the momentum of specific social processes. When sports on the one hand and the medial and economic interests on

43. Michael Meuser, "Körper-Handeln," in *Body Turn*, 108.
44. Thomas Alkemeyer, "Rhythmen, Resonanzen und Missklänge. Über die Körperlichkeit der Produktion des Sozialen im Spiel," in *Body Turn*, 265–95, 289–90.

the other hand merge, enormous dynamics following their own logic are set free. The subsystem of media and the subsystem of economy observe sporting events from their respective perspectives. Inevitably these observing subsystems affect sports. Thus, sport is forced to stage events in accordance with the requirements of media in order to further profit by gaining attention. To give an example: to boost media coverage, rules in table tennis and biathlon were changed, and thereby the face of these sports as well. This in turn is economically profitable. Attuning varying interests doesn't go smoothly though—neither in sport nor in other social realms. This is nothing to lament; our task is rather to diagnose.

These theoretical considerations have consequences for the question of what to do when certain developments are to be rejected on moral grounds. Here, we come across a basic problem not just of sport, but of moral responsibility in general.[45] How can various subsystems in a functionally differentiated society actually be coordinated?[46] How can systems be rerouted to make different decisions and take different actions? What influence on subsystems and their processes can individuals and social movements possibly have? These questions are vividly discussed. Yet, no solution to the problem is in sight—there is simply no authority to prescribe a solution. What can be said, however, is that only a combination of various forms of regulations (market, law, morals, experts) can adequately answer the complex problems of modernity. Consequently, moral appeal to concrete individuals can only be one strategy among others. To hope that single role models by themselves can bind the forces of systems turns out to be an illusion. Only if the rules of systems are altered, if the right course of

45. See Ludger Heidbrink, *Kritik der Verantwortung. Zu den Grenzen verantwortlichen Handelns in komplexen Kontexten* (Weilerswist: Velbrück, 2003).

46. See Franz-Xaver Kaufmann, Giandomenico Majone, and Vincent Ostrom, eds., *Guidance, Control and Evaluation in the Public Sector: The Bielefeld Interdisciplinary Project* (Berlin: Gruyter, 1986).

action of single actors is no longer played on, may improvements be in sight.

Likewise, insights deriving from Bourdieu's work help to sharpen our attention. Which sporting practices are of interest for us? Why these and why not others? Whom does the Church's engagement benefit? Raising these questions means questioning the options that orient Christian courses of action. How can the preferential option for the poor—conceived as a demand for justice in a broad sense—be realized in the realm of sport? Churches can demand and advance participation of those whose full participation in sports is denied or hindered: children, prisoners, the disabled, the aged, and the infirm.

Finally, we can reflect on what it means for Christian faith that religious life is evidently being developed by sporting communities. Does the Church realize what is going on? Does it realize the intensity of self-sense and self-awareness that unfolds when one participates in certain bodily practices? Even though demands to find a measured way to stop idolizing the body seem legitimate, they probably won't be far-reaching. Missionary efforts like the following are touching but seem quite helpless: a website in the United States offers little statues of Jesus playing football or baseball with kids as "a wonderful way to reinforce Jesus as 'friend' in everyday activities."[47]

Do bodily motivated communities and communities "on the go" represent a world that—contrary to the claims of the Second Vatican Council—does not raise an echo in the heart of the Church?[48] Has the Church lost contact with today's culture? It is not only the needs of the soul that are being expressed in sports. People want

47. See http://www.catholicshopper.com/products/inspirational_sport_statues.html (accessed on March 8, 2007).
48. Vatican Council II, "Pastoral Constitution on the Church in the Modern World," 903.

to sense and represent themselves bodily. They can do so in the stadium, halls, and streets—but rarely can they do so in churches. It seems therefore that we are encountering an emancipation of needs that we underestimate if we answer it solely with moral rejection. The real challenge for Christian faith that sport represents lies in the eminent meaning that sport has for people. Sport forms an experiential space that can be labeled religious and that exhibits a particular dignity while it cannot be governed by external authorities. To phrase it clearly: certain experiential spaces are no longer in the realm of the Church. The Church must therefore learn to connect to the creation of meaning that is taking place beyond its influence. The decisive question is: "Will the Church be able to critically acquire experiences of willful bodily movements?" Only if it manages to do so can it possibly explain the meaning Christian faith has to offer. First of all, it might be important that those people who develop their practical sense in the world of sport are allowed and able to interpret their practice in the context of Christian faith—because Christian faith announces the incarnation of God. And the incarnation means that also in the realm of religion, a "body turn" has taken place.

Bernhard Maier, S.D.B.

10 Sport as a Pastoral Opportunity

The Sports Chaplain

A Firm Anchoring in the Phenomenon of Sport

Before the team's departure for the 1984 Olympic Games in Los Angeles, a large Austrian daily paper ran the headline: "Austria's 'Good Shepherd' at the Olympics."[1] With the conferral of this honorable title on the top athletes' chaplain, the sports journalist made the right point: a sports chaplain must be a good shepherd for these elite athletes from whom is demanded so much—often more than what is actually good for them.

The task of taking care of the athlete's spiritual well-being in the midst of the ups and downs of sport is reminiscent of the opening paragraph of the Second Vatican Council's Pastoral Constitution states:

The joys and the hopes, the grief and the anxieties of the men of this age, especially those who are poor or in any way afflicted, these are the joys

---

1. "Österreichs guter Hirte bei Olympia," *Kurier*, July 28, 1984, 25, as reprinted in Bernhard Maier, *Olympia- und Spitzensport* (Vienna: VWG, 1993), 91.

and hopes, the grief and anxieties of the followers of Christ. Indeed, nothing genuinely human fails to raise an echo in their hearts. For theirs is a community composed of men. United in Christ, they are led by the Holy Spirit in their journey to the Kingdom of their Father and they have welcomed the news of salvation which is meant for every man. That is why this community realizes that it is truly linked with mankind and its history by the deepest of bonds.[2]

It is in this sense that a sport chaplain should be familiar with the "joys and hopes" of the athletes of our time. He should have a good knowledge of sport: he should either have an appropriate education or be proficient in a certain sport. A theoretical knowledge of the phenomenon of sport and a practical knowledge and direct contact with certain sporting events are also essential. All in all, it is necessary to have a fundamentally positive outlook toward sport and athletes.

In order to be accepted as a team's chaplain for the long term, it is extremely important to make an effort to establish relationships with the sports association, its officials, and its athletes. This can take years and requires no small amount of time and effort. A sociable and amiable nature certainly makes the contact-making process easier.

On the one hand the chaplain should never be too pushy, but on the other hand he should be able to carry out his pastoral duties and above all—where possible—to remind people of their Christian duties. Both of these things are facilitated by tact and a sense of humor.

Direct involvement as the chaplain in the life of an association or sports club should be striven for. But the pastor must be care-

2. Vatican Council II, "Pastoral Constitution on the Church in the Modern World: Gaudium et Spes," 922. This document was finished in 1965 after three years of work with 2,309 Yes votes against 75 No votes. See the introduction by Karl Rahner and Herbert Vorgrimler in *Kleines Konzilskompendium,* 2nd ed. (Freiburg: Herder, 1966), 423–47.

ful not to get bogged down into organizational work and should always keep his pastoral mission in view. Sometimes he will also have to fight against the feeling of being superfluous.[3]

So, a chaplain should have a certain liking for sport, a personal closeness to sport, and participation in it. Having a certain sensibility with regard to how one should react in cases of victory, defeat, disappointment, and injury, and in conflicts between athletes and trainers, is another valuable prerequisite for this type of pastoral work.

Longevity is also crucial, as it takes a lot of time to become fully acquainted with this area of pastoral work and to become accepted into it (at least fifteen to twenty years).

Next to personal prerequisites, there are also certain structural prerequisites for a chaplain to professional athletes so that sport and the Church can begin to work together. In Austria, this relationship is excellent. So the following explanation is not a call for immediate imitation, but should rather be understood as one way to find a creative path in the area of athletes' spiritual welfare.

In Austria, the spiritual attention that is directed to top athletes is rooted in the so-called Church and Sport apostolate that is carried out on the local level within the large association of diocesan sports communities. A priest and professor of ethics and social sciences, Dr. Rudolf Weiler, led the way for pastoral work in sport in Austria and foresaw the need for pastoral care since 1956. Yet, the first chaplain to Austrian Olympic team came in 1972: Rev. Fritz Pechtl, who was really a very talented pastor in this field. The Austrian Olympic Committee accepted the offer of cooperation with the Church at that time, and so there has now been pastoral care at the Olympics for forty years. Pastoral care to the Paralympics began in 2000, but it came about more by circumstance.

---

3. Cf. Maier, *Olympia- und Spitzensport*, 1993, 44.

The Austrian Sports Union, one of the three large umbrella organizations of Austrian sport, professes to Christian values in its preamble. As a result, a member of the clergy has formed part of the executive committee for decades; at the present moment, I tend to this.

The Austrian premiership football club VfB Admira Mödling has traditionally been close to a Christian-democratic standpoint. Club officials originally invited the newly appointed Olympic pastor to work with the club, and later even to be a chairperson.

The well-known women's handball team Hypo Niederösterreich—which is extremely successful in the Champions League—has also taken up this provision of a priest chaplain in the club since the 1984 Olympics. The famous trainer and manager Gunnar Prokop, a member of the Austrian Sports Union, is seen as responsible for this. His wife—who died unexpectedly—was the former Austrian home secretary, president of the Austrian Sports Union, and a former top athlete (silver medal in Mexico in 1968, and European champion and world record holder in the athletic pentathlon of 1969).

Membership into the Austrian Association of Physical Education Teachers requires that one assist a certain amount of classes, which I occasionally do, in order to continue to be up to date. Yet, the school authorities in Austria are extremely benevolent to me when it comes to missing classes in order to be chaplain at Olympic and Paralympic events!

In Austria there is a plan to include religious education and ethics in the curriculum for trainers. For a chaplain, teaching these lessons to the trainers could be simple way to come into contact with the top representatives of Austrian football.

Finally, there is also the possibility of being a guest speaker at a lecture series at the university level with the title "An Introduction to Sports Ethics."

An anchoring in many different clubs and associations is very useful for a professional sports chaplain. But that doesn't mean each chaplain should indulge in club-joining mania.

Being a chaplain is time consuming, because it means going to countless sports events regularly, especially where you have ties to a team. On the one hand, it is somewhat of a break compared with my everyday work as director of a high school. But on the other hand, it is tedious to hear the superficial comment after defeats: "Father, you didn't pray enough!"

So, a brief job description of a chaplain would include: visiting, observing, analyzing; expressing a position regarding sports ethics; calling attention to ethically doubtful incidents; taking a position based on moral principles that relates to a person's worth; showing care and understanding for the athletes and the pressure they are under to succeed. Some additional tasks could include writing books or articles, doing media interviews, and taking part in seminars on important questions in today's sport. All of this means being fully engaged in the phenomenon of sport. And it should be a source of fulfillment as well.

Egoism in Sport: An Antithesis to the Christian Paradigm

Moving along from the prerequisites of the chaplain, let us now square off with a chaplain's opponent in sport: egoism. Janez Drnovsek, the former president of Slovenia—a philosopher as well as a statesman—said regarding egoism:

The essence of life is awareness, being aware of yourself and of others. Only then begins the real life, of which I am writing; people who only think of themselves and of their ego have a low sense of awareness. When you look at the world you see a lot of suffering which is the result of low awareness. A higher awareness means overcoming your selfishness and not only thinking of yourself. You perceive the suffering of others, sympathise and try to help. For someone with low awareness, everything revolves around him and how he can get the most out of this life and this world. This is why we have had so many wars about power, wealth and prestige in the course of history—about everything to do with the ego. I want to convince you that it is [a] necessity for people to elevate their awareness. Otherwise the world will not survive for much longer.... Through our greed, we are destroying the world with our actions.... Especially in climate conservation we have seen that no-one cares about the welfare of mankind.... We need to finally wake up and raise our awareness, overcome our ego and act differently.[4]

In sports competitions, egoism is often mentioned. Because of this there is a certain tension for a Catholic priest who has to represent the ethical values of the Sermon on the Mount. Athletes themselves often claim that sport doesn't work without egoism. Yet, either they mean real egoism or are mixing it up with the "healthy" egoism of colloquial language. From the psychological standpoint, an egoist is rather the opposite of a strong person. He is constantly concerned with his usefulness—what others think of him—because he has an inferiority complex; he hasn't found his own self-worth and so compensates with a constant search for personal advantages. As he is lacking in self-recognition he can't see the positive in other people either.[5] Yet is this type of egoism really needed in sports competition?

Paradoxically, a well-known Austrian sports journalist wrote of the skiing star Michael Walchhofer in his moment of great triumph: "Michael Walchhofer is a good-natured giant, who in reality is missing just one (admittedly not unimportant) prerequisite for top-class sport: egoism."[6] In this sense, the dogma of egoism in sport is at least placed in question.

4. "Der slowenische Staatspräsident sagt über den Egoismus," in *Kurier*, Sunday ed., February 3, 2007; 6. Cf. also his book that became a bestseller in Slovenia: Janez Drnovsek, *Misli o življenju in zavedanju* [Thoughts on life and awareness] (Ljubljana: Mladinska knjiga, 2006).

5. Cf. Max Otto Bruker, Lebensbedingte Krankheit (Lahnstein: Bioverlag, 1997), 245.

6. "Michael Walchhofer nur eines fehlt: Egoismus," *Kurier*, Saturday, December 30, 2006.

The following formulation of Gunnar Drexel is not only taste-less and cynical, but it is also mistaken: "Sports competitors can't play a 'Mother-Teresa-game' of moral reasoning."[7]

Didn't Mother Teresa's heroic care of the sick and dying actually constitute hard work and not at all just a simple game of moral reasoning? The comparison of Mother Teresa's immeasur-able—and lasting—achievements that are recognized worldwide to a mere game, or to the "apparently seriously important" competition is ludicrous. The attempt of even equating egoism with a genuine fairness that recognizes the value and worth of the other person is like trying to reconcile fire and water.

Thus, in retrospect, it appears that extreme interest in win-ning is not actually the egoism of selfishness, but rather, a "sports egoism" that is therefore linked with the competitive or agonistic dimension of sport.[8] In fact, this concept has been adopted by utilitarian sport ethicists.[9] The fact that egoism does indeed ex-ist in sports has caused many to unjustly assume that it *must* ex-ist in sport. The egoism present in some sports success has made it a highly stylized moral principle, garnished with the adjectives "human" and "sporty." The wolf in the sheep's clothing is a sports egoism vested in a form of humanism. But it really constitutes a reciprocal tolerance of egoism.

Does this moral concept not come from the false idea that mor-als and morality are not made through philosophical and scientific ethics, but are rather created by a general pre-understanding and then reconstructed? Can "human" egoism be justified by moral feelings?

7. Gunnar Drexel, "Altruismus/Egoismus," in *Lexikon der Ethik im Sport*, 99, ed. Ommo Grupe and Dietmar Mieth (Schorndorf, Germany: Hofmann, 1998), 34.

8. Ibid., 34.

9. Claudia Pawlenka, *Utilitarismus und Sportethik* (Paderborn: Mentis, 2002), 177.

As I see it, Drexel does not succeed in the attempt to morally justify this "sports egoism." He confuses agonism with egoism and classifies genuine self-interest as egoism and therefore contradictory to altruism. Furthermore, he interprets the Golden Rule—biblically interpreted as the principle of balancing out love for thy self and for thy neighbor—not according to the subject, but instead, as a point in favor of egoism.

How is the term "egoism" actually defined? According to Peter Prechtl, egoism is "the characteristic of an ethical attitude that is only related to the pursuance of one's own aims."[10] However, self-interest and striving for one's own gain are part of the "the natural motives of man."[11] According to Otfried Höffe it is only immoral to make self-interest "the final measure in every action ... and to carry it out without considering the interests and rights of other people."[12] The definition of egoism as a "moral meaning that is set down in Kant's 'Anthropology' has become the only one."[13] It is differentiated from a natural striving for your own profit and from striving for self-preservation.

In conclusion to this brief excursus on egoism, we can see that there are varying "degrees of egoism."[14] As such, extreme egoism should not be accepted as something intrinsic to sport, where the idea of fairness should prevail. Consequently, this term should not be used in sport.

10. Peter Prechtel and Franz-Peter Burkard, eds., *Metzler Philosophie Lexikon* (Stuttgart: Metzler, 1995), 121.

11. Otfried Höffe, "Selbstinteresse," in *Lexikon der Ethik*, ed. O. Höffe (Munich: Beck, 2002), 227–28.

12. Ibid., 227.

13. Hans Reiner, "Egoismus," in *Historisches Wörterbuch der Philosophie*, ed. J. Ritter, vol. 2 (Basel: Schwabe, 1972), 302–15, 309.

14. Ibid., 312.

Specific Pastoral Care at the Olympics
and Paralympics

Pastoral care at the major sporting events is the culminating moment of the spiritual welfare program of Austria's top athletes. At the beginning, a part of this requires getting to know the athletes who have made the team. A top priority in your pastoral duties at the Olympic and Paralympic Games is to immediately surmise the available worship spaces in order to organize the liturgical services as conveniently as possible for your athletes. Organizing these activities requires a lot of experience as well as the direct involvement of those in charge of the teams. Being chaplain to the Austrian Olympic team and Paralympic pastor—as a result of a small team and a relatively homogenous confessional membership—is definitely easier than for the German Olympic team, which has both a Catholic and an Evangelical chaplain.

After the service, religious medals, rosaries, or devotional materials can be distributed. I recall that during the Winter Olympics in Turin, Austrian champion skier Christian Morgenstern explained to the media that he received his finger rosary from the Olympic pastor and that for him faith was an important part of his life.

No limits have been placed on fantasy when it comes to finding a starting point in top-class sport as regards offering help for athletes from a Christian motivation, for example offering a German language course for foreign athletes and their families.

The possibility of visiting those with injuries in a hospital—a very nice and gratefully received job—has decreased. In the case of most sports injuries the athletes can already go home the next day, or the one after that. So, you would often turn up too late.

Providing pastoral care for top-class athletes—even when it is possible to do so only in a voluntary capacity—is a major commitment and demands regular travel and attention, especially in the evening, in one's "free" time, or, yes, even during one's holiday or vacation.

When accompanying a community of athletes for a long time, as during the Olympics, there can be tense moments. The chaplain can help to reconcile things, radiate composure, listen, show understanding, provide humor, or even mediate in conflicts, and provide them with someone to talk to who has no vested interest in their success or failure, and remind them of God's mercy and his many blessings.

After a few years working as a chaplain for top-class athletes, you receive invitations to perform baptisms and weddings. I have also presided over funerals in the area of top-class sport, including funerals for top-class athletes.

The pastor is also often called upon for the ceremonial opening of sports halls and sports facilities. All of these provide opportunities to maintain the contacts that have been made in the past at these great events. Immediately after these big sporting events, there are also many invitations from clubs, parishes, and schools to come and give a presentation to the children about the experiences as chaplain to these top athletes.

Finally it is necessary to prepare for the annual sports day retreat and to come up with a new theme for this.

Dealing with the Press: Clarifying the Relationship between Sport and Religion

"Father, we lost because you didn't pray enough!" I have heard this countless times. Thankfully, also the opposite. One thing I have learned after all these years is that, in order to avoid the above reproach, the chaplain should always hold all his meetings with the athletes before the game or competition and afterward only if the team has been successful!

Is the faith of the athletes real, or is it to be understood as superstition?

There is a story that a priest goes to visit a friend and sees that there is a horseshoe hanging over the door. "What's the meaning of the horseshoe there? You don't really believe in good luck charms, do you?" "Of course not, Father," the friend answers, "but I found that it's also useful even when you don't believe in it!"

Again and again you are confronted with many questions regarding the rapport between faith and sport and some apparent similarities between sport and religion. I would like to briefly comment on some of these as they are the daily bread of a sports chaplain.

To what extent is God responsible for success in sport? According to one's degree of faith?

A difficult question! As far as that is concerned, God is the "creator" of every success because he has given us our particular talents and also the freedom to use and develop these talents. I imagine that God follows all our efforts with great "sympathy," that is, theological grace. Above all, God wants what is best for us—to be happy and to succeed in achieving this good. So I say to the top athletes in a homily or talk during the Olympics and Paralympics—which they gladly come to—that a complete failure or an injury is not the wish or desire of God. According to our Christian and biblical conviction, no prayer is meaningless. Every prayer is answered inasmuch as it serves the honor of God and our salvation. How, when, and where our prayer will be answered cannot be known. In this sense, I consider a wonderful, fairly achieved success as a gift of God.

A top athlete once said to me that God alone knows where and when in his life he will get back the 2/1000 of a second that lost him the gold medal. God lets the free game of nature and man's freedom and abilities take its course, to the point that an unfair victory might be achieved by a doped athlete while the athlete who played by the rules loses unfairly.

The following insight that athletes have formulated is also very important: "There are more important things in a person's life than success in sport or in work, in attaining wealth or a career." The Jewish philosopher Martin Buber once said: "Success is not another name for God." A happily married athlete once wrote to me: "If I hadn't lost the competition (at the Olympic Games), I wouldn't have gone off to the Bahamas out of frustration to distract myself and I wouldn't have met the woman with whom I want to spend the rest of my life!"

How does a sports chaplain attract athletes' attention and elevate it to religious questions when they are solely concentrated on the competition?

This is possible through a good relationship of trust that has been built up over the years and follows the approach of Saint Don Bosco in his preventive education. A certain sensibility is needed, so as not to be too blunt or overimposing. Timing is also important; a religious service is possible only when there are no other conflicting events. It is especially helpful if the team captain or coach can help in organizing these religious services.

Do top athletes question their faith when they experience setbacks or failures?

My impression is that athletes don't question their faith when a competition goes wrong. There are of course tears and disappointments. Many try to put the failure behind them quickly, because a top athlete is always fluctuating between success and failure, and so they focus on the next challenge. As a pastor, you try to help them with calm words that can help to build them up but also with a realism that tries to place all in its proper perspective.

Is the gesture of making the sign of the cross before a competition a personal expression of faith or rather something superstitious?

Personally, I like this sign—which is seen more and more—when athletes openly cross themselves as a open manifestation of their Catholic faith. I don't view it as superstitious, but rather as a religious ritual that has become a habit and that is often deepened with a thankful look toward heaven.

I have heard it said that soccer itself is a kind of religion and that the fans consider it as something "sacred." People see the stadium as analogous to a church and traveling to away games as going on pilgrimages. Outward similarities cannot be denied. However, if I personally had not been made aware of this comparison, I would never have come to see these analogies. I have never visited a stadium and had religious thoughts in this sense. Nor do I believe in the religion "soccer"; the so-called devotion to televised football and its heroes is often a compensation for the sadness and emptiness in people's lives. Sport or soccer or other mega-sports are just surrogate beliefs for an outlook on life, but have no connection to God. The German national soccer player Christoph Metzelder said that the so-called soccer religion doesn't help people with their problems because it is something worldly, finite, manmade, and not godly. Certainly I know fanatical fans, but no one who believes in the "holiness" of soccer. It is at best a sort of ideology and gives one a way of looking at the world.

Where then do we draw the line between soccer and religion? Or is it not at all necessary?

Sports are games that consist in rules, competition, physical confrontation, and an unknown result. In this way the game of sport, and particularly soccer, is a mirror of our life and its meaning. Everyone wants to win the top prize. But often people lose; in the end their dream of a successful life here on earth is not attained, and they are defeated by death. What does this mean? Is there a reasonable answer to this in history? Only in "God's athlete," Jesus Christ, who has conquered the greatest opponent, death, can we solve the mysteries of life.

In light of this, how should we consider sport: as a dangerous opponent for religion? Or could it serve the Church as "propaganda," so to speak, for its mission?

Sport is an opponent only in that it takes away time for the Sunday Mass. It can also, like business, tear us away from what is intellectual, spiritual, or demanding. Like all entertainment and the pursuit of mammon, it can distract us from more elevated things.

Those who don't know this also fail to fathom what long-lasting damage is being inflicted on man's soul. Our society, which is void of meaning and religion, is fragile and prone to ideologies that are fairly reckless and easily dominate. The opportunity for sport to be a means of promoting religion can come about only when top athletes are religious and true role models for their faith.

Sports give people a reason for living! What do you think of this comment?

Yes, of course, professional sport provides a livelihood for the trainers, the technicians, the professional players, the advertising and media industry, the people who sell hot dogs, and others. And in a broader sense, it is a source of lively entertainment for the fans in the stands or the people watching television.

What are the limits of the metaphor of sports heroes and Christian saints?

In theory a professional athlete can also be or become a Christian saint. But a key difference is that whether a player plays for fun or to earn a lot of money, they are primarily thinking of themselves. A Christian saint lives heroically for others: loving his fellow man and loving God above himself. For example, Saint John Bosco—a patron for youth work and the pastoral care of sport—asks us what good is it to simply cry about the evils in the world? He reminds us that it is better to channel this emotion into doing all that is in our power to eliminate these evils. A professional athlete can progress in the direction of a saint by generously engaging in charitable work, through fair play, through setting a good example, and even through gestures of devotion that acknowledge the presence of God in our lives.

The use of religious language in sport is becoming more and more common. What are your thoughts about this?

This is a disrespectful creation of journalists for poetic effect; they have no scruples in claiming "holiness" for motives that are purely success-orientated. It is tasteless and undignified to misuse religious language in sport or anywhere else. "Thou shalt not take the Lord's name in vain!"

Diego Maradona is a world-famous player; is it really so wrong to describe him as a soccer-god?

He was a brilliant soccer player and brought joy and gave many fans a sense of meaning in their lives, but in return he nearly suffocated his own life through drugs. In the world of soccer he was an artist (although not always fair). Perhaps one of the three to five best in the world. That he certainly earned the admiration of many, at least for a time, is unquestionable. Yet, Maradona has almost faded and lives a problematic life.

Is there such a thing as a soccer-god?

Of course not, but there are certainly enough transient things that are worshipped. Idolatry can be found throughout history;

prophets have tried again and again to speak against idolatry and to fight against it, but mostly in vain.

What do you think of chapels in stadiums?

Yes, it can be a good thing, when it is used for prayer and for church services. But when it encourages a superstition, then it is not good. As an expression of true piety and belief it is a good sign.

Before important games athletes pray for success. What do you think of this? Have you prayed together with athletes when you've been traveling with them?

Many athletes have told me that they pray more for the health of themselves and for their families. You can certainly also pray for success and for God's blessing. The temptation of superstition is always there. I have taken part in many prayer services with athletes for over thirty years in which I have preached sermons and prayed with them. These have been my most pleasant experiences in pastoral work with top athletes.

What do you think of athletes who openly profess their belief in God?

On the one hand, it is nice when it is genuine and not over-done with the purpose of advertising a particular religious group. In this area a lot of things are done with religion and beliefs that I don't like. The open confession or testimony of one's faith should be done in the right moment and should not come across as propaganda. In this regard, a nonverbal testimony is the best proof of an athlete's beliefs and is much more effective: going to services despite a hectic competition schedule, receiving the sacraments, praying, reading the Bible, being a model of fairness and goodness in sport, practicing teamwork and showing a readiness to help, and definitely not representing the so-called sports egoism.

What do you think of the claim that some sport associations that they are "not a club, but a religion"? In the Bible it states: what you attach your heart to, that is your God. So, this comment is true, isn't it?

Even though this maxim is quoted again and again, it doesn't make this unreasonable comment any better.

As we can see, a superficial amount of theology and a polemical interest easily provoke questions about the relationship between sport and religion from journalists and people interested in this field. The sports pastor needs to always make the effort to help the people to understand their faith and to help correct these misinterpretations and warn against superstitious practices.

Conclusion

A professional sports chaplain should dedicate himself wholeheartedly to his "flock" of athletes—to those who achieve in sport at the highest level, often with a not insignificant health risk. With these explanations, I have tried to only give ideas and not to demonstrate exactly how things should be done in each case. Here, you can see that there is plenty of room for creativity when it comes to the pastoral care of these athletes.

The bottom line is that each chaplain—for the love of top-class sport—must never accept an iota of instrumentalization or immorality and needs to present the morally upright action in his preaching. There are enough examples to show that sports egoism is not necessary to be successful. If this were the case, then it would not work with the Christian paradigm. Indeed, egoism is the greatest contradiction to Christian ethics. Consequently, it is worthwhile for a sport chaplain to work with the people who are exposed to this danger in sport. We must not let the existence of egoism in elite sport justify it as something necessary to sport. Rather, we must fight against it for the good of sport as well as for the good of the person.

Norbert Müller

11 Concrete Pastoral Action within Sport

"Sport is an important instrument of education and a way of spreading essential human and spiritual values."[1] As we have seen, for many decades now, the Church has given, not least due to the statements of the Popes, great value to sport for its contribution to Christian education, to the explanation and experience of values, and for what it lends to building a society characterized by reciprocal respect, fair behavior, and solidarity among all peoples and cultures.[2] Therefore, it is both an opportunity and a challenge to use this instrument and to help bring to the world of sport a Christian understanding of the human person that upholds their dignity and to seek to harmonize aspects of this prominent "body culture" of our day with the Christian way of life.

As a member of the scientific commission of the Church and

---

1. See "The Vatican Works to Humanize the Wide World of Sports," *L'Osservatore Romano*, weekly English ed., no. 46, November 16, 2005, 1.

2. See Benedict XVI, "Greeting to Representatives of the European and Italian Soccer Associations" (September 21, 2005), in *Insegnamenti di Benedetto XVI*, vol. 1 (Vatican: LEV, 2005), 567.

Sport working group that is under the auspices of the Catholic German Bishops' Conference, I wish to offer, as a segue to pastoral action, a synthesis of some relevant points from the document "Sport and Christian Ethos: A Joint Declaration."[3] This document was the specific fruit of many years of ongoing collaboration between Catholics and Evangelicals involved in sport ministry.

Challenges and Opportunities

A Critical Voice against Negative Tendencies and Abuses in Sport

First of all, it must be stated from the outset that not all manifestations and developments in modern sport can find approval from a Christian point of view. The Church shares with many other social institutions its criticism of various abuses in sport: its criticism of abuses such as doping, which is considered to be manipulation and treachery; its criticism of violence, racism, and nationalism; its criticism of the idolization of star athletes and of sport itself as a substitute religion; and its criticism of the exploitation of sport through interests that are alien to it; in a nutshell: the disregard and ruthless exploitation and abuse of human dignity and human rights.

In contrast to these pernicious tendencies, a Christian's understanding of the human person as invested with a unique personal dignity, as created in the image and likeness of God, has positive consequences for their concept of the body and for their activity in sport. Here the maxim is: "If human dignity is not the highest priority, sport cannot fulfill its social function."[4] In fact the joint declaration also states that "the Christian faith prompts people to op-

---

3. See "Sport und christliches Ethos," as found in the websites of the German Catholic Bishops' Conference: http://www.alt.dbk.de/schriften/data/3590/print_de.html, and the Evangelical Church of Germany: http://www.ekd.de/kirche-und-sport/daten/sport_und_christliches_ethos_EKD-Text_32.pdf .

4. "Sport und christliches Ethos," 2.4.

pose any idolization and exploitation of sport and also to oppose the commercialization of athletes. It motivates people to stand up for fairness, tolerance and solidarity."⁵

In light of this, all that in sport which is worthy of being called human, which has been practiced as such already, and which has potential to do so in the future calls for a deepening of commitment on the part of the Church.

Making Better Use of the Opportunities Afforded by Sport

There are many areas in modern society where the Gospel seems to have been thrust aside from the center of life. More than fifty years ago, Pope Paul VI said that "the split between the Gospel and culture is undoubtedly the tragedy of our time,"⁶ and this rift continues. But perhaps there are places and opportunities afforded by sport where this split between the Gospel and culture is not completely torn asunder. The practice of sport, and here I am referring especially to the practice of youth sports, offers some common ground where the values of the "sports culture" and many Gospel values intersect and can complement one another.

For example, youth sports offer real face-to-face social interaction and team experience—something rare in an age of "virtual reality." In an age of individualism, sports still involve team play. Community sports provide places where people can work together toward a common goal such as playing a game. In an age of comfort if not all-out hedonism, sports still speak about making sacrifices. While licentiousness is in vogue, sports propose rules and restraint. Thus, we must not underestimate the opportunities sport offers the youth in today's media-dominated culture. Rather, we must capitalize on the many opportunities implicit in sport.

5. "Sport und christliches Ethos," 2.6.
6. Paul VI, Apostolic Exhortation *Evangelii Nuntiandi* (Vatican: Tipografia Poliglotta Vaticana, 1975), 27.

Many opportunities are within the reach of everyone, as the foremost sphere of action is youth education as carried out by the family and in the school. Christian schools and universities must be leading institutions in the practice of carrying out a sport ethos in the spirit of an integral Christian education in close cooperation with families. This concept assumes teachers who know how to put their faith into practice in the ethos of sports—coaches and instructors who can contribute to an ongoing awareness of the ethical and sport values at the grassroots level.

Christian sport associations play an important role in everyday practice if over and above the sport activity itself they take Christian moral values seriously, and fulfill them through voluntary service to the community with its social, educational, and sociopolitical tasks.[7] To achieve this, educational efforts of the Christian churches need a clearly focused profile. Church-run academies, educational institutions, and other facilities ought to keep in mind sports' formative potential and be open to ethical themes that are implicit to sport. Those topics should not be missing in the formation of priests, of pastoral workers, and of youth workers. The practice of youth sport is the best way to begin this.[8]

Here again, the great opportunity of the youth coach should not be underestimated. While children might not be as easily motivated to attend catechetical instruction, they might participate in a school-, parish-, or club-related sports program, where adult volunteers are helping them to perfect physical, human, and social skills. In doing so they become ipso facto role models for the youth.

Youth seek confirmation outside the home of the values that are taught to them by their parents. Here, the special role of a coach is evident, as he or she spends more time with children than

7. See "Sport und christliches Ethos," 4.5.
8. See ibid., 4.3.

their parents and other teachers. The coach's role must be understood as complementary to the work of parents.

Pope Benedict XVI pointed out how "the task of education passes through freedom but also requires authority."[9] Education is not the mere transmission of data but rather a responsibility entrusted to both parents and teachers. Thus, the Holy Father went on to note how "especially when it is a matter of educating in faith, the figure of the witness and the role of witnessing is central."[10] The use of the title "coach" is a sign of respect, yet it is also a great responsibility to be a positive influence in the players' lives.

In this respect we must be grateful to lay organizations and to other initiatives within the Church that have brought a Christian spirit to sport. Pope John Paul II clearly defined his high regard for sport: "Sport is not only a source of well-being but also an ideal in life; it stands for courage and optimism." A truly Christian impulse in sport can lead to a revival of values and to accessibility to the meaning of life. Because of this, we not only could consider sport as a modern Areopagus, but also should consider youth sports as a type of "youth ministry."

A profound role-model function that goes beyond the resonance they get in the media is fulfilled by extraordinary athletes, who manage to combine high performance in sport with an ethical attitude and to maintain the connection to other fields of life: family and friends, studies and professional life, politics and religious life. Thus, pastoral attention to professional athletes should also be given due importance.[11]

All those working in national and international sport organizations can bring their humane ethos, stimulated by Christian be-

9. Benedict XVI, "Letter to the Diocese of Rome on the Urgent Task of Educating Young People," (January 21, 2008) L'Osservatore Romano, English ed., no. 6, February 6, 2008,10.

10. Ibid.

11. See "Sport und christliches Ethos," 3.7

lief, to bear on their work, where the values and moral principles of sports need a consequent realization in everyday life. Through their commitment they can fit Christian convictions into a humane set of rules that uphold human dignity and defend it against instrumentalization, technocracy, and heteronomy, and additionally engage themselves in the sporting business in favor of transparency and an orientation toward values.

Concrete Fields of Action
The Promotion of Sports Virtues and Values

Once a sports instructor or coach or an organization or association is conscious of the responsibility in forming the youth through sporting activities, the question immediately arises: what values or virtues? Here, I would like to propose fairness as a global virtue that can be learned through sport.

Through sport, this important ethical impulse of fairness is introduced into society. It has always been a principle of the Olympic Movement, and through it fairness in sport has been proclaimed around the world. Fairness not only implies respecting the rules, but also stands for a basic human attitude: the unconditional respect of the opponent and the protection of his right to remain bodily and mentally un-harmed. The opponent is a partner in sport and, as a fellow human being, wants to develop his or her abilities in freedom. As the joint declaration notes: "Sportswomen and sportsmen have asserted fairness as a virtue with global esteem. As a virtue, fairness reaches far beyond the realm of sport into politics and economy and into the field of human social intercourse."[12]

Fairness finds its biblical basis in the so-called Golden Rule: "Do unto others as you would have others do unto you" (Mt 7:12).

---

12. "Sport und christliches Ethos," 2.4.

This rule has its numerous counterparts in other religions, and in sport on a global level its universal ethical claim is accepted. Dialogue in peace between the various religions and cultures can only be carried out in this spirit of fairness.[13]

Respecting the Rules

Sport can take place successfully only when the rules that are self-imposed and binding for all are respected by all, and furthermore when violations are punished. This categorization requires, however, that the rules be contrary neither to moral principles nor to human dignity. Respecting the rules is an indispensable part of the educational task in sport.[14]

Service to Peace

Fairness as a disposition and practice is an important contribution to peace. Sport obviously does not automatically bring about peace. Nevertheless, a universal understanding of the world can be achieved through sport. This is especially true for international gatherings such as world championships or the Olympic Games, where athletes who come into contact with foreigners and a greater sensitivity is fostered. These encounters provide opportunities for a "temporary period of peace" and can help to encourage work toward peace.[15] Under the banner of fairness and peace, sport can and must fulfill its self-imposed task of constructing a more peaceful and better world (see Olympic Charter), "in which respect, loyalty and solidarity between the peoples and cultures prevail."[16] Therefore, sport organizations have to take their task of supporting peace seriously.

---

13. Ibid., 3.4.   14. Ibid., 3.7.
15. Ibid., 3.5.
16. Benedict XVI, "Greeting to Representatives of the European and Italian Soccer Associations," 567.

Service to the Weak and Excluded

For Christians particularly, sport can also be seen as a ministry to the weak and segregated. Through sport they gain new hope and may return or be included into the community. This practical commitment to foreigners, immigrants, and the unemployed, and especially to the physically and mentally disabled, is an act of solidarity and a contribution to social integration. They all "are able to gain a variety of new experiences in sport and in clubs, they can gain pleasure from their own activity and become better equipped for life through achieving a sense of effort and achievement. Meetings of persons with and without disabilities free them from their isolation, take them seriously and endow them with recognition as persons."[17] The cooperation of sport and Church institutions is especially helpful in the endeavors to help these particularly deprived neighbors.

Fields of Common Sports Ministry

"The human being who has been created as a unity of body, soul and mind stands at the center of the ministry of the Church."[18] This ministry can bear fruit particularly well in ecumenical and interreligious cooperation.

Defending the Culture of Sunday

Pope Benedict XVI pointed out at the World Youth Day in Cologne that Sunday must remain an important day of rest from work. "Yet this free time," said the Holy Father, "is empty if God is not present."[19] Thus the need to protect a "culture of Sunday," which

17. "Sport und christliches Ethos," 3.6.
18. Ibid., 4.1.
19. Benedict XVI, "Homily at the World Youth Day Gathering in Cologne, Marienfeld" (August 21, 2005), *L'Osservatore Romano,* English ed., no. 34, August 24, 2005, 12.

is threatened, amongst other things, by sports. Here the effort on the part of all Christians is important to preserve Sunday as the day of the week "which liberates us from the fetters of constraints and which makes us feel that our life is more a gift than an achievement ... families, parishes and sports clubs are all called upon to develop a new 'culture of Sunday' through an appropriate arrangement of events."[20] In the realm of sport schedules, appointed times have to be reconsidered in order to make it possible for athletes to take part in the celebration of the Sunday Mass. "Those working in the ministry should keep in mind what sport means to man nowadays. Therefore they are asked to open up to sport more than has already been the case."[21] Accordingly, religious services could be facilitated to accommodate those attending these major sport events.

Pastoral Ministry at Sport Events

A proven form of Church presence is to be found in the institution of the ministers (the so-called sport chaplain) at national and international sport events, such as the Olympic Games, the Paralympics, and the world championships. It is often the case that such pastoral ministry in ecumenical collaboration reaches not only believers but also those who are aloof to the Church and non-Christians.

Ongoing Cooperation and Collaboration

Because of their different structures and specific goals the relations between the Catholic and Protestant Church and Sport organizations has not been free from occasional tensions in Germany. Nevertheless, the multitude of common interests and aims calls for continuous improvement in their cooperation with each other.

20. "Sport und christliches Ethos," 4.7
21. Ibid.

This can be enhanced by joint committees, joint activities, and conferences with their respective representatives from the field of sport, from the national level to the level of the parishes and local sports clubs. The Church representatives, for example, priests and ministers, both salaried and voluntary pastoral workers, should not hesitate to take the first step in approaching the sport authorities.[22]

In order to achieve a "new evangelization" a coordinated collaboration within the Church structures is needed. The Christian sport associations, which are usually embedded in Church organizations, build bridges to the realm of sport. Both Church-run educational institutions and charity organizations have to cooperate with them when sport is involved in the social field. Sportive elements can be included into these activities, as in the Church's development aid programs for example. These minor investments could result in a high humane yield return.

The national and continental bishops' conferences can play a helpful role. Through their authority and aid they are able to give important support to the efforts and initiatives. They can strengthen those who work for ideal motives in this field, most of them on a voluntary basis. They can support the efforts to spread the Christian message and ethos in the various areas of sport.

Conclusion

Our times are both momentous and fascinating. While on the one hand people seem to be pursuing material prosperity, on the other hand we are witnessing a desperate search for meaning, the quest for an inner life, and a desire to learn new forms and methods of meditation and prayer. Even in secularized societies, the spiritual dimension of life is being sought after as an antidote

22. Ibid., 4.4.

to dehumanization. This so-called religious revival represents an opportunity.

Depending on our receptivity, the Church's institutions within the field of sport can be an occasion for instilling spiritual values beneficial in defending the dignity of human person and helping them to mature. The Church has to convince people that with regard to sport and to the athletes it is necessary to take one's bearings from a Christian ethos. This orientation can be a help, "as it is exactly the Christian message that allows us to be human in a deepened and extensive sense"[23] and participates in helping sports to fulfill its values, which are often rooted in Christianity.

23. Ibid., 5.

Bibliography

Alkemeyer, Thomas. "Bewegen als Kulturtechnik." In *Neue Sammlung:* Vierteljahres-Zeitschrift für Erziehung und Gesellschaft 43 (2003): 347–57.

Ambrose of Milan. "Expositio Evangelii Secumdum Lucam," in *Santus Ambrosius Mediolanensis*. J. P. Migne Patrologia Latina 15 (1815–75): 1527D–1850D.

———. "On the Death of His Brother Satyrus: Oration II." In *Funeral Orations by Gregory Nazianzein and Ambrose*. Translated by John Sullivan and Martin McGuire, 199–245. New York: Fathers of the Church, 1953.

Ammicht Quinn, Regina, and Elsa Tamez. "The Body and Religion." *Concilium: International Journal for Theology* 2 (2002).

Aquinas, Thomas. *Summa Theologica*. Vol. 1. Translated and edited by the Dominican Fathers of the English Province. New York: Benzinger, 1947.

———. *Thomae Aquinatis Iuxta Editionem*. Edited by Joannis Francisci Bernardi de Rubeis. Madrid: Tipographia Viduae Elisaei Sanchez, 1769.

Arendt, Hannah. *Vita activa: oder Vom tätigen Leben*. Munich: Piper 1992.

Auer, Alfons. *Autonome Moral und christlicher Glaube*. 2nd ed. Düsseldorf: Schnell & Steiner, 1984.

———. *Umweltethik Ein theologischer Beitrag zur ökologischen Diskussion*. Düsseldorf: Patmos, 1984.

———. *Zur Theologie der Ethik*. Freiburg: Herder, 1995.

Augustine. *The Soliloquies*. Translated by Rose Elizabeth Cleveland. Boston: Little, Brown, 1910.

Balthasar, Hans Urs von. *Theo Drama: Theological Dramatic Theory: The Dramatis Personae Man in God*. Vols. 2 and 3. San Francisco: Ignatius Press, 1990.

Bamberg, Corona. "Von Wert und Würde menschlicher Muße." *Geist und Leben* 57 (1984): 12–23.

Baranzke, Heike. *Würde der Kreatur? Die Idee der Würde im Horizont der Bioethik Epistemata Philosophie*. Würzburg: Königshausen & Neumann, 2002.

Barkhaus, Annette, and Anne Fleig, eds. *Grenzverläufe, der Körper als Schnittstelle.* Munich: Fink, 2002.

Barthes, Roland. *Mythologies.* New York: Noonday Press, 1972.

Basil the Great. "On the Use of Pagan Authors." In *The Fathers, Historians and Writers of the Church: Literally Translated,* 443–47. Dublin: W. B. Kelly, 1846.

Benedict XVI. "Address to Civil and Political Authorities in Prague" (September 26, 2009). *L'Osservatore Romano,* Italian edition, no. 224, September 28–29, 2009, 5.

———. "Address to the General Assembly of the Italian Bishops' Conference" (May 29, 2008). *L'Osservatore Romano,* English edition, no. 23, June 4, 2008, 5.

———. "Angelus Greeting of December 18, 2005." In *Insegnamenti di Benedetto XVI,* 1:1004. Vatican: LEV, 2005.

———. "Angelus Greeting of February 12, 2006." In *Insegnamenti di Benedetto XVI,* 2:180. Vatican: LEV, 2006/1.

———. "Angelus Greeting of July 8, 2007." In *Insegnamenti di Benedetto XVI,* 3:32. Vatican: LEV, 2007/2.

———. "Sunday Angelus: 3 August." *L'Osservatore Romano,* English edition, no. 32, August 6, 2008, 1.

———. "Ansprache an Die Österreichische Alpine Skinationalmannschaft" (October 6, 2007). In *Insegnamenti di Benedetto XVI,* 3:422–23. Vatican: LEV, 2007/2.

———. *Deus Caritas Est.* Vatican: LEV, 2006.

———. "Greeting to Professional Soccer Referees at Wednesday General Audience, January 25, 2006." In *Insegnamenti di Benedetto XVI,* 2:105. Vatican: LEV, 2006/1.

———. "Greeting to Representatives of the European and Italian Soccer Associations" (September 21, 2005). In *Insegnamenti di Benedetto XVI,* 1:567. Vatican: LEV, 2005.

———. "Homily at the World Youth Day Gathering in Cologne, Marienfeld" (August 21, 2005). *L'Osservatore Romano,* English edition, no. 34, August 24, 2005, 12.

———. "Homily during the Inaugural Mass of His Petrine Ministry" (April 24, 2005). *L'Osservatore Romano,* English edition, no. 17, April 27, 2005, 9.

———. "Letter to the Diocese of Rome on the Urgent Task of Educating Young People" (January 21, 2008). *L'Osservatore Romano,* English edition, no. 6, February 6, 2008, 10.

———. "Meeting with Clergy of Rome" (February 29, 2009). *L'Osservatore Romano,* English edition, no. 10, March 11, 2009, 4.

———. "Message to Cardinal Severino Poletto, Archbishop of Turin in Occasion of the Upcoming Winter Olympic Games" (November 29, 2005). *L'Osservatore Romano,* English edition, no. 6, February 8, 2006, 2.

———. "Message to the President of the Pontifical Council for the Laity on Sports,

Education and Faith" (November 3, 2009). *L'Osservatore Romano*, English edition, no. 46, November 18, 2009, 5.

————. "Non siate solo competitori sportive…" [Be not only competitive athletes…] (October 6, 2007). *L'Osservatore Romano*, Italian edition, no. 41, October 12, 2007, 4.

————. "A Spectacle of Humanity and Tenacity That Teaches Important Lessons for Life: Speech to the Participants of the World Swimming Championship" (August 1, 2009). *L'Osservatore Romano*, English edition, no. 31, August 5, 2009, 12.

————. "Wednesday General Audience: Greeting to the Athletes of the European Taekwondo" (April 9, 2008). In *Insegnamenti di Benedetto XVI*, 4:48. Vatican: LEV 2008/1.

————. "Wednesday General Audience of October 5, 2005." In *Insegnamenti di Benedetto XVI*, 1:636. Vatican: LEV, 2005.

————. "Wednesday General Audience of August 1, 2007." *L'Osservatore Romano*, English edition, no. 32/33, August 8/15, 2007, 4.

————. "Wednesday General Audience of January 9, 2008." In *Insegnamenti di Benedetto XVI*, 4:48. Vatican: LEV, 2008/1.

————. "Wednesday General Audience of May 7, 2008." In *Insegnamenti di Benedetto XVI*, 4:732–34. Vatican: LEV, 2008/1..

Benjamin, Walter. "Erfahrung und Armut." In *Gesammelte Schriften*, vol. 2, pt. 1, 213–19. Edited by R. Tiedemann and H. Schweppenhäuse. Frankfurt: Akademie, 1977.

Bitter, Gottfried, et al., eds. *Neues Handbuch religionspädagogischer Grundbegriffe*, 2nd ed. Munich: Kösel, 2006.

Bourdieu, Pierre. *Distinction: A Social Critique of the Judgement of Taste*. Translated by Richard Nice. Cambridge, Mass.: Harvard University Press, 1984.

————. *In Other Words. Essays Towards a Reflexive Sociology*. Translated by Matthew Adamson. Stanford, Calif.: Stanford University Press, 1990.

————. "Sport and Social Class." In *Social Science Information* (Paris) 17, no. 6 (1978): 810–40.

Bobba, Giovanni, and Fratesco Mauro, eds. *Scritti Alpinistici del Sac. Dott. Achille Ratti*. Milano: Bertieri-Vanzetti, 1923.

Bruker, Max Otto. *Lebensbedingte Krankheit*. Lahnstein: Bioverlag, 1997.

Carter, John, and Arnd Krüger, eds. *Ritual and Record: Sports, Records, and Quantifications in Pre-Modern Societies*. New York: Greenwood Press, 1990.

Cassirer, Ernst. *Versuch über den Menschen*. Hamburg: Felix Meiner, 1996.

Catechism of the Catholic Church. London: Geoffrey Chapman, 1994.

Chrysostom, John. *Saint Chrysostom's Homilies on Corinthians I and II*. Vol. 12 of *Nicene and Post-Nicene Fathers of the Christian Church*. Edited by Alexander Roberts and James Donaldson. Peabody, Mass.: Hendrickson Publishers, 1995. [The

Ante-Nicene Christian Library was originally published in Edinburgh between 1867 and 1873 by T&T Clark and edited by Rev. Alexander Roberts and James Donaldson.]

———. *Saint Chrysostom's Homilies on Galatians, Ephesians, Philippians*. Vol. 13 of *Nicene and Post-Nicene Fathers of the Christian Church*. Edited by Alexander Roberts and James Donaldson. Peabody, Mass.: Hendrickson Publishers, 1995.

———. *Saint Chrysostom's Homilies on the Acts of the Apostles and the Epistle to the Romans*. Vol. 11 of *Nicene and Post-Nicene Fathers of the Christian Church*. Edited by Alexander Roberts and James Donaldson. Peabody, Mass.: Hendrickson Publishers, 1995.

———. *Saint Chrysostom's Homilies on the Gospel of St. John, Hebrews*. Vol. 14 of *Nicene and Post-Nicene Fathers of the Christian Church*. Edited by Alexander Roberts and James Donaldson. Peabody, Mass.: Hendrickson Publishers, 1995.

———. *Saint Chrysostom's Homilies on the Gospel of Saint Matthew*, Vol. 10 of *Nicene and Post-Nicene Fathers of the Christian Church*. Edited by Alexander Roberts and James Donaldson. Peabody, Mass.: Hendrickson Publishers, 1995.

———. *Saint Chrysostom's Homilies on the Priesthood, Ascetic Treatises, and the Statues*. Vol. 9 of *Nicene and Post-Nicene Fathers of the Christian Church*. Edited by Alexander Roberts and James Donaldson. Peabody, Mass.: Hendrickson Publishers, 1995.

Clement of Alexandria. *Clement of Alexandria*. Vol. 2 of *Ante-Nicene Fathers*. Edited by Alexander Roberts and James Donaldson. Peabody, Mass.: Hendrickson Publishers, 1995.

Commissione ecclesiale pastorale del tempo libero turismo e sport. *Sport e vita cristiana: nota pastorale 50*. Bologna: Edizione Dehoniane, 1995.

Cyril of Jerusalem. *Cyril of Jerusalem, Gregory Nazianzen*. Vol. 7 of *Nicene and Post-Nicene Fathers: Series II*. Edited by Alexander Roberts and James Donaldson. Peabody, Mass.: Hendrickson Publishers, 1995.

Danto, Arthur. *Narration and Knowledge*. New York: Columbia University Press, 1985.

De Finance, Joseph. *Citoyen de deux mondes: la place de l'homme dans la création*. Rome: Università Gregoriana Editrice, 1980.

Deleuze, Gilles, and Félix Guattari. *A Thousand Plateaus: Capitalism and Schizophrenia*. Translated by Brian Massumi. London: Continuum, 2004.

Demmer, Klaus. *Gottes Anspruch denken: Die Gottesfrage in der Moraltheologie*. Freiburg: Herder, 1995.

Diem, Carl. *Olympiaden 1964: Eine Geschichte des Sports*. Stuttgart: Cotta Verlag, 1994.

Drnovsek, Janez. "Der slowenische Staatspräsident sagt über den Egoismus." *Kurier*, Sunday edition, February 3, 2007, 6.

―――. *Misli o življenju in zavedanju* [Thoughts on life and awareness]. Ljubljana: Mladinska knjiga, 2006.

Duque Salas, Luis Alberto. "El Valor Humano y Cristiano del deporte según el Magisterio Pontificio: de Pio XII a Juan Pablo II." PhD dissertation, Pontificium Athenaeum Santacae Crucis, 1997.

Ebertz, Michael N. "Sport-Treiben als (Er)Lebensstil." I*Religionsunterricht an höheren Schulen* 5 (1997): 291–99.

Elias, Norbert, Stephen Mennell, and Johan Goudsblom. *Norbert Elias on Civilization, Power, and Knowledge: Selected Writings*. Chicago: University of Chicago Press, 1998.

Ellero, Babini. *L'antropologia teologica di Hans Urs von Balthasar*. Milan: Jaca Book, 1988.

Enz, Franz. *Sport im Aufgabenfeld der Kirche*. Munich: Barth, 1970.

Foucault, Michel. "Afterword." In Hubert Dreyfus and Paul Rabinow, *Michel Foucault: Beyond Structuralism and Hermeneutics*. 2nd ed. Chicago: University of Chicago Press, 1982.

Feeney, Robert. *A Catholic Perspective: Physical Exercise and Sports*. Marysville, Wash.: Aquinas Press, 1995.

Feuerbach, Ludwig. "Grundsätze zur Philosophie der Zukunft." In *Feuerbach-Studienausgabe*, 3:248–319. Edited by Erich Thies. Frankfurt: Suhrkamp, 1975.

Flasch, Kurt. *Meister Eckhart. Die Geburt der "Deutschen Mystik" aus dem Geist der arabischen Philosophie*. Munich: Beck, 2006.

Flusser, Vilém. *Die Schrift. Hat Schreiben Zukunft?* 4th ed. Göttingen: Immatrix, 1992.

Gebauer, Gunter. "Die Mythen-Maschine." In *Sportphilosophie*, edited by Volker Caysa, 290–317. Leipzig: Reclam, 1997.

―――, ed. *Olympische Spiele—die andere Utopie der Moderne. Olympia zwischen Kult und Droge*. Frankfurt: Suhrkamp, 1996.

Gehlen, Arnold. *Der Mensch. Seine Natur und seine Stellung in der Welt*. Wiesbaden: Aula, 1986.

Gierer, Alfred. *Die Physik, das Leben und die Seele*. Munich: Piper, 1985.

Grabmann, Martin, and Joseph Mausbach, eds. *Aurelius Augustinus: Festschrift der Görres-Gesellschaft zum 1500*. Cologne: Bachem, 1930.

Greganti, Alberto, ed. *Cent'anni di storia nella realtà dello sport Italiana*, Vol. 2. Rome: Centro Sportivo Italiano, 2006.

Gugutzer, Robert, ed. *Body Turn: Perspektiven der Soziologie des Körpers und des Sports*. Bielefeld, Germany: Transkript Verlag, 2006.

Gumbrecht, Hans Ulrich. *In Praise of Athletic Beauty*. Cambridge, Mass.: Harvard University Press, 2006.

———. *Production of Presence: What Meaning Cannot Convey.* Stanford, Calif.: Stanford University Press, 2003.

Grupe, Ommo, and Dietmar Mieth, eds. *Lexikon der Ethik im Sport.* Schorndorf: Hofmann, 1998.

Haegel, Pascal. *Le corps, quel défi pour la personne?* Paris: Fayard, 1999.

Haker, Hille. "The Perfect Body: Biomedical Utopias." *Concilium: International Journal for Theology* 2 (2002): 9–18.

———. "Selbstkonzepte aus feministisch-ethischer Sicht." *Freiburger Zeitschrift für Philosophie und Theologie* 116 (2002): 126–43.

Haslinger, Herbert, ed. *Handbuch Praktische Theologie.* Vol. 2. Mainz: Grünewald, 2000.

Haug, Walter, and Dietmar Mieth, eds. *Religiöse Erfahrung: Historische Modelle in christlicher Tradition.* Munich: Fink, 1992.

Heidbrink, Ludger. *Kritik der Verantwortung. Zu den Grenzen verantwortlichen Handelns in komplexen Kontexten.* Weilerswist: Velbrück, 2003.

Henrich, Dieter. *Bewußtes Leben. Untersuchungen zum Verhältnis von Subjektivität und Metaphysik.* Stuttgart: Reclam, 1999.

Hesiod. *The Theogony, Work and Days, and The Shield of Heracles.* Translated by Hugh Evelyn-White. Stillwell, Kans.: Digireads.com Publishing, 2008.

Höff, Ottfried. "Selbstinteresse." In *Lexikon der Ethik,* edited by O. Höff, 227–28. Munich: Beck, 2002.

Hübenthal, Christoph. "Der menschliche und religiöse Sinn des Sports." *Diakonia* 36 (2005): 235–41.

———. *Grundlegung der christlichen Sozialethik: Versuch eines freiheitsanalytisch-handlungsreflexiven Ansatzes.* Münster: Aschendorff, 2006.

Huizinga, Johan. *Homo Ludens: A Study of the Play Element in Culture.* Boston: Beacon Press, 1971.

Illich, Ivan. *Tools for Conviviality.* New York: Harper & Row, 1973.

Jakobi, Paul, and Heinz-Egon Rösch, eds. *Sport und Religion. Schriftenreihe Christliche Perspektiven im Sport* 8. Mainz: Topos-Taschenbücher, 1986.

John Paul II. "Address to Italian Olympic Medal winners" (November 24, 1984). *L'Osservatore Romano,* English edition, no. 50, December 3, 1984, 4.

———. "Address to Participants of Athletic World Championships" (September 2, 1987). *L'Osservatore Romano,* English edition, no. 36, September 7, 1987, 5.

———. "Address to the International Convention: 'The Face and Soul of Sport'" (October 28, 2000). *L'Osservatore Romano,* English edition, no. 46, November 15, 2000, 9.

———. *Christifideles Laici: On the Vocation and the Mission of the Lay Faithful in the Church and in the World.* Vatican: LEV, 1988.

———. "Discorso ad atleti italiani ed argentini" (May 25, 1979). In *Insegnamenti di Giovanni Paolo II*, 2:1347–48. Vatican: LEV, 1979/1.

———. "Homily at the Mass for Sports Men and Women" (October 29, 2000). *L'Osservatore Romano*, English edition, no. 44, November 1, 2000, 1.

———. "International Jubilee of Sport: Homily at Olympic Stadium" (April 12, 1984). *L'Osservatore Romano*, English edition, no. 17, April 24, 1984, 4–5.

———. *Redemptor Hominis*. Milano: Ancora, 1979.

———. "Speech to Catholic Federation of Sports and Physical Education" (April 3, 1986). *L'Osservatore Romano*, English edition, no. 17, April 28, 1986, 5.

———. "Wednesday General Audience" (February 6, 1980). *L'Osservatore Romano*, English edition, February 11, 1980, 1.

John XXIII. *Pacem et Terris*, 40th anniversary edition. Vatican: LEV 2003.

Joisten, Karen. "Der Mensch im Spiegel der Olympischen Idee." In *Olympischer Dreiklang: Werte-Geschichte-Zeitgeist*, series 6, edited by M. Messing, 21–34. Kassel: Agon Sportverlag, 2004.

———. *Philosophie der Heimat—Heimat der Philosophie*. Berlin: Akademie, 2003.

———. "Wenn Gott den Ball versenkt." In *Abseits denken: Fussball in Kultur, Philosophie und Wissenschaft*, edited by Andreas Hütig and Johannes Marx, 8–86. Kassel: Agon Sportverlag, 2004.

Jüthner, Julius. "Die athletischen Leibesübungen der Griechen." In *Einzelne sportarten: Lauf, Sprung und Wurfbewerbe*, edited by Friedrich Brein, 2:195–201. Vienna: Hermann Böhlaus, 1968.

Kamper, Demmer. *Geschichte und menschliche Natur: Die Tragweite der gegenwärtigen Anthropologiekritik*. Munich: Hanser, 1973.

Kant, Immanuel. *Werke in sechs Bänden*. Edited by W. Weischedel. Darmstadt: Wissenschaftliche Buchgesellschaft, 1983.

Karrer, Leo, ed. *Handbuch der Praktischen Gemeindearbeit*. Freiburg: Herder, 1990.

Kästner, Erich. *Der tägliche Kram: Chansons und Prosa 1945–1948*. In *Werke*. Edited by Hermann Kurzke, 2:7–185. Frankfurt: Deutscher Taschenbuch, 1998.

Kaufmann, Franz-Xaver, Giandomenico Majone, and Vincent Ostrom, eds. *Guidance, Control and Evaluation in the Public Sector: The Bielefeld Interdisciplinary Project*. Berlin: Gruyter, 1986.

Kemp, Peter. *Das Unersetzliche. Eine Technologie-Ethik*. Berlin: WiehernVerlag 1992.

Koch, Alois. "Das biblische Menschenbild und seine Bedeutung für die Wertung der Leiblichkeit und der Leibesübungen." In *Begegnung: Christentum und Sport*, edited by Willi Schwank and Alois Koch, 2:51–78. Aachen: Meyer und Meyer 2000.

———. *Johannes Chrysostom und seine Kenntnisse der antiken Agonistik*. Hindesheim: Weidmann, 2007.

König, Eugen. "Ethik und Zweckrationalität des technologischen Sports." In *Sportethik: Regeln—Fairness—Doping*, edited by Claudia Pawlenka. Paderborn: Mentis, 2004.

Korff, Wilhelm. *Norm und Sittlichkeit*. Mainz: Grünewald, 1975.

Kraus, Karl. *Pro Domo et Mundo*. Munich: Langen, 1912

Kremer, Jacob. *Der Erste Brief an die Korinther*. Regensburg: Pustet 1997.

Krüger, Michael. *Einführung in die Geschichte der Leibeserziehung und des Sportes*, Vol. 1. Schorndorf: Hofmann, 2004.

———. *Einführung in die Geschichte der Leibeserziehung und des Sportes*. Vol. 2. Schorndorf: Hofmann, 2005.

Landmann, Michael. *Fundamental-Anthropologie*. Bonn: Bouvier, 1979.

Langness, Anja. "Jugendliche Lebenswelten: Familie, Schule, Freizeit." In *Jugend 2006*, edited by Shell Deutschland Holding, 49–102, 94ff. Frankfurt: Fischer, 2006.

Lehmann, Karl. "Neue Zeichen der Zeit. Unterscheidungskriterien zur Diagnose der Kirche in der Gesellschaft und zum kirchlichen Handeln heute." Inaugural address to assembly of the Germans Bishops' Conference (September 19, 2005). In *Der Vorsitzende der Deutschen Bischofskonferenz 26*. Bonn: Sekretariat der Deutschen Bishofskonfeenz, 2006.

Maier, Bernhard. *Olympia- und Spitzensport*. Vienna: VWG, 1993.

Martin, Emily. *Flexible Bodies: Tracking Immunity in American Culture from the Days of Polio to the Age of AIDS*. Boston: Beacon Press, 1994.

Mazza, Carlo. "Sport as Viewed from the Church's Magisterium." In *The World of Sport Today: A Field of Christian Mission*. Edited by Pontificium Consilium Pro Laicis, 55–73. Vatican: LEV, 2006.

Mette, Norbert, and Folkert Rickers, eds. *Lexikon der Religionspädagogik*. Neukirchen-Vluyn: Neukirchener Verlag, 2001.

Metz, Johann. "Seele." In *Lexikon fur Teologie und Kirche*, edited by Michael Buchberger, 9:570. Freiburg: Herder, 1964.

Metz, Johann, and Francis Fiorenza. "El hombre como unidad de alma y cuerpo." In *Mysterium Salutis*, edited by J. Feiner and M. Löhrer, 4:680–704. Madrid: Ed. Cristianidad, 1970.

Mieth, Dietmar. "Anthropologie und Ethik." In *Was ist der Mensch? Theologische Anthropologie im interdisziplinären Kontext*, edited by Michael Graf, 351–67. Stuttgart: Metzler, 2004.

———. "Das Reich Gottes bei Johann Sebastian Drey und die Begründung einer Katholischen Soziallehre." In *Theologie als Instanz der Moderne*, edited by Michael Kessler and Ottmar Fuchs, 315–32. Tübingen: Francke, 2005.

———. "Das Weltverhältnis des christlichen Glaubens am Beispiel der theologischen Ethik." In *Fundamente der Theologischen Ethik. Bilanz und Neuansätze*, edited by Adrian Holderegger, 290–312. Freiburg: Herder, 1996.

————. "Die Folgen des Fouls: Ethische Verantwortung im und für den Sport." *Herder Korredspondenz* 58 (2004): 397–402.

————. "The Ethics of Sport." *Concilium: International Journal for Theology*, English edition, no. 205 (1989): 79–92.

————. *Moral und Erfahrung.* Vol. 1. 4th ed. Freiburg: Herder, 1999.

————. "Mystik–theologiegeschichtlich" [Mysticism in the history of theology]. In *Neues Handbuch theologischer Grundbegriffe*, edited by Peter Eicher, 3:135–45. Munich: Koesel Verlag, 2005.

————. "Towards an Ethic of Sport in Contemporary Culture." In *The World of Sport Today: A Field of Christian Mission*, edited by Pontificium Consilium Pro Laicis, 23–43. Vatican: Vatican: LEV, 2006.

Müller, Norbert, ed. *Olympism: Selected Writings of Pierre de Coubertin.* Lausanne: I.O.C., 2000.

Neswald, Elizabeth. *Medien-Theologie: Das Werk Vilém Flussers.* Cologne: Böhlau Verlag, 1998.

Nietzsche, Friedrich. *Die fröhliche Wissenschaft.* Vol. 3 of *Sämtliche Werke: Kritische Studienausgabe.* Edited by Giorgio Colli and Mazzino Montinari. Berlin: Deutscher Taschenbuch Verlag, 1980.

Pass, Manfred, and Klaus Peter Weinhold. "Kirche und Sport." In *Lexikon der Ethik im Sport*, 99, edited by Ommo Grupe and Dietmar Mieth, 289–92. Schorndorf: Hofmann, 1998.

Paul VI. Apostolic Exhortation *Evangelii Nuntiandi.* Vatican: Tipografia Poliglotta Vaticana, 1975.

————. *Ecclesiam Suam.* Vatican: Tipografia Poliglotta Vaticana, 1964.

Pausanius. *Pausanias's Description of Greece.* Translated by James G. Frazer. London: Macmillan, 1898.

Pawlenka, Claudia, ed. *Sportethik: Regeln—Fairness—Doping.* Paderborn: Mentis, 2004.

————. *Utilitarismus und Sportethik.* Paderborn: Mentis, 2002.

Pende, Nicola, and Raimondo Spiazzi. *Unità e grandezza dell'uomo.* Brescia, Italy: Morcelliana, 1956.

Philostratus, Flavius. "On Gymnastics." In *Sources for the History of Greek Athletics.* Translated by R. S. Robinson, 202–38. Ann Arbor, Mich.: Cushing-Malloy, 1955.

Pironio, Eduardo. "Lo Sport nei documenti pontifici." In *Lo Sport nei Documenti Pontifici*, edited by G. Gandolfo and Luisa Vassallo, 251–65. Brescia, Italy: La Scuola, 1994.

Pius XII. "Agli uomini della Azione Cattolica" (September 7, 1947). In *Discorsi e Radiomessaggi di Pio XII*, vol. 9. Vatican: Tipografia Poliglotta Vaticana, 1947.

———. "Education and Sport" (November 8, 1952). In *A Catholic Perspective: Physical Exercise and Sports*, edited by Robert Feeney, 43–56. Marysville, Wash.: Aquinas Press, 1995.

———. "Fundamental Principles Governing Sporting Activities" (November 10, 1951). In *A Catholic Perspective: Physical Exercise and Sports*, edited by Robert Feeney, 42–43. Marysville, Wash: Aquinas Press, 1995.

———. "La verità della seconda parte del simbolo apostolico" (February 17, 1942). In *Discorsi e Radiomessaggi di Pio XII*, vol. 3. Vatican: Tipografia Poliglotta Vaticana.

———. "Le Virtù per una Cristiana Educazione Ginnica Atletica e Agonistica" (October 9, 1955). In *Discorsi e Radiomessaggi di Pio XII*, vol. 17. Vatican: Tipografia Poliglotta Vaticana, 1955.

———. "Lessons of the Mountain" (September 26, 1948). In *A Catholic Perspective: Physical Exercise and Sports*, edited by Robert Feeney, 37–40. Marysville, Wash.: Aquinas Press, 1995.

———. "Paterni voti ed auspice per le olimpiadi di Melbourne" (October 24, 1956). In *Discorsi e Radiomessaggi di Pio XII*, vol. 18. Vatican: Tipografia Poliglotta Vaticana, 1956.

———. "Speech to the Central Sports School of the U.S Armed Forces" (July 29, 1945). In *Discorsi e Radiomessaggi di Pio XII*, vol. 7. Vatican: Tipografia Poliglotta Vaticana, 1945.

———. "The Sporting Ideal" (May 20, 1945). In Robert Feeney, *A Catholic Perspective: Physical Exercise and Sports*, 27–35. Marysville, Wash.: Aquinas Press, 1995.

Plato. *The Collected Dialogues of Plato*. Edited by Edith Hamilton and Huntington Cairns, 14th ed. Princeton: Princeton University Press, 1989.

Plessner, Helmuth. *Die Stufen des Organischen und der Mensch. Einleitung in die philosophische Anthropologie*. Vol. 4. Frankfurt: Gruyter, 1981.

Poliakoff, Michael. *Combat Sports in the Ancient World*. New Haven, Conn.: Yale University Press, 1995.

Pontificium Consilium Pro Laicis. *Sport: An Educational and Pastoral Challenge*, Vatican: LEV, 2008.

———. *The World of Sport Today: Field of Christian Mission*. Vatican: LEV, 2006.

Poplutz, Uta. *Athlet des Evangeliums*. Freiburg: Herder, 2004.

Prechtel, Peter, and Franz-Peter Burkard, eds. *Metzler Philosophie Lexikon*. Stuttgart: Metzler, 1995.

Pontifical Council for the Laity. "The Vatican Works to Humanize the Wide World of Sports." *L'Osservatore Romano*, English edition, no. 46, November 16, 2005, 1.

Prieto, Leopold. "El hombre, el animal y la antropologia." *Ecclesia* 19, no.1, (2005): 43–56.

Pröpper, Thomas. *Evangelium und freie Vernunft: Konturen einer theologischen Hermeneutik*. Freiburg: Herder, 2001.

Rahner, Karl. "Para un teologia del símbolo." In *Escritos de Teologia*, edited by J. Feiner et al., 4:283–321. Madrid: Taurus Ediciones, 1964.

Rahner, Karl, and Herbert Vorgrimler. *Kleiner Konzilskompendium*. 2nd ed. Freiburg: Herder, 1966.

Ratzinger, Joseph. *Co-Workers of the Truth: Meditations for Every Day of the Year*. San Francisco: Ignatius Press, 1992.

————. *Gottes Glanz in unserer Zeit. Meditationen zum Kirchenjahr*. Freiburg: Herder Press, 2005.

————. *Milestones: Memoirs 1927–1977*. San Francisco: Ignatius Press, 1998.

————. *Mitarbeiter der Wahrheit, Gedanken für jeden*. Vol. 1. Edited by Irene Grassl. 3rd ed. Würzburg: Naumann Press, 1992.

————. *Suchen, was droben ist. Meditationen das Jahr hindurch*. Freiburg: Herder Press, 1985.

Reiner, Hans. "Egoismus." In *Historisches Wörterbuch der Philosophie*, edited by J. Ritter, 2:302–15. Basel: Schwabe, 1972.

Rigauer, Bero. "Die Erfindung des menschlichen Körpers in der Soziologie. Eine systemtheoretische Konzeption und Perspektive." In *Body Turn: Perspektiven der Soziologie des Körpers und des Sports*, edited by Robert Gugutzer, 57–79 (Bielefeld, Germany: Transkript Verlag, 2006.

Ruiz de la Pena, José. L. *Imagen del hombre. Antropologia teologica fundamental*. Santander, Spain: Sal Térrea, 1988.

Scheler, Max. *Man's Place in Nature*. Translated by Hans Meyerhoff. Boston: Beacon Press, 1961.

Schilling, Othmar. *Das biblische Menschenbild*. Cologne: Wort und Werk, 1961.

Schöbel, Heinz. *Olympia und seine Spiele*. 7th ed. Berlin: Uranaia, 1988.

Schroer, Markus, ed. *Soziologie des Körpers*. Frankfurt: Suhrkamp, 2005.

Schulze, Bernd. "Körperbewegung als Formbildung. Ansätze einer systemtheoretischen Bewegungskonzeption." In *Body Turn: Perspektiven der Soziologie des Körpers und des Sports*, edited by Robert Gugutzer, 81–93. Bielefeld, Germany: Transkript Verlag, 2006.

Schwank,Willi. "Christentum und Sport." In *Lexikon der Ethik im Sport*, edited by Ommo Grupe and Dietmar Mieth, 84–91. Schorndorf: Hofmann, 1998.

Seel, Martin, "Die Zelebration des Unvermögens. Aspekte einer Ästhetik des Sports." In *Ethisch-ästhetische Studien*, edited by Martin Seel, 188–200. Frankfurt: Suhrkamp, 1996.

Seneca, Lucius Annaeus. *Moral Epistles*. Translated by Richard M. Gummere and edited by the Loeb Classical Library. Vol. 2. Cambridge, Mass.: Harvard University Press, 1920.

Snell, Bruno. *Die Entdeckung des Geistes: Studien zur Entstehung des europäischen Denkens bei den Griechen*. Göttingen: Vandenhoeck & Ruprecht, 1993.

Splett, Jörg. "Der Mensch zwischen Freiheit und Zwang aus der Sicht der philosophischen Anthropologie." In *Sport zwischen Freiheit und Zwang, Christliche Perspektiven im Sport 5*, edited by Paul Jakobi and H. E. Rösch, 118–33. Mainz: Matthias-Grünewald-Verlag, 1981.

"Sport: Spiel und Kampf." Special issue, *Diakonia* 36, no. 4 (2005).

"Sport und christliches Ethos: Gemeinsame Erklärung der Kirchen zum Sport." In *Arbeitshilfe des Sekretariats der Deutschen Bischofskonferenz*, no. 80. Bonn: Sekretariat der Deutschen Bishofskonferenz, 1990.

Tanner, Jakob. "Be a Somebody with a Body—Die Körpermaschine der Arbeitsgesellschaft." In *Wieviel Körper braucht der Mensch?* edited by Gero von Randow, 43–53. Hamburg: Koerber-Stiftung, 2001.

Tertullian. *Latin Christianity: Its Founder Tertullian*, Vol. 3 of *Ante-Nicene Fathers*. Edited by Alexander Roberts and James Donaldson. Peabody, Mass.: Hendrickson Publishers, 1995. [The Ante-Nicene Christian Library was originally published in Edinburgh between 1867 and 1873 by T&T Clark and edited by Rev. Alexander Roberts and James Donaldson.]

Vatican Council II. "Pastoral Constitution on the Church in the Modern World: Gaudium et Spes." In *Vatican Council II: The Conciliar and Post Conciliar Documents*. Revised ed. Edited by Austin Flannery, 1:903–1001. Dublin: Dominican Publications, 1988.

Vogt, Martin. "Der Sport im Mittelalter." In *Ge-schichte des Sports aller Volker und Zeiten*, edited by G. Bogeng, 163–237. Leipzig: Seemann, 1926.

Wacquant, Loic. *Body and Soul: Notebooks of an Apprentice Boxer*. New York: Oxford University Press, 2004.

Weiler, Rudolf. *Sportethik: Aufrufe zu Gesinnung und Bekenntnis*. Graz: Austria Medien Serv., 1996.

Contributors

Pedro Barrajón, L.C., is a priest of the Legionaries of Christ from Spain. He is currently the rector of the Pontifical Athenaeum Regina Apostolorum in Rome, where he teaches anthropology.

Bishop Josef Clemens a priest, originally from Paderborn, was the personal secretary to Cardinal Josef Ratzinger from 1984 to 2003. Since being elevated to bishop in 2004, he serves as the secretary of the Pontifical Council for the Laity.

Stephan Goertz has been professor of Christian social ethics and pastoral theology at the Saarland University, Saarbrücken, since 2004. He was appointed head of the faculty of Catholic Moral Theology at the Johannes-Gutenberg University in Mainz in 2010.

Christoph Hübenthal is assistant professor of theological ethics at the Radboud University, Nijmegen, and member of the scientific commission of the Church and Sport working group of the Catholic German Bishops' Conference.

Karen Joisten is assistant professor of philosophy at the Johannes-Gutenberg University, Mainz. She specializes in narrative philosophy, anthropology, ethics, and philosophy of culture.

Alois Koch, S.J., dedicated the later part of his life as a Jesuit priest to researching the theme of sport in the Fathers of the Church. He died in 2009 in Cologne.

Kevin Lixey, L.C., is a priest of the Legionaries of Christ from the United States. Since 2004 he has headed the Church and Sport section within the Pontifical Council for the Laity.

Bernhard Maier, S.D.B., is a Salesian priest who has been the chaplain to the Austrian National Olympic team since 1982. He balances this position with his main apostolate with youth as the high school principal of the Don-Bosco-Gymnasium in Unterwaltersdorf (Austria).

Bishop Carlo Mazza headed the office for pastoral care in sport and leisure within the Italian Bishops' Conference, which also included being chaplain to the Italian Olympic Team. Since 2007 he has been the bishop of Fidenza (Italy).

Dietmar Mieth is professor of theological ethics at the Eberhard-Karls University, Tübingen. He is author of numerous books on moral ethics, and a member of the scientific commission of the Church and Sport working group of the Catholic German Bishops' Conference.

Norbert Müller is professor of sports science at the Johannes-Gutenberg University. He is an expert in Pierre de Coubertin and a member of the scientific commission of the Church and Sport working group of the Catholic German Bishops' Conference.

Index

Koch, Ernst, 64
König, Eugen, 102
Korff, Wilhelm, 162–63
Kraus, Karl, 189
Kremer, Jacob, 87n12
Krüger, Arnd, 68n14
Krüger, Michael, 26–28, 30n27
Küng, Hans, 160

Landmann, Michael, 65n7, 66
Lehmann, Karl, 190
Liber creaturarum, 161, 166, 176
Liber revelationis, 161, 176
Lixey, Kevin, xii, 5, 104–20
locus theologicus, 157
Losing, 20, 99, 114, 217–18. *See also*
    Defeat
Loyalty, 3, 114, 229
Lübbe, Hermann, 171n23
Lukacs, Georg, 33
Luke, Gospel of, 92, 137
Luhmann, Niklas, 202
Luther, Martin, 166

Maccabees, Book of, 82
Maier, Bernhard, xi, xv, xvi, 206–22
Maradona, Diego, 35, 220
Mark, Gospel of, 137
Martin, Emily, 174n25
Martyrdom, 115
Matthew, Gospel of, 98, 171–72, 177,
    228
Mazza, Carlo, xiii, 121–38, 190n4
Meister Eckhart, 161n4, 176, 182, 185
Mercurialis, "De arte gymnastica,"
    30
Merry del Val, Cardinal, 104
Mette, Norbert, 189n2
Metz, Johann, 53– 55

Metzelder, Christoph, 218
Meuser, Michael, 200n39, 201–2
Middle Ages, x, 25–27, 30, 161
Mieth, Dietmar, vi, ix–xvi, 73n18,
    86n9, 156–85, 191n8–9, 198n28,
    212n7, 213n12
Mokrosch, Reinhold, 213
Morgenstern, Christian, 214
Mother Theresa, 212
Mounier, Emanuele, 39–40
Mountain: climbing, 104, 108, 117;
    lessons of the, 118–19, 197
Müller, Norbert, xv, 104n1, 172, 177,
    223–33
Myth: animals, 49;
    demythologization, 171;
    machineries, 35n38, 36;
    mythologies, 192n10, 236; of the
    self-reliant, 196. *See also* Hesiod

Neoplatonism, 50
Neo-scholasticism, 161
Neswald, Elizabeth, 34n36
New evangelization, 232
New Testament, 53, 83–86, 103
Nietzsche, Friedrich, 33
Nostra Aetate, 170
Novatian, 81

Official. *See* Referee
Old Testament, 24, 53, 84–85, 103
Olivi, Peter, 54
Olympia, 83, 97
Olympic: chaplain, 188, 206–22;
    Charter, 229; Committee, 106,
    208; Congress, 154; discipline, 69;
    Games, 83, 96–98, 102, 149–51,
    198, 206, 209, 214, 217, 229, 231;
    gods, 18, 21; idea, 102, 164, 170;

Sport and Christianity: A Sign of the Times in the Light of Faith was designed in Meta Serif, with Meta Sans display type, by Kachergis Book Design of Pittsboro, North Carolina. It was printed on 55-pound Natures Natural and bound by Sheridan Books of Ann Arbor, Michigan.